The Ethics of Swagger

The Ethics of Swagger
Prizewinning African American Novels, 1977–1993

Michael DeRell Hill

The Ohio State University Press
Columbus

Library of Congress Cataloging-in-Publication Data
Hill, Michael D., 1971–
Ethics of swagger : prizewinning African American novels, 1977–1993 / Michael DeRell Hill.
p. cm.
Includes bibliographical references and index.
ISBN 978-0-8142-1214-1 (cloth : alk. paper)—ISBN 978-0-8142-9315-7 (cd)
1. American fiction—African American authors—History and criticism. 2. American fiction—
20th century—History and criticism. 3. Bradley, David, 1950—Criticism and interpretation. 4.
Gaines, Ernest J., 1933—Criticism and interpretation. 5. Johnson, Charles (Charles Richard),
1948—Criticism and interpretation. 6. Morrison, Toni—Criticism and interpretation. 7. Naylor, Gloria—Criticism and interpretation. 8. Walker, Alice, 1944—Criticism and interpretation.
9. Wideman, John Edgar—Criticism and interpretation. I. Title.
PS374.N4H55 2013
813'.5409896073—dc23
2012041797

Cover design by Laurence J. Nozik
Text design by Juliet Williams
Type set in Adobe Bembo and Wilke

♾ The paper used in this publication meets the minimum requirements of the American National Standard for Information Sciences—Permanence of Paper for Printed Library Materials.
ANSI Z39.48-1992.

9 8 7 6 5 4 3 2 1

Contents

acknowledgments

This book proves that insight demands both conspicuous and invisible collaborations. While the list will never be complete, I would like to acknowledge some folks who kept the faith.

James Keil arrested my attention when I was an undergraduate. By demanding discipline and encouraging dreams, he clarified my academic calling and convinced me to pursue it. I will forever be grateful that he took the time to care. While at Howard University, I also was blessed to meet E. Ethelbert Miller. His gentle prodding launched me into archival research, and our conversations reminded me to include the human dimension as I analyzed literature. Like Frederick Douglass, poet Miller is defined by the lives sprouting from his own. I count mine as one among many. By hiring me as his research assistant, R. Baxter Miller showed a kindness that has never waned. He introduced me to African American writing as a praisesong of survival and extolled the CLA, MELUS, and other landmark institutions in the study of black literature. Because of his tutelage, I can see the textures that braid my efforts into a venerated history. His gift of perspective grows in value daily.

Elaine Scarry enlivened my graduate education by untying the cordons of intellectual curiosity. While teaching me that the mind should roam, she also insisted that I make my wending coherent. Her example ever spurs me toward a more epic outlook. With graceful erudition, Lawrence Buell modeled analytical rigor. He empathized with my scholarly exhaustion, yet he motivated me to look anew and to do so scrupulously. Through his lived testimony, I have learned that a potent work ethic is the best complement to talent. From the moment that I met him, Henry Louis Gates, Jr., bolstered my confidence. He empowered me to trust my instincts and persuaded me to express as much of the truth as I could discern. His admonitions define my professional practice; I appreciate the light touch of his guidance.

This project began in classes that I taught at Wake Forest University. For the chance to enhance my thinking about African American novels, I owe a debt to the faculty, staff, and students of that fine institution. The University of Iowa has also supported me wondrously. From the College of Liberal Arts and Sciences, I have received summer research money, a semester leave, travel stipends, and a course reduction. The English Department and the Program in African American Studies have generously provided funds for my trips to literary archives, a research assistant, and the purchase of critical texts. If this administrative aid proved valuable, then the munificence of my colleagues touched me equally. Iowa's neighboring reflects a community defined by sincere concern. While this concern is evident at work, it permeates all of my life. Being amid such conviviality made it easier to finish this book.

Several people read early drafts of this project, and I am especially grateful for the feedback of Dolan Hubbard, John Jackson, Herman Beavers, Lawrence Jackson, Adam Bradley, Darryl Dickson-Carr, and Lawrence Buell. Kathleen Diffley made copious notes that helped refine my thinking, and Garrett Stewart and Ed Folsom advanced my grasp of central concepts. Through conversations with Matt Brown, Loren Glass, and Harry Stecopoulos, I realized how broader developments in Reagan-era America resonated with prizewinning black novelists. The acuity of Deborah Whaley, Richard Turner, Gene Jarrett, Imani Perry, Tim Havens, Marc Connor, Evie Shockley, Fredrick Woodard, Venise Berry, and Sydné Mahone added depth to my interpretations of black cultural production.

Horace Porter vetted no fewer than three full drafts of this manuscript, and his expert guidance took the mystery out of the publication process. When I think of his selfless mentoring, I can only hope to shine for others the way that he lit the path for me. He epitomizes the fact that we do indeed walk on the shoulders of our elders. In a world rapidly retreating from hospitality, he shows the fruits that can be harvested through graciousness. I cannot imagine where I would be without his steadying influence. At The Ohio State University Press, I received brilliant feedback from two anonymous readers and boundless enthusiasm from Sandy Crooms. I do not take these efforts for granted; thank you all.

The Bethel AME Church family buoyed me with their prayers, words, and deeds. To the Hill and Moore clans, I say that the road and the sky that you have covered profoundly attest your love. My daughter Caitlyn lived with this book from the moment that she began kindergarten to her entry into fourth grade. Although she remains suspicious of nonfiction, I hope that she finds this project a worthy reason to have had to share her Daddy. My son Michael Carl was mostly oblivious to my toil, yet he appreciates his expanded ability to monopolize my iPad. To my wife Lena, I dedicate this book to you. You sift my ideas, returning them to me intact, yet improved. At the center of maelstroms, your resolve frees me to forge ahead. You remain my latest and my greatest inspiration.

A New Attitude

Upon being asked whether she experienced "a sense of triumph" when she received the Nobel Prize, Toni Morrison replied, "I felt the way I used to feel at commencements where I'd get an honorary degree: that it was very important for young black people to see a black person do that, that there were probably young people . . . who weren't quite sure that they could do it. But seeing me up there might encourage them . . . That made me happy. It gave me license to strut" (Dreifus 99). In many ways, her sentiments were not new. She echoed a chorus of blacks who viewed their respective firsts as potential spurs to future generations.[1] If her commitment to youth empowerment put her on familiar terrain, then her mention of strutting complicated matters. Strutting is "to walk with an affected air of dignity" or "to . . . swagger" ("Strut," def. 7a, 5a). Although these definitions imply garishness, Morrison's remarks revealed a blend of responsibility, achievement, and style that fueled late twentieth-century black artistic freedom. Her attitude and the era that it captured mark a crucial development in African American literature.

Black writing has long been a tool for fighting racial injustice, and after the Black Arts Movement, this obligation remained a high priority.

---

1. The cultural first has a long tradition in African American experience. For analyses and examples, see Joan Potter's *African American Firsts: Famous Little-Known and Unsung Triumphs of Blacks in America* (2009) and Jessica Carney Smith's *Black Firsts: 4,000 Ground-Breaking and Pioneering Historical Events* (2002).

While most authors agreed that portraying black life required aesthetic and ethical attentiveness, the 1970s debates about such attentiveness revealed a hunger for more autonomy. This hunger reflected a belief that despite America's persistent devaluation of black "moral personality," communities still existed where ethical "codes and sanctions of conduct" were being negotiated (Wilson xix, viii). Although these codes did not eschew Eurocentric influences, they made black cultural values their golden mean.[2] This evolution heralded a declaration of independence. By subordinating white literary expectations to their aims, black writers not only questioned prevailing aesthetics but also the moralities that informed them. This questioning unsettled traditional humanistic assumptions, yet instead of repudiating humanism, authors sought to redeem its virtues while shedding its vices.[3] Among the former, they treasured "justice, brotherhood, and love" (R. Jackson 62). One thing they rued was humanism's misreading of flair.[4]

John Edgar Wideman observes that regardless of the activities, making "a unique statement" is "an Afro-American cultural inheritance." He continues, "'Dr. J' plays basketball very well, but he also uses basketball as a means of self-expression. He has mastered the techniques. So not only do you see basketball (the game) being played, but you see 'Dr. J.' Ideally, that is . . . the way I would like to write a novel" (Samuels 23). With this allusion, the writer suggests swagger—a boldly innovative self-presentation—as a retort to racial prejudice. Swagger here involves more than just ego; it entails cultural recovery. Because slavery and segregation threatened parts of black life, especially aggression and flamboyance, swagger, in the post–civil rights era, became "a way to both reclaim and celebrate viscerally . . . aspect[s] of self that ha[d] historically been eroded" (Bey 153). This idea emerges clearly when the dunk, one of Dr. J's iconic shots, is considered. Defining not just scoring but also master-

2. James S. Hans's *The Sovereignty of Taste* (2002) presents artistic independence as "a quest for personal expression." This quest interacts with market forces, but it adopts taste as "the golden mean,'" "the mechanism on basis of which humans make sense of the world" (2). Hans's perspective clarifies prizewinning black novelists' recalibration of America's literary appetites.

3. Heather Love concludes that even though "African American studies . . . critiqued humanism by pointing to its founding exclusions," the discipline still affirmed "key humanist values" (372). In earlier research, Richard Barksdale, R. Baxter Miller, and George Kent all suggested something similar. See Barksdale's *Praisesong of Survival: Lectures and Essays, 1957–1989* (1992), Miller's *Black American Literature and Humanism* (1981), and Kent's *Blackness and the Adventure of Western Culture* (1972).

4. Describing the "New Humanists of the 1930s," R. Baxter Miller asserted, "Emphasizing gentility, they condemned American naturalism as a 'barbaric' style" (*Black* 2). His reasoning influences my claim about humanism's distrust of flair.

fully improvised identity, Dr. J's dunks embraced black styles and revised the agendas of basketball's white creator.[5] This combination of cultural affirmation and institutional critique showed his expressive authority. By the late twentieth-century, Wideman and other novelists were writing books that heeded Dr. J's cues. Their efforts consolidated the work of prior generations.

Describing his Oklahoma City childhood, Ralph Ellison highlighted "expert players of the 'dozens,'" "old ladies . . . who were defiant of white folk and black alike," and "Negro hustlers . . . who wore Stetson hats, expensive shoes with well-starched overalls" (*Collected* 201). Because they "successfully" fused "form . . . with function," these people—for him—exemplified "elegance" (Ellison, Harper, and Stepto 426). His vision affirmed vernacular panache; nonetheless, his writing presaged the distance from elegance to swagger. Ellison's essay "Change the Joke, Slip the Yoke" (1958) credited T. S. Eliot and James Joyce as inspirations for his use of folk materials.[6] Denying any mimicry, he suggested that these craftsmen emboldened his creative experiments. While his attempts were classic, his executions were dogged by doubt. The mountainous drafts of *Invisible Man* (1952) and the sheer girth of *Three Days Before the Shooting* (2010) attest epic ambition and a genius's agon. If Ellison's talent wrung from black life an ethics of elegance, then a group of post–civil rights novelists brandished an ethics of swagger. This cohort helped secure African American literature's place in the academy, and their prolific prize-winning accelerated the canonization.

---

5. While today's much-hyped contests mask the history, the dunk has interesting racial dimensions. Julius Irving enrolled at the University of Massachusetts in 1968, and for his entire collegiate career, the dunk was illegal. Although this rule could be attributed to many causes, John Edgar Wideman, an all–Ivy League forward at Penn in the early 1960s, claimed that mainstream college basketball sought to curb the improvisatory aspects of the black street game. For more on these issues, see Jeff Greenfield's "The Black and White Truth About Basketball" (1975), Nelson George's *Elevating the Game: Black Men and Basketball* (1992), and Todd Boyd's *Young, Black, Rich, and Famous: The Rise of the NBA, the Hip Hop Invasion, and the Transformation of American Culture* (2003).

6. Ellison observed, "I use folklore in my work not because I am Negro, but because writers like Eliot and Joyce made me conscious of the literary value of my folk inheritance" (*Collected* 111–12). Implicitly engaging this idea, John Edgar Wideman confessed: "I think I had my priorities a little bit mixed up. I felt that I had to prove something about black speech for instance, and about black culture, and that they needed to be imbedded within the larger literary frame. In other words, a quote from T. S. Eliot would authenticate a quote from my grandmother. Or the quote from my grandmother wasn't enough, I had to have a Joycean allusion to buttress it" (Bonetti, "Interview with John" 51). Wideman's misgivings led him to study a black literary tradition that Ellison sometimes deprecated. While bucking that tradition empowered Ellison, his artistry suffered some because he foreswore a vital fellowship.

Until 1953, no black novelist had ever won a major American literary prize.[7] Ralph Ellison ended this drought when he received the National Book Award for *Invisible Man*. During the almost twenty-five years that followed, no other black fiction writer was given a major award.[8] A seventeen-year span near the close of the twentieth century changed this situation. From 1977 to 1993, four tightly grouped clusters of precedent-setting performance occurred. *Song of Solomon* (1977), Toni Morrison's third novel, captured the National Book Critics Circle Award in 1977. Five quiet years ensued, but then the accolades began to pile up. From 1982–84, David Bradley collected a PEN/Faulkner for *The Chaneysville Incident* (1981), Alice Walker earned a National Book Award and a Pulitzer Prize for *The Color Purple* (1982), Gloria Naylor snagged a National Book Award (First Novel) for *The Women of Brewster Place* (1982), and John Edgar Wideman's *Sent For You Yesterday* (1983) also netted a PEN/Faulkner.[9] After a lull, Toni Morrison claimed the 1988 Pulitzer Prize for *Beloved* (1987), while Charles Johnson's *Middle Passage* (1990) became only the fourth African American novel to be honored with a National Book Award. The next year John Edgar Wideman's *Philadelphia Fire* (1990) secured for its writer a second PEN/Faulkner. The final stretch included the single year of 1993 when Ernest Gaines won the National Book Critics Circle Award for *A Lesson Before Dying* (1993) and Toni

7. This study considers the Pulitzer Prize, the National Book Award (NBA), the National Book Critics Circle Award (NBCCA), and the PEN/Faulkner as major American literary prizes. It also takes into account the Nobel Prize, the acme of recognition for writing. While the Nobel, the Pulitzer, and the NBA have been around since 1901, 1918, and 1950, respectively, the NBCCA was first presented in 1974, and the PEN/Faulkner was created in 1981. I acknowledge the arbitrariness of this group, yet I believe that each of the awards signifies the relationship between black novelists' ambitions and white literary standards. In addition, the differences in the sizes, constituencies, and practices of the selections committees means that taken together, these prizes gloss black fiction writers' interactions with the literary marketplace.

8. Although black writers did not win major prizes before the 1940s, segregated awards, especially those sponsored by the NAACP and the National Urban League, played an integral role in promoting artistic expression. For more on these prizes, see Lou-Ann Crouther's "*Crisis, The: Literary Prizes*" (2004) and Abby Arthur and Ronald Mayberry Johnson's *Propaganda and Aesthetics: The Literary Politics of African American Magazines in the Twentieth Century* (1979).

9. A shared moniker generates confusion regarding Alice Walker and Gloria Naylor's honors. During the early 1980s, the National Book Awards were renamed the American Book Awards. The Before Columbus Foundation, a multicultural collective, also conferred what they called the American Book Award. In *The Economy of Prestige: Prizes, Awards, and the Circulation of Cultural Value* (2005), James English states that in "three successive years, the National Book Award went to Gloria Naylor, Paule Marshall, and Alice Walker" (237). Aside from mixing up the chronology of these awards—Naylor and Walker won in 1983, English also confuses Marshall's 1984 Before Columbus Foundation American Book Award with Naylor and Walker's erstwhile National Book Awards. Carol Iannone makes a similar mistake in "Literature By Quota" (1991) when she attributes to Naylor both an NBA and an ABA (51). See Darryl Dickson-Carr (44–45) for more on the Before Columbus Foundation and English (149–52) for a brief history of the National Book Awards.

Morrison was chosen as the first African American ever to win a Nobel Prize in Literature. In conferring this award, the Nobel Committee honored all of Morrison's works, but the proximity of its publication makes *Jazz* (1992) a special case.[10]

The Ethics of Swagger explores how prizewinning novelists between 1977 and 1993 signaled the end of black writers' journeys through insecurity toward autonomy. Identifying these prizewinners—David Bradley, Ernest Gaines, Charles Johnson, Toni Morrison, Gloria Naylor, Alice Walker, and John Edgar Wideman—as a literary class, this monograph focuses on the complex choices that granted these writers creative liberty and contends that black novelists' modernist and postmodernist experiments began succeeding because these authors shed anxieties regarding Eurocentric literary ideas and recovered their own literary traditions. This recovery involved extensive reading of prior African American authors and scrupulous study of their contemporaries' works. By steeping themselves in aesthetics and themes from their own cultural archives, black novelists resolved the quandaries that had vexed post–World War II African American writing. These resolutions inspired evocative attempts to express "the uncreated conscience of democracy," and amid a conservative revolution, their skills garnered them awards that were linked to white control (Henry 191). Award-winning black novelists from 1977–93, a group that I call the Black Archivists, shaped national dialogues about merit, and along the way, they not only altered literature but also the options for black identity. Their efforts responded to civil rights era referendums on racial destiny.

Debating Literary Morals

During the 1960s and 1970s, African American novelists faced a dilemma regarding the representation of black life.[11] Their predicament reflected

---

10. Although I briefly engage novels by Morrison that are either outside of this study's chronology—*The Bluest Eye* (1970) and *Sula* (1973)—or bereft of singular distinction—*Tar Baby* (1981)—these works are somewhat separate from the considerations that I chart in *The Ethics of Swagger*.

11. Dana Williams describes the dilemma that I identify: "Despite having survived Jim Crow and having made significant, though limited, strides during the civil rights movement, African Americans in the 1970s were still largely uncertain about their futures. A leading cause of this uncertainty was the question of personal and, to some degree, communal identity. Previously, African American cultural institutions, including literature, had failed to address this subject adequately. This void became especially pronounced in the post–Jim Crow world, where options for new black identities should have abounded" (x).

uncertainties about writing in a "presumably racially integrated society" (Barksdale 170). While these uncertainties registered mainstream demands that black authors be "properly schooled in Euro-Western techniques and practices," the attitudes also showed fundamental suspicions about all white evaluations of black skill (170). Ralph Ellison and the theorists of the Black Arts Movement vigorously debated the grounds for such suspicions. Ellison acknowledged America's racist legacies, but his faith in democracy convinced him that blacks' suffering made them poignant symbols of the nation's freedom.[12] He thus advocated for a literature that embraced an American tradition including Mark Twain, William Faulkner, T. S. Eliot, and Ernest Hemingway.[13] Convinced that white supremacy threatened truthful representations of African American experience, BAM gainsaid mainstream America's relevance to its literary ethics and advocated art guided by black cultural values.[14] BAM not only vilified the denial of black humanity but also advanced racial solidarity as a creative principle. Although Ellison and BAM disagreed about tone, their vitriol actually registered different notions of vocation.

Ellison and BAM agreed that writing was a moral enterprise; thus, neither lied about America's history of racial injustice. Despite their shared beliefs about the writer's role in searching for truth, they diverged in their notions of what such searching meant for black literature. Disdaining any suggestion that blacks were not heirs of democracy, Ellison concluded that the minority author's first and foremost responsibility was honoring the "quality of the American language" (*Collected* 744). He felt that disciplined craftsmanship provided the most responsible indictment of racism. Wary of a technically refined yet soulless art, proponents of BAM claimed that accurate depictions required tapping into "racial memory, a collective unconsciousness" (N. Harris 6). They were convinced that genuine social progress required "'positive' black images" that challenged white America's moral failures (M. Neal 4). These conflicting notions of vocation extended into disputes about genre.

Black artists, whose formative experiences included segregation, the Great Depression, and World War II, grew disenchanted with the bal-

12. Ellison fully elaborates his thoughts about black suffering and American freedom in "What America Would Be Like Without Blacks" (1970).
13. For evidence of Ellison's affinity for Twain, Faulkner, Eliot, and Hemingway, see the essay "Twentieth Century Fiction and the Black Mask of Humanity" (1953).
14. Larry Neal—a leading spokesman—observed, "The Black Arts Movement is radically opposed to any concept of the artist that alienates him from his community" (1960). Offering more acerbic sentiments, Amiri Baraka contended, "The Black Artist's role in America is to aid in the destruction of America as he knows it" ("State/meant" 169).

kanized narratives produced by sociology and psychology.[15] Intent on exploring the "sentiments sanctioning the processes" of racial oppression, several writers believed that the novel was a perfect form for portraying the individuated impressions and the shared cultural experiences that influenced the African American psyche (L. Jackson, *Indignant* 190). Ellison in *Invisible Man* showcased the novel's truth-telling capacities by capturing "the ambiguities of . . . the racial world" (Byrd, *I Call* 93).[16] If he attended to the moral merits of extended fiction, then influential BAM thinkers such as Amiri Baraka and Maulana Karenga questioned the genre's bourgeois preoccupations. Madhu Dubey explains, "The Black Aesthetic decree that . . . art should address and affirm a unified black community motivated its privileging of certain literary forms over others. Drama and poetry were the preferred genres, for they facilitated direct oral communication between artist and audience" (*Black* 22).[17] This tension between Ellison and BAM's genre choices revisits issues about writing and readership that have long impacted African American literature.

Ellison's emphasis on the shared values of black and white Americans reflects, among other things, his sensitivity to an interracial readership for his publications.[18] If, as scholars have argued, black novelists, since the nineteenth century, have struggled with a racially "divided audience, an audience made up of two elements with differing and antagonistic points of view," then Ellison's situation seemingly lacks novelty

15. In *The Indignant Generation: A Narrative History of African American Writers and Critics, 1934–1960* (2010), Lawrence Jackson explores Horace Cayton as an example of a black intellectual who turned from social sciences and embraced literature. One could argue that writers such as Ralph Ellison, Richard Wright, Ann Petry, and Chester Himes hovered along the boundaries between positivist and creative accounts of black life.

16. Charles Johnson applauds Ellison's contributions in "Where Fiction and Philosophy Meet" (1988), and John Edgar Wideman makes a similar point in "The Language of Home" (1985).

17. Rolland Murray reinforces Dubey's observation: "Breaking with a longer tradition that foregrounded the novel as a vital tool in improving the social standing of the black public, nationalists routinely construed drama, poetry, and autobiography as the preferred modes for disseminating their ideology" (7). Keith Gilyard complicates Dubey and Murray's perception: "The tendency is indeed to think of BAM as largely an outpouring of poems and plays. That's an understandable perception . . . But . . . I think the novel is a larger part of the Black Arts Movement that many folks assume" (R. Lewis). For Ellison's view on BAM and the novel, see (Ellison, Harper, and Stepto 424–25).

18. Ellison's early publishing in leftist journals probably affected his comfort with writing for a racially mixed audience. By connecting his 1950s authorial persona to democratic pluralism, he produces a smooth yet intriguing shift in his conception of racial integration. See Barbara Foley's *Wrestling With the Left: The Making of Ralph Ellison's Invisible Man* (2010) for a sustained discussion of these transitions.

(J. Johnson, "Dilemma" 378).[19] What makes his position so significant is the expectant atmosphere of the civil rights struggle. Where once the black author risked limiting himself to the "monotypical, glorified, and race-proud" fictions expected by blacks or "the old stereotypes" demanded by whites, Ellison, BAM authors, and other black writers encountered a 1960s and 1970s world where richer possibilities flourished (L. Jackson, *Indignant* 271). Ellison saw these opportunities as support for his integrationist stance, but BAM remained skeptical about black entry into the American mainstream. If their skepticism reflected paradoxes such as the concomitant growth of the black middle class, poverty, and incarceration,[20] then it also suggested their wrestling with the idea that without "white . . . commitment to imposing black inferiority, African American literature would not have existed as a literature" (Warren 17).[21] These musings on white oppression's role in black literature prompted Ellison and BAM to engage the New Critical underpinnings of American aesthetics.

Stressing the literary text as a self-contained product, the New Critics rose to prominence between the 1930s and the 1950s.[22] Ralph Ellison appreciated their attention to form and was quite friendly with Robert Penn Warren, one of the movement's early advocates. If Ellison embraced some of the method's mandates, then BAM sought to uncover "the covert ideological agenda" of New Criticism and to discount its dismissal

19. Claudia Tate's *Domestic Allegories of Political Desire: The Black Heroine's Text at the Turn of the Century* (1992); Ann DuCille's *The Coupling Convention: Sex, Text, and Tradition in Black Women's Fiction* (1993); Robert Reid-Pharr's *Conjugal Unions: The Body, The House, and the Black American* (1999); and Caroline Gebhard and Barbara McCaskill's edited collection *Post-Bellum, Pre-Harlem: African American Literature and Culture, 1877–1919* (2006) all engage the efforts of early African American novelists to make their works meaningful not only for their "first readers—middle-and working class-black men and women" but also for white audiences (Tate, *Domestic* 5). Their analyses suggest that James Weldon Johnson's 1928 essay, "The Dilemma of the Negro Author," arises from a well-defined lineage.

20. These facts struck black writers not only through headlines but also personally. In particular, the Black Archivists often struggled with their own better-heeled lifestyles and their interactions with impoverished or imprisoned family members. In *Brothers and Keepers* (1984), John Edgar Wideman juxtaposes his plight and that of Robby, his brother who is serving a long-term jail sentence. These juxtapositions are not confined to the late twentieth century. As recently as CNN's 2008 series "Black in America," Michael Eric Dyson was interviewed with his brother, Everett, who is incarcerated.

21. Addison Gayle observed that the white ability "to define the terms in which the Black artist will deal with his own experience" had bedeviled black writing throughout its history (105).

22. John Crowe Ransom, a major expositor of New Criticism, presented his early views on the self-contained literary text in "Criticism, Inc" (1937), writing that the literary work, specifically the poem, should be analyzed as "a desperate ontological or metaphysical manoeuvre" (601). By 1941, he offered a more expansive version of his ideas in *The New Criticism*.

of black expression (Dubey, *Black* 9).[23] BAM felt that notwithstanding the purported objectivity of New Criticism, its interpretations were prejudiced. Even though Ellison maligned BAM's mindsets as "provincialism," the radical writers remained anxious about his deep commitment to incorporating Edmund Wilson's commentaries on symbolism and Andre Malraux's ideas about ideological art (*Collected* 212).[24] The impasse here seems methodological, but more profoundly the disagreement centers on who defines and confers esteem. These meditations have intriguing intraracial dimensions, but with the push toward integration, their interracial aspects are amplified. Nowhere is this clearer than in prizewinning.

Notwithstanding the few blacks that served on the selection committees for major American literary awards during the late twentieth century, these entities still existed as purveyors of white cultural taste. Because prize committees had that reputation, black writers maintained an uneasy relationship with mainstream awards. This uneasiness stemmed from ironic attitudes toward recognition. If "artistic activities" demand assessments that go beyond "material profit," then prizes become a "system" for estimating "the quality of" creative "work" and for determining the "esteem" that should be "granted to the work's creator" (Heinich 89). Major American literary awards claimed this systematic function; nonetheless, the legacy of racism colored their actions. While black writers noticed racial bias in mainstream awards, many remained invested in the prize system. Their investment reflected a simple truth of combatting inequality. Because white supremacy impugns the black ability to compete with whites, freedom for blacks requires addressing such imputations. The most effective response overwhelms injustice with virtuosity. Although this outlook casts racism as a pliable force, it also gives the prize-grantor immense power over the recognition process. Shifts from this prestige-oriented model to an esteem-based concept set the stage for

23. For more on how the black literature/New Criticism saga impacted the atmosphere in which prizewinning black novelists from 1977–93 honed their artistry, see John Edgar Tidwell's "The Birth of a Black New Criticism" (1979), Ronald A. T. Judy's (*Dis)forming the Canon: African-Arabic Slave Narratives and the Vernacular* (1993), and Joyce Ann Joyce's *Richard Wright's Art of Tragedy* (1991). Lawrence Jackson deals with New Criticism and mid-twentieth-century black writing in *The Indignant Generation*.

24. Ellison's comment on provincialism takes place during his *Paris Review* interview, and his charges emanate from precise developments in 1930s intellectual history. Despite such precision, they reflect his general preference for engaging white Western criticism, a preference that rankled Black Arts Movement thinkers. See John S. Wright's *Shadowing Ralph Ellison* (2006), especially the chapter "Ellison's Spiritual Technologies," and Lawrence Jackson's *Ralph Ellison: Emergence of Genius* (2002) for meticulous accounts of Ellison's encounters with the writings Edmund Wilson and Andre Malraux.

the Black Archivists, and the history of blacks winning literary awards shows why.[25]

Beginning in 1950 with Gwendolyn Brooks's Pulitzer Prize for *Annie Allen* (1949), several black writers won major awards. These achievements, in the early days of the civil rights movement, were often seen through the lens of what Pierre Bourdieu calls "a domination effect" (Heinich 102). Because white prize-granting bodies controlled honor, black prize seekers received recognition when they met those bodies' expectations.[26] African American writers, particularly poets and dramatists, garnered mainstream awards from the 1950s through the end of the twentieth century, but as the century advanced, they called into question white prize-grantors' postures toward evaluation.[27] Although black writers of the 1960s often viewed mainstream awards as instruments that

25. Prestige-based analyses view prizes as "a matter of power-relations among others" whereas esteem-driven models see awards as "a matter of personal identity and social interdependency" (Heinich 86). Pierre Bourdieu pioneers the prestige template, and James English and Ashraf Rushdy apply his ideas about the "field of cultural production" (Rushdy, *Neo-Slave* 8). Although my study benefits from their insights, I also rely on Nathalie Heinich's notion of esteem to sketch the relationship between the Black Archivists' experiences with white literary expectations and their uncovering of black artistic traditions. Heinch's ideas show that "the antagonistic, competitive, and unequal dimensions of recognition" involve awards juries, peer judgment, and creative confidence (103). Since the late twentieth century marks prizewinning black novelists' movement from a "weak socialization" in their artistic activities to a stronger one, the interrelatedness of these agents' roles in recognition increases (Heinich 92). *The Ethics of Swagger* considers that phenomenon via artistic fellowship.

26. Brooks's beliefs about how domination impacted her pre-1960s work surfaced in a 1971 interview. Analyzing her award-winning verses, she said that she "could not imagine herself [in the 1970s] writing the kind of poem whose theme was a pleading of her humanity to a larger white society" (Henderson 17–18). Her sentiments recalled a 1954 interview in which Ralph Ellison warned that black writers should not "indulge" the "false issue" created by "white people" questioning black "humanity" (*Collected* 213). These outlooks show a heightening independence among black writers that crests with the Black Archivists.

27. In both poetry and drama, black writers have had consistent success in getting nominated for and winning major awards. Alice Walker was a finalist for the 1974 National Book Award in poetry. In addition to serving as national poet laureate, Rita Dove won the Pulitzer Prize for poetry in 1987. Since then, Yusef Komunyakaa has won the 1994 National Book Award, and Lucille Clifton received that same prize in 2000. Recently, Natasha Trethewey won the Pulitzer Prize in 2007, and Nikky Finney received the National Book Award in 2011. Black dramatists boast an even more extensive record of accomplishment. In 1956 Alice Childress's play *Trouble in Mind* (1955) won an Obie, making her the first black woman to be so honored. In 1959 Lorraine Hansberry's *A Raisin in the Sun* (1959) won the New York Drama Critics Circle Award. By 1964 two black playwrights received Obies, Adrienne Kennedy for *Funnyhouse of a Negro* (1962) and Amiri Baraka for *Dutchman* (1964). *No Place to be Somebody* (1969) by Charles Gordone won the Pulitzer Prize in 1970, marking the first time that a black playwright had ever gained that distinction. Ed Bullins received Obies in both 1971 and 1975 for *The Fabulous Miss Marie* (1971) and *The Taking of Miss Janie* (1975) respectively. The latter play also won the New York Drama Critics Circle Award. In 1974 Ntozake Shange's *For Colored Girls Who Have Considered Suicide When the Rainbow Is Enuf* (1975) also collected an Obie. Since the early 1980s, August Wilson and Suzan-Lori Parks have cemented black playwrights' places in the pantheon of American award winning.

"the motley crew of little white fathers" used to police American literary excellence, later authors acknowledged that prizes were not necessarily evidence of submission to white creative values (Killens 30).[28] This acknowledgment dawned dramatically among black novelists, and their sense of vocation blended esteem and cultural conservation. This blending occurred because writers clarified their creative legacies and strengthened their professional fellowship. Resulting in a slew of major awards, these two developments revealed the impact of discovering black literary archives.

Repositories of Wonder

The present availability of books such as *The Norton Anthology of African American Literature* (1997) makes it hard to remember that the study of black writing only blossomed fully in the 1980s.[29] Although a host of factors caused this blossoming, prizewinning novelists played pivotal roles. These roles not only reflected their efforts after receiving awards but also their actions beforehand. Of these precursor actions, few resonated as powerfully as their revitalization of black literary traditions. The debates between Ellison and BAM bedeviled aspiring black novelists from 1960 well into the 1970s, and because of their acrimony, the belief in a coherent if diverse history of black writing yielded to a vision of polarized encampments. Propelled by teaching obligations, editing responsibilities, and unconfirmed hunches, David Bradley, Ernest Gaines, Charles Johnson, Toni Morrison, Gloria Naylor, Alice Walker, and John

28. John Oliver Killens once mockingly expressed how the white mainstream would attempt to bribe black writers: "You'll never win the prizes or the critics' adulation unless you cool your anger . . . Keep criticizing society and you'll . . . incur the wrath of us white reviewers, who . . . would really like to bring you into the fold. Oh yes, in spite of the fact that you are a Negro, you too can join the club if you'll just play down your Negro-ness." While Killens's remark captures the irreverent wit that pervades his 1965 essay collection *Black Man's Burden*, it also articulates his opinion regarding his novel *And Then We Heard The Thunder* (1962), which was nominated for the Pulitzer Prize. He suggests that "a writer who writes to . . . win National Book Awards" runs the risk of forgetting his obligation to "tell as much of the truth as he knows the painful truth to be" (31).

29. Preceding *The Norton Anthology of African American Literature* (1997) by more than two decades, landmark works such as Richard Barksdale and Kenneth Kinnamon's *Black Writers of America* (1972) made "it possible to teach African American literature survey courses without assigning multiple texts" (Dickson-Carr 59). *Negro Caravan* (1941), *Calvacade* (1971), and *From the Dark Tower* (1974) joined *Black Writers of America* as pioneering early attempts to package African American literature for college curriculums. For more on the importance of these efforts, see the introductions to *Call and Response: The Riverside Anthology of the African American Literary Tradition* (1998) and *The Norton Anthology of African American Literature*.

Edgar Wideman examined the literary past and concluded that it held something more than fractures. These novelists felt that prior black writings constituted rich archives of themes and aesthetics. Convinced that these archives could promote resonant artistries, Bradley, Gaines, Johnson, Morrison, Naylor, Walker, and Wideman crafted novels that juxtaposed white expectations and black traditions. Their results showed fellowship's contribution to creative accomplishment.

Alice Walker's mid-1970s search for Zora Neale Hurston's grave literalizes the digging that precedes the unearthing of black literary legacies. If this kind of intragender recovery is well documented, then other late twentieth-century impulses toward restoring artistic elders are underappreciated.[30] Walker championed Langston Hughes as a nurturing predecessor, and Wideman's study of Phillis Wheatley aided his understanding of vernacular language. While these novelists studied the African American literary past for complicated and distinct reasons, each was convinced that such study would enrich her or his art. Their award-winning peers shared these convictions. The label Black Archivists appropriately names prizewinning African American novelists between 1977 and 1993 because they scoured academic collections and touted skillful writers such as Hurston, Hughes, Wheatley, Jean Toomer, Dorothy West, and Wallace Thurman.[31] If trips to libraries familiarized the Black Archivists with their forbears, then complementarily these authors also began looking to their contemporaries for camaraderie, criticism, and inspiration. These searches produced an imagined and an imaginative community that featured meticulous readings, resourceful promotion, and rigorous critiques.[32] Generating many benefits, this communion diversified the novelists' artistic approaches. These diversifications showed how black literary archives vitiate the impact of white creative standards.

Whether one considers the gothic postmodernism of *Beloved,* the epistolary frame of *The Color Purple,* the ship's log structure of *Middle*

30. Michael Awkward and Karla Holloway have identified a black female literary tradition, and their work builds upon earlier studies by Barbara Christian, Gloria Wade-Gayles, and Claudia Tate. These analyses have companion texts by Jeffrey Leak and Keith Clark that explore masculinity. Though gendered interpretations provide insights, they sometimes reify distorting divisions. The Black Archivists illustrate the rich if spirited exchanges that enlivened both inter- and intragender artistic interactions in late twentieth-century African American writing.

31. For authors such as Morrison, Wideman, and Walker, discovering a black literary tradition meant completing extensive research in repositories such as the Schomburg Library or the Moorland-Spingarn Center. Johnson and Naylor respectively parlayed academic research and professional curiosity into a scholarly monograph and a creative writing thesis.

32. My phrasing and thinking owe a debt to Benedict Anderson's *Imagined Communities: Reflections on the Origin and Spread of Nationalism* (1991).

Passage, or the observer-hero dynamic in *A Lesson Before Dying,* the
Black Archivists' technical diversity is considerable. One could argue
that this variety seems derivative. For example, after reading Edgar Allan
Poe's *The Fall of the House of Usher* (1839), Morrison might have decided
that gothic conventions made sense for her next novel. Likewise, Charles
Johnson's perusal of Herman Melville's *Moby Dick* (1851) might have
convinced him that narration in the form of a ship's log would work
well. Some literary criticism emphasizes the cosmopolitan sensibilities
of late twentieth-century black writers and speculates about this sort of
cross-cultural influence. Even as such scholarship's "intertextual readings"
effectively chart black-white collaboration in the service of a pluralistic "American consciousness," these analyses run the risk of "once more
subsuming the particularities of experiences written as black beneath an
occupying force of white determinations" (Nielsen 22).[33] Prizewinning
black novelists between 1977 and 1993 resist such occupations through
their choice of themes.[34]

Novels such as *The Chaneysville Incident, Jazz,* and *Philadelphia Fire*
consolidate slavery, segregation, the Great Migration, and urban blight as
prisms through which post–civil rights black existence should be examined.[35] Though these books bear the respective imprints of Robert Penn
Warren's historical imagination, F. Scott Fitzgerald's urban lyricism, and
Don DeLillo's technological anxiety, their engagements with elemental
aspects of twentieth century black life stifle explanations that seek to
read them exclusively through the "central norm" of white literary aesthetics (Nielsen 21). Late twentieth-century black novelists felt that part
of their art's power stemmed from the shared rituals underlying their
book's themes. As they commemorated these traditions, their blending
of aesthetic influences and recurring experiences produced a significant
collection.

33. bell hooks observes that American pluralism's demands that its black citizens "forsake attachment to race and/or cultural identity and be 'just humans'" often represents a call to adopt
"the values and beliefs of privileged-class whites" (*Killing* 266).

34. Simon Gikandi observes that Robert Hayden's major works probed "the black subject,
confronted by the harsh realities of everyday life." This individual dealt with "cultural negativity,"
but through "creative imagination," he, like his author, strove "to bring some of the . . . ugliness—
of modern life into a measure of control" (318–19). Gikandi's remarks explain the negotiations
that the Black Archivists make with their choices of themes (322).

35. Several studies of the African American novel explore how changes in late 20th century
historiography impacted narrative techniques and the choices of themes. For a sampling, see Keith
Byerman's *Remembering the Past in Contemporary Fiction* (2005), Ashraf Rushdy's *Neo-Slave Narratives: Studies in the Social Logic of a Literary Form* (1999), and Philip Page's *Reclaiming Community in
Contemporary African American Fiction* (1999).

Xiomara Santamarina, in "'Are We There Yet?': Archives, History, and Specificity in African American Literary Studies" (2008), argues that the scrutiny of Diasporic interactions has obscured vital domestic developments in black literature.[36] She concludes that "literary periodization" must be examined for discrete African American genres to receive "the close readings and the historical analyses that [their] texts demand" (309). Prizewinning black novels from 1977–93 underscore her point. While the proportions of attention differ, all of the award-winning texts by the Black Archivists have provoked careful critical analysis. These analyses, for the most part, lionize poststructuralist, postmodern, or cosmopolitan versions of these novels' sophistication, but these studies have overlooked the collective dimensions of the Black Archivists' achievements.

The Black Archivists and their peers represent the last class of African American novelists that witnessed as opposed to heard about the civil rights movement. Understanding segregation's structural oppression, these writers considered racism's etchings on black character. Those markings, while integral, did not hide other contours of identity. From these experiences, the collective shaped an art defined by ""true literacy" that is "not just the contemplative awareness of, and cowardly escape from, the fictions that others would impose on [African Americans] but the assertion of [their] own fiction[s], namely . . . an assertion that enables [them] to redefine the conceptual and cultural dictates of [their] world" (R. Miller, "Deeper" 52). Nowhere is this literacy more evident than in the group's multivalent yet galvanizing commitment to creative autonomy. By attending to swagger, black prizewinning novelists from 1977 to 1993 signaled their profound aims.

You Don't Know My Style

During the late twentieth- and early twenty-first centuries, athletes such as Florence Griffith Joyner, Michael Jordan, the Williams Sisters, and Michael Vick, along with rappers, especially Jay Z and Lil Wayne, made swagger something more than just confidence. These performers linked the concept to creative freedom, and their linkage produced paradoxical effects. If swagger expressed transcendent talent, then it also registered an

---

36. Bernard Bell's *The Contemporary African American Novel: Its Folk Roots and Modern Literary Branches* (2005) similarly critiques the transnational impulses in the criticism of the African American novel.

audacity that could be deemed offensive.[37] This ambivalence betrayed not only a peculiar racial history but also a longer American struggle with styles of success. Prizewinning novelists from 1977 to 1993 joined a wave of black achievers that had been gaining momentum since the 1950s. While the civil rights movement turned all black accomplishments into propaganda, developments in the post–civil rights era caused onlookers to question mainstream recognition.[38] Skeptical blacks suspected that cultural assimilation demanded draconian sacrifices. In the 1980s, white commentators fed up with affirmative action, multiculturalism, and political correctness contended that excellence had been compromised. Black novelists wrote in this climate in which the meaning of their skills was indecipherable, and they used swagger to refine their aesthetics. Their choices recalled earlier moments in American literary history.

The Black Archivists sought to transform the novel. Although their respective approaches ranged from renovating philosophical fiction to revising modernist indeterminacy, they were united in the belief that fattening one's style could resolve black writings' ethical dilemmas. Their attitudes returned the nation to its uneasy truces with Walt Whitman and William Faulkner. Complaining in 1859 that the poet affected "swagger" and confused "vulgar impertinence" with "originality," one of Whitman's reviewers named the anxieties stoked by bold, unorthodox artistry (Anonymous, "Walt"). The same daring that granted Whitman "the swagger of a prophet" prompted others to associate him with American "rowdyism" (Buchanan 218; Price 166).[39] Between these poles of prophecy and bluster, a moral conundrum festered. Faulkner illuminated this problem in his portrait of *Absalom, Absalom!*'s Thomas Sutpen. While

37. In 2011, Touré stated that Michael Vick's playing style lampooned "the whole regimented militaristic ethos" of football ("What"). This description evokes the transformative impact of Flo-Jo in track and field, Jordan in basketball, Venus and Serena in tennis, and Jay Z and Lil Wayne in pop music. Although these eccentrics gain admiration, their arrogance when wedded to black expressive styles often riles mainstream commentators. For evidence of such controversy, see David Zirin's "The Women GQ Ignored" (2011), Nat Charles' "The Williams Sisters: Reveling in the Richness of Black Beauty" (2002), Delia Douglass' "To Be Young, Gifted, and Black" (2002), Rick Reilly's "Be Like Michael Jordan, No Thanks" (2009), and Touré's "What If Michael Vick Were White?" (2011). Jay Z and Lil Wayne, in songs like "All I Need" (2001) and "Dr. Carter" (2008), cleverly allude to the collisions between their expressive skills and mainstream tastes.

38. Ralph Bunche's 1950 Nobel Peace Prize, Althea Gibson's 1957 Wimbledon singles title, and Sidney Poitier's 1963 Best Actor Award epitomized the dignified black triumph that affirmed the civil rights movement's integrationist goals. If these events captured black autonomy as a nonthreatening enterprise, then Tommie Smith and John Carlos' black power salute at the 1968 Olympics showed victory as an intimidating possibility. These paradoxical perspectives suggest the conundrums posed by black achievement in the late twentieth century.

39. Warm thanks to Ed Folsom for guiding to me to these nuggets regarding Whitman and swagger.

the southern gentry appreciated Sutpen's willfulness, his "swagger" made him suspect (Faulkner 10). He transgressed social codes, but more than that, his self-possession shook the community's sense of itself. Revising Whitman and Sutpen's circumstances, the Black Archivists used encounters between replete personality and censoring society to show America's myopia. They made the nation's difficulty with the ethics of swagger a part of their creativity and, in so doing, provoked alternate views of talent, recognition, and independence.

The Black Archivists understood that by the late 1970s, social changes were diversifying the material conditions of African Americans. Despite accepting this fact, they also noted that America's history of oppression exerted immense pressure on black culture. Their novels attempted to relieve this pressure through swagger. With works whose aesthetics and themes reflected rigorous study of multiple literary traditions, the Black Archivists crafted a canon that subjected judgments regarding taste and skill to black culture's rich imperatives. A scene from John Edgar Wideman's *Sent For You Yesterday* suggests swagger's place in this development. Pondering what to do with a "souvenir," Doot—a narrator—muses: "My grandfather's brown hat rests in the top of my cupboard . . . I don't know what to do with it . . . Should I consider wearing it? Would John French like the idea of his hat reborn, his grandson wearing his swagger, his country-boy, city-boy lid?" (116–17). If swagger here denotes the hat, then is autonomous black expression merely a matter of accessorizing? Does Doot's ability to don his grandfather's swagger mean that he inherits his independence?

Wideman's depiction alludes to the intimate choices of style that enrich identity; thus, John French's hat, an emblem of the rural/urban, nurturing/dangerous fusion within his character, marks his presence in an effacing world. If French's lid is indeed a souvenir, then it is one that commemorates the deep meanings inscribed in black life. Doot, the aspiring writer, wonders what to do with his grandfather's hat because he has not yet claimed authority over his family's or his culture's experiences. Such authority commences with the recovery of traditions. Like Doot, the Black Archivists discover possibilities for literary innovation in their histories, and by analyzing these histories the novelists can reject "unintentional bribes from the whites" even as they compel mainstream critics toward admiring estimates of their work (Hughes 1270). This admiration translates into prizes, and prizewinning signaled a key byproduct of swagger. A look at a writer who never won a major prize, Ishmael Reed, proves illustrative of that development.

Reed, on the strength of his third novel, *Mumbo Jumbo* (1972), was one of twelve finalists for the 1973 National Book Award.[40] During the 1960s, the committees that decided the Pulitzer Prize and the NBA virtually ignored black novelists; thus, his distinction could have been viewed as progress.[41] Despite that perspective's allure, Reed did not believe that the mainstream American literary establishment had undergone a change of heart. He proclaimed, "When you look at the Pulitzer Prize committee, there's a president from Dow Jones on it, and mostly white males— [the situation is the same with] the American Book Awards." According to Reed, once a black writer knew "these things," then he could "see the motivation" behind both these prize committee's choices and the concessions that an artist might make to get these kinds of recognitions (Martin 180).[42] Reed's cynicism perhaps reflected spite that he had never got his due from American prize granting agencies. Still, his contentions carry interesting clues for understanding black novelists who won prizes.

Contemplating the shift from segregation to integration, the Black Archivists concluded that swagger demanded less a renunciation of pluralistic democracy, à la the Black Arts Movement, or deference to white Western aesthetics, à la Ralph Ellison, and more the responsible attention to the full contents of black America's literary archives. Whether via the transition from slavery to freedom or the move from rural to urban spaces, black prizewinning novels between 1977 and 1993 addressed epochal historical crises.[43] These books examined America's willingness

40. Between Ralph Ellison's 1953 triumph and Alice Walker and Gloria Naylor's breakthroughs in 1983, James Baldwin, Reed, and Barry Beckham are among the few black nominees for the National Book Award. Baldwin was nominated in 1957 for *Giovanni's Room* (1956), and Beckham's *Runner Mack* (1972) received a nomination in 1973. Joe Weixlmann talks about the latter's nomination in "The Dream Turned 'Daymare': Barry Beckham's *Runner Mack*" (1981).

41. An exception to these committees' general neglect of black fiction, John Oliver Killens's novels *And Then We Heard The Thunder* (1962) and *The Cotillion, or One Good Bull is Half the Herd* (1971) were both nominated for the Pulitzer Prize. Killens's nominations were intriguing because to some, he "will always be associated with the Black Arts Movement" and art that emphasizes "activism" (R. Lewis).

42. Reed's most vitriolic claims regarding black novelists' selling out are directed at Alice Walker and *The Color Purple*. He contends, "I call these black feminists, people like Alice Walker, the kind of novels they write, I call them 'neoconfederate' novelists, the kind of writing that Thomas Dixon wrote in *The Clansman*. This kind of plantation literature, they're just reviving these notions, whipping up hysteria, and they're supported by people like Gloria Steinem—Susan Brown Miller was a judge on the committee which gave Alice Walker the American Book Award, and this was her reward for being the intellectual midwife of Susan Brown Miller's terrible and really fallacious ideas about black men" (Martin 179). When Reed mentions the American Book Award, he is referring to what is most widely known as the National Book Award. See note above for more on this issue.

43. Handling slavery in *Beloved* and *Middle Passage*, segregation in *The Color Purple* and *A Lesson Before Dying*, the Great Migration in *Jazz* and *The Women of Brewster Place*, and ambivalent

to exploit as opposed to confront black life and considered the consequences of the nation's indifference toward those who struggled to affirm its myths. Sensing in this situation not the rabid prejudice that typified pre–civil rights black life but an absurd outlook on black existence, the Black Archivists questioned received wisdom in ways that differentiated them from both the post–World War II and the Black Arts Movement classes of writers. Their questioning apprehended "the forms of things unknown" and exposed those forms to the ethics of swagger.[44]

The Black Archivists rejected a blind faith in democracy and moved beyond anxiety about Eurocentric models of artistry. Nevertheless, even as they struggled to achieve artistic autonomy, they rejected oversimplifications. They did not try to create, like Amiri Baraka, a literature enraptured by "the destruction of America" ("Revolutionary" 1902). Nor did they seek, like Ralph Ellison, to "reduce the chaos of living to form" (*Collected* 229). Instead, they refined their understanding of the irreconcilable complexity of black American existence and sought an "uncompromised" way of "making the statement[s]" they "wanted to make" (Baraka, Liner). This book chronicles that process and its indelible legacy for African American literary history.

Scaffolds

This study has two parts: Part I, "White Expectations," and Part II, "Black Traditions." Part I considers how Toni Morrison's *Beloved,* Alice Walker's *The Color Purple,* Charles Johnson's *Middle Passage,* and Ernest Gaines's *A Lesson Before Dying* explore the pressures that white opinions exert on black novels. By focusing on prize granting, mentors, and narration, this part shows that white authority shaped black novelists' investment in the ethics of swagger.

Analyzing Morrison's portrayal of Sethe and Paul D's love affair in *Beloved,* chapter 1 argues that the triangle formed by the couple, their

---

urbanity in *Song of Solomon, The Chaneysville Incident, Sent For You Yesterday,* and *Philadelphia Fire,* the Black Archivists evoked key touch-points of twentieth-century African American life.

44. Taken from Shakespeare, the phrase "the forms of things unknown" has been used prominently by Richard Wright in *White Man, Listen!* (1957) and Stephen Henderson in *Understanding the New Black Poetry: Black Speech & Black Music as Poetic References* (1972). For Wright and Henderson, this phrase becomes shorthand for the vital resources of black folk experiences, especially those related to music. See John Carpenter's chapter, "'The Forms of Things Unknown': Richard Wright and Stephen Henderson's Quiet Appropriations" (2008), for more on this phrase's history in black critical writings.

former slaveholders, and their black elders symbolizes Morrison's struggles to balance the demands of her life experiences, prize selection committees, and the black literary past. Initially, white forces distort her and the couple's respective projects, but eventually both agents discover how black cultural memory can transform desire. While these discoveries promise no deliverance from white influences, whether slave-owners' legacies or awards juries' deliberations, they do reveal that black ethical priorities can sublimate mainstream attitudes.

In chapter 2, white authority figures haunt the protagonists of *The Color Purple* and *Middle Passage,* as these black orphans cast about for roots, families, and coherent selfhood. Linking the central characters' situations to their plights as novelists, Walker and Johnson suggest how their white mentors inspired these novels' back-to-Africa plots. Just as their protagonists cannot abandon America's multiracial democracy, Walker and Johnson find that Africa, while it aids moral clarity, cannot resolve black American uncertainty about white cultural power. Such resolution, for them and their characters, entails authorizing one's self to select from multiple, potentially edifying traditions.

Chapter 3 avers that *A Lesson Before Dying* connects its protagonists' searches for dignity in Jim Crow America to late twentieth-century black novelists' interactions with putatively white styles of representation. If segregation limited black personality, then white narrative strategies likewise threatened to enervate black writing. While Gaines acknowledges this threat, he contends that creative control requires resisting artistic trends and honoring black rural grace. He, like his characters, grounds self-expression in black humanism's critique of American democracy.

If part I stresses how prizewinning black novelists' depictions of slavery, Reconstruction, and segregation reflect their struggles with white expectations, then part II ponders how Gloria Naylor's *The Women of Brewster Place,* Toni Morrison's *Jazz* and *Song of Solomon,* David Bradley's *The Chaneysville Incident,* and John Edgar Wideman's *Sent For You Yesterday* and *Philadelphia Fire* use black literary traditions—especially communion without consensus, ambivalent inheritance, and fruitful failure—to refine the ethics of swagger.

Examining *Women* and *Jazz*'s accounts of the Great Migration, chapter 4 contends that the urban lostness in these novels is a metaphor of late twentieth-century black fiction writing. Naylor and Morrison present nourishing communities that are not conflict-free. By critiquing facile unity, their books imply that fellowship hinges less on consensus and more on communion. Naylor's and Morrison's aggressive revisions of one another's works also discount unanimity, yet they provide discriminating scrutiny in place of voyeurism, a benefit that offers a firmer, if more challenging, foundation for black literature.

In chapter 5, the protagonists of *Song of Solomon* and *The Chaneysville Incident* battle with bourgeois inheritance in the post–*Brown v. Board* urban city. Connecting these characters' dilemmas to their own 1970s attempts at writing fiction, Morrison and Bradley suggest that taking full possession of the black past requires blending northern and southern sensibilities. This blending, for characters and writers, recalls love's crucial role in confronting America's dispossessions. Emphasizing the possibilities that earlier sacrifices earned, these books and their authors change commemoration from a burden to a benefit.

Chapter 6 analyzes *Sent For You Yesterday* and *Philadelphia Fire*'s depictions of failed artists. Placing Wideman's discovery of black literature against the backdrop of his family tragedies, this chapter asserts that his books' proper topics are losses that threaten empathy. Wideman meets such losses with urgent experimentation and shapes a melancholy yet commanding expression. Despite his command, his apprehensions about art's inadequate impact on black fate feed his measured perspective on achievement. Wideman's outlook registers misgivings that his fellow prizewinners share; nonetheless, sober undertones do not diminish the refulgence of the ethics of swagger.

While critics such as Stanley Crouch and Carol Iannone see Reagan era black prizewinning as evidence of "the soft bigotry of low expectations," the Black Archivists combine strong cultural identification and prodigious skills to demand notice of their excellence.[45] They are varied voices candidly expressing American blackness. Even when diverse constituencies, sometimes even competing ones, find their justifying narratives in the Black Archivists canon, they still confront these writers' artistic authority, authority that is not impervious to but is unperturbed by the agendas of others. Claudia Tate enhances our grasp of these developments by identifying "the tension between . . . personal desire

45. Stanley Crouch claims that Ellison's 1953 National Book Award is especially significant because "it preceded nearly every citation of excellence being overwhelmed by or selling out to the politics of race, class, sex, and sexual preference" ("Ralph"). Carol Iannone likewise derides the awards received by Toni Morrison, Charles Johnson, and Alice Walker as concessions to political correctness. Quoting Chinua Achebe, she says that she believes that these race-sensitive awards selections promote "a dictatorship of mediocrity" ("Literature" 53). The phrase "the soft bigotry of low expectations" is often associated with President George Bush, and as early as a July 20, 2000 speech to the NAACP, he used it to identify the mindset of those who would provide preferential treatment to unqualified blacks and other minorities.

and political demand" as a crucial site in black literature (*Psychoanalysis* 5). The Black Archivists noted the vast political significance of winning major prizes; however, their artistries also prominently reflected cravings after resplendent performance. Thus, their desire signals not just the yearning for cultural progress but also the pursuit of artistic improvement. These blended appetites defined the ethics of swagger and led the late twentieth-century African American novel to unparalleled distinction.

White Expectations

one

Beloved and
Black Prizewinning

In the twenty-first century, Toni Morrison's lofty stature seems almost preordained. Her writing epitomizes serious fiction, and she is that rarity, a black literary celebrity. Although her popularity remains high, her career inspires dissent. Some critics extol her as innovative while others dismiss her as imitative. If this disagreement, given the subjectivity of artistic judgments, is predictable, it also hints at how racial realities influence creativity. Morrison, more than any of the Black Archivists, noted the profits and the perils that attended black novels' broader circulation in white mainstream channels. Because of her careful cost/benefit analysis, certain commentators deem her an opportunist. Such detractions are whispered today, but when her fifth novel, *Beloved,* was published in 1987, they were voiced raucously. Since criticism about *Beloved* often concentrates on post-publication events, Morrison's mindset before she completed the novel rarely gets full scrutiny. Such neglect obscures her encounters with white literary expectations. When these encounters are examined, her plight along with that of other Reagan era black novelists crystallizes.

Beloved is usually viewed as the crowning text of Morrison's literary rise,[1] and by the 1980s, when she planned and wrote this book, her career

---

1. A 2006 *New York Times Book Review* poll recognized *Beloved* as "the single best work of American fiction published in the last 25 years" (Anonymous, "What"). This accomplishment recalled Ralph Ellison's distinction when in 1965, the *New York Herald Tribune* recognized *Invisible*

was ascending. Despite the ascendancy, she felt uncertain about black fiction. She believed that the novel was becoming an important genre for African Americans, yet she found too few writers who were recording the legacies that integration threatened to erase.[2] She feared that this disregard for cultural preservation would rob the black novelist of her moorings. If Morrison sought to thwart such robberies and challenge mainstream America's distorted portraits of black life, then her interest in literary prizes, an interest born in the 1970s, suggested her complex relationship with white aesthetic judgments. Notwithstanding the voluminous criticism that *Beloved* has inspired, not much attention has been paid to how the book's themes dramatize its author's grappling with the black novelist's pursuit of artistic autonomy. This grappling emerges via a black couple's search for love in the context of white supremacy. Reflecting both her interest in cultural history and her meditations on black fiction and prizewinning, Morrison's linkage of heterosexual romance and literary work reveals how desire and satisfaction are contorted by America's racial past. She uses love and labor to reveal the moral convictions that can affirm black life in this nation; these convictions inform the ethics of swagger.

While many of the more than six hundred articles, chapters, dissertations, essays, and monographs that *Beloved* has inspired analyze its title character, only a handful engage Sethe and Paul D's love affair.[3] This novel undeniably has a lot to do with Beloved the character; nevertheless, fully understanding the book requires a sustained look at the

---

Man as "the most distinguished single work published" since 1945 (Walling 4). Though united in esteem, these two books and their authors sound different major chords.

   2. Morrison, in 1986, observed, "I was talking to a woman writer a couple of years ago and she said that all her hopes in her work were in the future. And I said that all mine were in the past, meaning that . . . there were things already there that had either been buried, discredited, or never looked at and I feel it particularly strongly with black literature." Extending that thought, she suggested that the black novel, despite its nineteenth-century roots, remained a "new" enterprise: "The examination of it, the experimentation within it, the information that has to surface from it, the play in it—it's still very, very young and new and that's all right because I think it's only been very recently that it was important to have black novels really, for black people at large" (McCluskey 40).

   3. See Deborah Ayer Sitter's "The Making of a Man: Dialogic Meaning in *Beloved*" (1992), Mary Paniccia Carden's "Models of Memory and Romance: The Dual Endings of Toni Morrison's *Beloved*" (1999), and James Frank Walter's *Reading Marriage in the American Romance: Remembering Love as Destiny* (2008) for explorations of how *Beloved*'s "romance plot" raises questions about "the normalized expectations and rules that mold male and female subjectivities" (Carden 402). In *The Cambridge Companion to Toni Morrison* (2007), Deirdre J. Raynor and Johnnella E. Butler's "Morrison and the Critical Community" chart major trends in analyses of Toni Morrison's work. Linden Peach's introduction to *Toni Morrison: Contemporary Critical Essays* (1998) also discusses critical reactions to Morrison.

odd couple at its center. Aside from offering an example of hard-won intimacy, this pair also expresses a crucial metaphor. Sethe and Paul D occupy a nineteenth-century world of slavery, emancipation, and Reconstruction. Though they seem divorced from the 1980s, their relationship involves single motherhood, child killing, and imprisonment, three poignant themes from the Reagan era, during which Morrison wrote the book.[4] This resonance could be understood as an instance of contemporary readers being forced "to reconsider the traumatic past" (Page, *Dangerous* 157). While Morrison admitted such intentions, she stated that it was only after *Beloved*'s publication that she sensed the book's demand for a memorial that could "summon the presences of, or recollect the absences of slaves" ("A Bench" 44). Her earlier ambitions for the novel were less epic. She explains, "[*Beloved*] was not about the institution—Slavery with a capital S. It was about these anonymous people called slaves. What they do to keep on, how they make a life, what they're willing to risk, however long it lasts, in order to relate to one another" (Angelo 257). Emphasizing pleasure amid distress, the novelist's decision to make Sethe and Paul D's relationship a metaphor of her quest for creative independence suggests the unevenness of black access to happiness. This unevenness spawns resentment, emulation, and new experiments in self-definition, a trio of responses that captures Morrison's movement through confounding and then revising prejudice.

Focusing Sethe and Paul D's chase after intimacy through the lens of Morrison's encounters with New Criticism and American prize-granting committees, this chapter argues that *Beloved* betrays its author's bouts with "whitefolks on the brain" (A. Walker, *In Search* 35).[5] It links the text's depictions of self-determined love with Morrison's struggle to find the proper attitude toward mainstream approval. Contending that Sethe and Paul D's alliance shows the inter- and intraracial entanglements that precede healing, this analysis concludes that in *Beloved,* Morrison revealed how deeply white calculations of literary value influenced her even as she finally discovered the folly of such investments. Her experiences and

4. Welfare, abortion, and the prison industrial complex are mainstays of black analyses of Ronald Reagan's presidency. For a succinct statement, see Michael C. Dawson and Lawrence D. Bobo's "The Reagan Legacy and the George W. Bush Era" (2004).

5. In 1972, Alice Walker stated that critics inexplicable preference for Richard Wright's *Native Son* (1940) rather than Zora Neale Hurston's *Their Eyes Were Watching God* (1937) boiled down to each novel's position on "worrying about white folks" (*In Search* 35). Her folksy phrase captured the importance of black thrall to white expectation, and her use of Hurston and Wright suggested why knowing the black literary tradition might simplify the post–civil rights writer's creative tasks.

those of her characters illustrate the dangers of a facile subscription to received standards. Whether in a post-Emancipation or a post–civil rights world, black confrontations with white expectations demand sophisticated decisions about what should and should not be kept. Making those decisions starts with discovering an ethical compass.

Creative Risks and Intimacy's Lessons

Sethe and Paul D represent two of the black community's more controversial members—the single mother and the ex-convict.[6] Although these types raised moral concerns throughout African American history, during the late 1970s and the 1980s, impassioned speeches about family values and black male criminality made putative "welfare queens" and "Willie Hortons" the objects of more intense scrutiny.[7] For Morrison, such "pariah figures" had long been central to her art (Tate, "Toni" 168).[8] Not-

6. Sethe, even under slavery, does not experience an out of wedlock childbirth, the moral breach that often pushes discussions of black single motherhood toward sanctimony. Nonetheless, her female-headed household provokes a related acid discourse. See Stanley Elkins's *Slavery: A Problem in American Institutional and Intellectual Life* (1959) and Daniel Patrick Moynihan's *The Negro Family: The Case for National Action* (1965) for castigations of black matriarchy. For analyses of how Morrison's portrayals of slavery engage these discourses, see James Berger's "Ghosts of Liberalism: Morrison's *Beloved* and the Moynihan Report" (1999) and Michelle Pagni-Stewart's "Moynihan's 'Tangle of Pathology': Toni Morrison's Legacy of Motherhood" (1997).

7. Focusing on the case of a woman from Chicago, Ronald Reagan coined the term "welfare queen" to evoke what he felt was a widespread abuse of the welfare system (Douglas and Michaels 185). Eventually, his phrase pejoratively marked black, female-headed households. For more on black single motherhood, see Susan Douglas and Meredith Michaels's *The Mommy Myth: The Idealization of Motherhood and How It Has Undermined All Women* (2005), Sharon Hays's *Flat Broke With Children: Women in the Age of Welfare Reform,* Ellen Reese's *Backlash Against Welfare Mothers: Past and Present* (2005), and Frank Gilliam's "The 'Welfare Queen' Experiment: How Viewers React to Images of African American Mothers on Welfare" (1999). If welfare dominated public perceptions of black femininity in the 1980s, then criminality played a crucial role in how black males were depicted. In 1988, an infamous conflation of black men with criminality occurred when George H. W. Bush's campaign used William "Willie" Horton to illustrate the threat that a dark menace might pose to innocent people. See Roger Simon's "The Killer and the Candidate: How Willie Horton and George Bush Rewrote the Rules of Political Advertising" (1990) and Jack W. Germond and Jules Witcover's *Whose Broad Stripes and Bright Stars: The Trivial Pursuit of the Presidency, 1988* (1989). Charles Johnson commented on Willie Horton in his essay "A Phenomenology of the Black Body" (Byrd, *I Call* 119–21).

8. Morrison had depicted female-headed households through the characters of Eva and Hannah Peace, Nel Wright, and Pilate and Reba Dead in *Sula* and *Song of Solomon,* respectively. Ex-convicts such as *The Bluest Eye*'s Cholly Breedlove and *Sula*'s Shadrack also received sustained portrayals. These characters reflected Morrison's belief that "the black community is a pariah community" (Tate, "Toni" 168). John Edgar Wideman admired Morrison's interest in outlaw characters; in fact, Bonnie TuSmith suggests that Wideman sees a "call-and-response between his works and those of Toni Morrison" (*Conversations* ix). The Black Archivists solve many problems of black representation because they use one another to grow on.

withstanding these precedents, her focus on outcasts in *Beloved* explored how slavery and its aftermath required dealing with white authority and black subordination. Her point was not that bondage caused single motherhood or incarceration; rather, she contended that these judgmental labels in themselves assaulted black cultural complexity. During a testy exchange, Morrison critiqued such assaults. Regarding teen pregnancy and single motherhood, she stated, "Neither of those things seems to me a debility. . . . I don't think anybody cares about unwed mothers unless they're black—or poor. The question is not morality, the question is money" (Angelo 260, 261). She also claimed that black male employment and criminality aroused "comic-book solutions" rather than a "vigorous attack on the wrongness" (Angelo 259).[9] Although Morrison impugns the hypocrisy of family-values rhetoric and law-and-order ideals, her remarks illustrate the problems that arise when mainstream morality flattens black experiences to assert white superiority. She knew that such gestures were not confined to sociopolitical discussions, and her attitude toward New Criticism suggests how completely she grasps the stakes.

Morrison did not begin publishing until 1970, yet she acquired her idea of a writer's function during the heyday of New Criticism. Talking about that moment, she observed, "In the fifties, when I was a student, the embarrassment of being called a politically minded writer was so acute, the fear of critical derision for channeling one's creativity toward the state of social affairs so profound, it made me wonder . . . What could be so bad about being socially astute, politically aware in literature?" (*Sula* xi).[10] She offered the previous comment in 2004, but she made a similar point in 1984 while she was working on *Beloved*:

> I am not interested in indulging myself in some private, closed exercise of my imagination that fulfills only the obligation of my personal dreams— which is to say yes, the work must be political. It must have that as its thrust. That's a pejorative term in critical circles now: if a work of art has any political influence in it, somehow it's tainted. My feeling is just the opposite: if it has none, it is tainted. (Morrison, *What* 64)

9. Nancy Peterson discusses the alarmed response to Morrison's remarks on teenage pregnancy and black male criminality in her 1993 article "Canonizing Toni Morrison."

10. Morrison's statement not only evoked New Criticism but also the more pernicious specter of Joseph McCarthy, the Wisconsin senator whose allegations wreaked havoc in the 1950s. For more on McCarthy, see David Oshinsky's *A Conspiracy So Immense: The World of Joe McCarthy* (1985) and Arthur Herman's *Joseph McCarthy: Reexamining the Life and Legacy of America's Most Hated Senator* (2000).

From the 1950s, when she was in college, through the 1980s, when she was already an award-winning writer, Morrison remained convinced that white aesthetic judgments generally and the formalist mandates of New Criticism specifically unduly influenced black literary expression.[11] Her response was to try to be both "a careful . . . craftswoman" and a novelist who reflected a reality "beyond the story told at the center of the text" (Morrison, *What* xiv). *Beloved*'s accounts of Sethe and Paul D's relationship suggest how skillfully she achieved this combination.

Sethe and Paul D as a couple signal Morrison's willingness to politicize her depiction of romantic love. Although debates surrounding female-headed households, serving prison time, and shacking-up define post–civil rights America, her engagement with these loaded discourses is evident in the contrast between Sethe's marriage to Halle and her affair with Paul D. When Sethe arrived at Sweet Home, the Kentucky plantation where she met Paul D in 1848, she was a young girl who was struggling with her mother's death and the meaning of her own survival. After twelve months of patient observation, she chose Halle to be her husband. Morrison's portrayal of this slave union emphasizes tenderness and naïve expectancy. Upon telling her mistress Mrs. Garner that Halle had proposed, Sethe innocently asked, "Is there a wedding" (27). Her sentiment partially reflects the inability to destroy human desire. Beyond that though, Sethe betrays an idealization of both Halle and their marriage. Her efforts to make slave life normal show a penchant for "fluidly turning her dream into the truth" (Mayberry 164). If this penchant prompts Mrs. Garner's bemused condescension, then by the time she reunites with Paul D, more than two decades later, her dreams have met much crueler fates.

Sethe and Paul D's reunion reflects slow-steeping lust. By all accounts, she has not been dating since she left Sweet Home in 1855, and he, though not celibate, was still driven by "the sex with her [he] had been imagining off and on for twenty-five years" (25). The two do not jump into bed as soon as they see each other; however, their lovemaking is not long delayed, and its implications are complicated. Paul D's sexual desire for Sethe helped him endure a chain gang in Alfred, Georgia, where he was forced to perform fellatio on prison guards. While she carried no fantasies during the interim between 1855 and 1873, she does see

11. In *The Negro Novel in America* (1965), Robert Bone classically expressed the view that political content was a handicapping force for the black novel. Lawrence Jackson concisely documents the New Critical roots of Robert Bone's study (*Indignant* 473). For more on Bone and New Criticism, see Clarence Major's *The Dark and Feeling* (1974).

him as someone whose affection can blunt the murderous impulses that landed her in jail and in a haunted house. The realities that surround Sethe and Paul D's lives invest their consummation and their decision to live together with felicity, but other factors taint their circumstances.

No one in *Beloved* protests the immorality of Sethe and Paul D's situation, yet Morrison allows a collision of Reconstruction era behavior and late twentieth-century narratives of black deviance to inform her novel's events. Noting among other things Sethe's status as "a single mother working a low-paying job," James Berger concludes that her "family is certainly dysfunctional, if not (to use a loaded term from the Moynihan report) pathological" (411). Berger's gloss suggests *Beloved*'s engagement with demonizing narratives of black family life, and his broader argument explicitly links these narratives to white attempts to study the putative mysteries of black behaviors. This exploration of white totalizing narratives and the way that they condition black experience becomes crucial not only to *Beloved*'s presentation of family but also its depictions of love. By examining the interplay between Sweet Home's two male slaveholders and Sethe and Paul D's respective searches for identity, the full implications of white expectations and black desire can be seen.

The basis of Sethe and Paul D's familiarity is their shared enslavement. On Sweet Home, the two experienced first the enlightened ownership of Mr. Garner and then the spirit-rending superintendence of Schoolteacher, two very different white men. Garner identified respect rather than coercion as the crux of mastery and deemed his slaves "men" because they complied with his wishes out of reason, not intimidation (220). When Garner died, leaving his plantation to his wife, her cousin, Schoolteacher, restructured Sweet Home instituting a dehumanizing regime steeped in "*measurement, analysis,* and *classification*" of black life (McGurl 346). Notwithstanding Garner and Schoolteacher's differences, both men distorted Sethe and Paul D's options for selfhood.

Before she ever met Mr. Garner or encountered his "special kind of slavery," Sethe experienced life with a mother who died trying to escape from a plantation and who protested being raped by throwing her children away "without names" (140, 62). This lineage explains some of her later attitudes. At Sweet Home, Sethe initially attempted to beat back white authority with delicate ornamentation such as myrtle and mint sprig. These embellishments were meant as subtle buffers against the arbitrary power of whiteness, a power she associated with her mother's hung corpse and her siblings who were murdered as a "resistance tactic" (Bouson 139).[12] While its form was decorative, her act was essentially evasive. Paul D's accounts of his time on the plantation hint at why. Unlike Sethe, he has no parents. His only family is his brothers, Paul A and Paul F, and his close friends, Sixo and Halle. While Paul D and his siblings happily take Garner's word that they are men, Sixo and Halle raise questions about black freedom and white authority. Garner's presence allows the Pauls to claim if not liberty then at least distinction. When Garner dies and Schoolteacher's reign begins, everyone on Sweet Home gains perspective.

The lenience that defined Garner's stewardship lulled Sethe and the Pauls into complacency. Knowing the costs of seeking true freedom, namely running away, they all equivocated. Their isolation in the "wonderful lie" that was the plantation ended when Schoolteacher taught them what Garner had only implied—the absoluteness of white authority (221). Although his methods were ostensibly objective and scientific, Schoolteacher's dispassionate practices not only yielded profitability but also emotional harrowing. His techniques inspired the slaves to hatch an escape plot. Because it broke up Sethe's marriage and sent Paul D to the chain gang, this escape attempt exemplifies the wreckage that accompanies the pursuit of black independence. Sethe and Paul D's relationship begins with these fateful steps toward freedom, and this origin complete with the twenty-five year gestation, the unequal consequences, and the distinct personalities symbolizes Morrison as she attempted to make sense of how white aesthetic assumptions fit into her art.

In 1977, Morrison stated, "I was . . . aware that there was an enormous amount of apology going on, even in the best [black] writing. But more important than that, there was so much explanation . . . the Black writers always explained something to somebody else. And I didn't want to explain anything to anybody else!" (Bakerman 38). Three years later, the novelist specified who she meant by "anybody": "I'm always a little disturbed by the sociological evaluations white people make of Black literature . . . It's demoralizing for me to be required to explain Black life once again for the benefit of white people" (Koenen 67). Morrison wanted to document the complexity of black existence, yet after studying the African American literary tradition, she felt that indulging an unin-

---

12. In *Stolen Childhood: Slave Youth in Nineteenth Century America* (1998), Wilma King states that slave women could not "make decisions about their bodies" and thus often "became pregnant through forced cohabitation or rape" (4). These facts suggest that Sethe's mother possessed a rebelliousness that she did not relinquish even when facing death. While Sethe reprises that trait, her desire for an enduring refutation of white authority influences her choices.

formed white audience caused lapses in creativity. She explained, "I was preoccupied with books by black people that approached [black experience], but I always missed some intimacy, some direction, some voice. Ralph Ellison and Richard Wright . . . were saying something . . . to white people, to men.[13] Just in terms of the style, I missed something in the fiction that I felt in a real sense in the music and poetry of black artists" (Ruas 96).[14] Throughout her career, Morrison attempted to free her art from the bonds of assuming a white readership, but at the same moment, she was increasingly invested in prizewinning, a designation of merit that is largely mediated by whites. Her attitude recalls Sethe and Paul D's pre-Schoolteacher mindsets.

Just as Sethe idealizes her marriage and Paul D romanticizes his manhood, Morrison uses prizewinning to gauge the value of black autonomy in America. The room that Garner gives for self-expression seems immense, particularly when measured against past experiences (i.e., hung corpses) and other alternatives (i.e., the brutality of neighboring slaveholders). Despite providing this license, Sweet Home is still a plantation; thus, Sethe and Paul D are defining themselves within a space designed for slavery. Mark McGurl connects *Beloved*'s plantation imagery to Morrison's teaching career as a university professor.[15] While that connection is insightful, the link between Sweet Home, the plantation, and the American prize-granting establishment illuminates the ethical issues that inform Morrison's aesthetic practice. Specifically, it conveys her attempt to decide whether mainstream awards were orienting marks in a pluralistic society or shibboleths meant to distract and distort. Morrison's history with prizes and awards prior to *Beloved* clarifies her pursuit of the ethics of swagger.

Morrison believed that the lack of prizewinning black novels implied lingering mainstream doubts about African American creativity. Although

13. Laura Doyle suggests that Morrison's reactions to her black male predecessors deeply condition her fiction. See her chapter, "'To Get to a Place': Intercorporeality in *Beloved*," in *Bordering on the Body: The Racial Matrix of Modern Fiction and Culture* (1994) for an expansive treatment of Morrison's response to Ralph Ellison.

14. Regarding black writers and black musicians, Ntozake Shange affirms Morrison's point: "We, as a people, or as a literary cult, or a literary culture have not demanded singularity from our writers . . . a black writer can get away with abscond and covet for him or herself the richness of his or her person long before a black musician or singer cd" (3). John Edgar Wideman makes a similar point about black musical virtuosity in "Stomping the Blues: Rituals in Black Music and Speech" (1978).

15. See the "Plantations and Campuses" section of chapter 6 in *The Program Era* (2009) for McGurl's analysis of *Beloved*. A classic comparison of post–*Brown v. Board* black American existence to life on a plantation occurs in Malcolm X's 1963 speech, "Message to the Grassroots."

she considered such sentiments ignorant, she also felt that without a record of achievement, any objection to white literary judgments would be viewed as a case of sour grapes. As the jewelry that accessorized "qualities of [literary] greatness," awards not only negotiated "transactions between . . . cultural and political capital" but also provided tremendous leverage in the black artist's psyche (Black Creation 4; English 10).[16] Morrison's demands for prestige, however, are initially as barren as Sethe and Paul D's slave-borne attempts to normalize black hope. Notwithstanding a temporary relief from bondage's severity, they submit to white authority, and their efforts become trivial aberrations that prove the norm. With her runners-up for the 1974 (*Sula*) and the 1978 National Book Awards (*Song of Solomon*), and even her 1977 National Book Critics Circle Award triumph, Morrison felt the pressure exerted by that reality. *Beloved* reflects her discoveries about such pressure and her investment in esteem rather than prestige.

When *Sula*, her second novel, was shortlisted for the NBA, Morrison manifested concerns about black artistic authority and creative concession. She suggested that in the book's opening, she had tried to close the "threshold between the [white] reader and the black-topic text" by constructing a "safe, welcoming lobby" (*Sula* xv). Although her sensitivity to white readers yielded a defensible adjustment, her decision revealed a willingness to subordinate black values to white expectations. When her next book *Song of Solomon* was nominated for both the NBCCA and the NBA, Morrison's engagement with the ethical consequences of writing to meet white standards grew even more complicated.[17] She won the NBCCA and lost the NBA, yet her reaction, tempered dissatisfaction, betrayed less a competitive personality and more the belief that prizewinning held crucial, if convoluted significance for her and for black novelists.[18] Sethe and Paul D's Sweet Home

16. My reading of Morrison's attitude toward prizes captures this study's dual focus on mainstream recognition and intraracial vocation. Although she covets the former and thus fits English's model of prestige, her evolving outlook requires embrace of the latter, a sign of esteem.

17. First presented in 1974, the National Book Critics Circle Award featured wide polling of book reviewers and a jury of twenty or more judges. The NBA had been around since 1950 and was selected by a committee of five. Because the NBA had a history that dated to the civil rights movement and had last been won by Ralph Ellison, Morrison's nominations for that award seem to have registered with special intensity for her.

18. The 1977 National Book Critics Circle Award represented a breakthrough, but Morrison's reaction to the announcement of the 1978 National Book Award winner suggested her complex engagements with white literary expectations. When Collette Dowling traveled with Morrison shortly after the announcement, she speculated that the novelist's disappointment at not winning might have caused a "bad mood" during the trip. Dowling writes, "Many people in the publishing industry had considered Toni Morrison a shoo-in [for the NBA] . . . Perhaps this bad news had accounted for her bad mood earlier" (55). Dowling's opinions are a dubious basis for

experiences of failed and successful plans for liberty clarify Morrison's reasoning.

Sethe and Paul D remember Sweet Home nostalgically because of marriage and brotherhood, yet the plantation acquires its most profound meaning as a catalyst for their freedom. While Schoolteacher's brutality eloquently expressed his control over their bodies and minds, his viciousness also moved them toward bolder experiments in self-assertion. His roles in their escape efforts are illustrative. On the one hand, he installs the measures that convince Sweet Home's slaves to risk running away. This negative consciousness-raising moves the slaves toward solidarity, yet his lessons become even more textured. When Sethe joins the escape plot, she dreams of reconstructing her family beyond Schoolteacher's reach. Paul D's ambitions lack that precision, yet they share the same spirit. Revealing thoughts about a future, these sentiments customize their rebellion against white authority. In the aftermath of this foiled attempt, Schoolteacher allows his nephews to suckle from Sethe and places a collar on Paul D, thus trying to destroy both their specific intentions and their general will. This perversity becomes the excess that hurtles Sethe and Paul D along different paths toward freedom, yet it also haunts their calculations of identity. This interrelationship of black autonomy and white surveillance sutures the couples' post–Sweet Home reunion and romance to Morrison's meditations on the black novelist, "social death," and literary prizewinning (Patterson 39).[19]

By 1873, when Sethe and Paul D see each other after a more than twenty-year absence, their lives are all about managing enslavement's spillover into their post-Emancipation worlds. She strives to come to grips with murdering her daughter,[20] and he tries to decipher the

---

judging Morrison's mentality, but she does register the writer's interest in prizewinning. Morrison brought up the NBA announcement; she wanted Dowling, who thought that the winners would not be chosen for another few days, to know the results.

19. In *Slavery and Social Death: A Comparative Study* (1982), Orlando Patterson argues that the authority of the slaveowner was buttressed by defining the slave as "a socially dead person." This social death marked "a secular excommunication" that completed the subjugation of the slave (5). Convinced that this subjugation survived beyond enslavement, Morrison in part uses *Beloved* to explore how such survivals boomerang through history.

20. A good starting point for the vast criticism that analyzes Sethe's murder of her daughter is Kathleen Marks's *Toni Morrison's Beloved and the Apotropaic Imagination* (2002). Marks examines Sethe's deed through the lens of "apotropaic" actions, "those gestures" that lead one to do "what one finds horrible so as to mitigate its horror" and neutralize its "threat" (2). Other illuminating treatments include Christopher Peterson's "*Beloved*'s Claim" (2006), Jennifer Fitzgerald's "Selfhood and Community: Psychoanalysis and Discourse in *Beloved*" (1993), Mae G. Henderson's "Toni Morrison's *Beloved:* Re-membering the Body as Historical Text" (1991), and Elizabeth House's "Toni Morrison's Ghost: The Beloved Who is Not Beloved" (1990).

"tobacco tin" that has replaced his "red heart" (72–73).[21] Signaling the reclaiming of black selfhood from dehumanizing white value systems, their attempts are the foundations of survival. Nonetheless, their beliefs in the singularity of their efforts produce a problematic exceptionalism. While former slaves know that bondage's effects were disperse, their preoccupation with their own wounds blunts one of the best weapons that they possess against "social death," community. The tension between distorting individuation and healing togetherness becomes the subtext of Sethe and Paul D's romance, and this part of their interactions ties them to Morrison's pre-*Beloved* outlook on black prizewinning.

By the early 1980s, Morrison had experience and laurels, yet like black novelists from time immemorial, she wondered whether white aesthetic judgments were gumming up her creativity. Her musings were particularly ironic since mainstream prizes, powerful apparatuses in maintaining white tastes, were her favorite metric of success. For more than a decade, she had taken responsibility for legitimizing African American fiction, and she remained convinced à la James Weldon Johnson that "the amount and standard of the literature" that blacks produced would do much to determine their greatness (*Book* vii). Despite this conviction, as she surveyed the literary landscape anew, she concluded that she had a lot of help. Alice Walker, Gloria Naylor, David Bradley, and John Edgar Wideman had all won major literary prizes by the time Morrison started *Beloved*. Their achievements clarified for her that one key to confronting white aesthetic judgment was recognizing that you were not alone. With her clear if belated understanding, Morrison began registering how black creative fellowship, both actual and metaphorical, could speed her attainment of the ethics of swagger. This realization emerged in *Beloved* through her exposing Sethe and Paul D's paralyzed affections to the wisdom of Baby Suggs and Stamp Paid, two elders who failed in their attacks on slavery and still endured as vital tutors.

21. Riffing off of the Tin Man in Victor Fleming's *The Wizard of Oz* (1939) and perhaps more likely in Sidney Lumet's *The Wiz* (1978), Toni Morrison portrays Paul D as one who "plunge[s] into reticence and the solitary life, suppressing his memories . . . and masking the sexual repression . . . of his necessary asceticism" (Kang 847). Though critics fervently analyze the metal for flesh substitution that embroiders Paul D's pursuit of survival, *Beloved* offers another symbol of his adjustment to bondage's violations: "After Alfred he had shut down a generous portion of his head, operating on the part that helped him walk, eat, sleep, sing. If he could do those things—with a little work and a little sex thrown in—he asked for no more" (41). The heart/mind binary that grounds Paul D's management of his life reinforces Nancy Kang's contention that he is a figure of "an isolated, incommunicable self in multiform combinations" (847).

Elders and the Black Novelist's Psyche

Three years before she published *Beloved,* Morrison wrote a famous essay, "Rootedness: The Ancestor as Foundation" (1984). There she concluded that an elder or an ancestral figure often determined a character's fate in African American writing. Although concerned with plot and narration, Morrison's remarks really centered on the differences between how black and white writers defined their roles. She explained that white critics often viewed the artist as the "supreme individual"; thus, they believed that the writer was "always in confrontation with his society." Though such conflict can exist for black authors, she felt that it was rarer because they were not "isolated" projections of an "ivory tower" but instead representative of "an implied 'we'" (*What* 62). Many commentators have analyzed Morrison's novels and black women's writing more broadly with these observations in mind. Despite these attentions, the specific relationship between her statements about elders and her professional strivings has been underexamined. In particular, her sense of what ancestors might mean for a canon of black prizewinning has been neglected.

Given the resurgent interest that black women's fiction inspired in the 1970s, the critical concentration on "Rootedness" and gender is understandable. Morrison repeatedly emphasized her desire to combat the erasure of black women's experiences, and she stated forthrightly that her art originated in an attempt to explore "being a little black girl" in America (Naylor, "Conversation" 198). While gender is a powerful part of her creative identity, she also craves resplendent performance, an aim that for her involves artistic competition.[22] Morrison is not naïve about the deficiencies of awards and prizes as markers of aesthetic accomplishment; nevertheless, she sees within them significant chances to force white judgment into contact with black talent. Because of this perception, her observations about elders have intriguing implications for black prizewinning.

In 1974 when she made the shortlist for the National Book Award, the only black novelists who had ever been nominated for any major prize were Ralph Ellison, James Baldwin, John Oliver Killens, Ernest Gaines, Barry Beckham, and Ishmael Reed. Of this group, Ellison

---

22. Expanding Michael Awkward's perspective, George E. Lewis argues that analysis of African American cultural production must privilege "the promulgation of new cooperative, rather than competitive, relationships between artists" (xi). While an uncritical focus on competition could be distorting, the Black Archivists address creative anxiety precisely by competing; thus, ignoring these realities would obscure key parts of their success. See Awkward (7–8) for his take on competition and the difference between black male and black female literature.

remained the sole winner. Morrison knew of his status as a literary lumi-
nary, and occasionally, in her capacity as a Random House editor, she
would seek his aid. Regarding these requests, she explained, "[Ellison]
was unhelpful when I tried to enlist him on behalf of new or younger
[black] writers . . . Ralph had no interest in rallying" for them (Rampersad 487). His lack of support registered sharply in Morrison's mind. As
she considered elders and the black literary tradition in "Rootedness,"
her suggestion that older, more experienced characters could control the
fate of younger ones not only noted fictional creations but also the realities of American publishing. One cannot prove that Morrison blamed
the dearth in black prizewinning on Ellison's indifference; however, her
opinions about how blacks could win prestigious prizes repudiated his
posture. More evocatively, her convictions about ancestors, black identity,
and white practices surfaced through *Beloved*'s portrayals of Baby and
Stamp's impact on Sethe and Paul D.

Positioned at the beginning of *Beloved,* Sethe and Paul D's 1873
reunion features exorcism, lovemaking, and a trip to a carnival. These
activities fuel a growing romantic attraction, and the couple's intimacy
hints at the richest options for Reconstruction era black life. If happiness
threatens during their relationship's early days, then soon moral dilemmas
and infidelity challenge its hopeful start. More precisely, Sethe's defiant
uncertainty regarding her 1855 murder of her daughter joins with the
sexual repression born during Paul D's 1856 chain gang bid to rob their
courtship of its momentum. Sethe's infanticide and Paul D's cheating
are direct legacies of Sweet Home and an Alfred, Georgia chain gang,
two spaces where black identity proceeds from the perverse whims of
white authority. Although such perversion informs the deeds' origins,
their consequences are confined to black environments where fragile
experiments in liberated living are running. White tyranny's ability to
live beyond its direct manifestation seemingly perpetuates oppression.
In addition, such concealed power spawns explanations that stress black
behavior rather than white causality. Sethe and Paul D's scarred souls do
not distinguish them from other blacks in postbellum Cincinnati, but
their sensitivity to their burdens blinds them to the fullest legacies of the
community. These legacies involve a woman whom both of them knew
well and a man whose generosity opens doors.

Baby, Sethe's mother-in-law, and Stamp, a longtime resident of black
Cincinnati, are not romantically linked, but they are tandem emissaries in
a community where former slaves struggle to make their "hearts . . . free
to love" (Griesinger 691). While Baby preaches to help folks with "claim-

ing ownership of" their "freed sel[ves]," Stamp took as his "clear and holy purpose" provision for "the contraband humans that he ferried across the river" (*Beloved* 95, 169).[23] These characters epitomize the elders that Morrison described in "Rootedness." In addition to securing material wellbeing for recently escaped blacks, they also tutored them in full appreciation of liberty. Baby, from her birth in 1790 to her arrival at Sweet Home in 1838, experienced "the nastiness of life" (23). Mothering eight children by six different men, she watched as all of them save one were sold away. She was abused because of a busted hip and concluded that God burdened her with deprivation. Despite these realities, she transformed misfortune into witnessing. Her sermons rebuffed misery, counseling love as a reinvigorator of formerly enslaved black lives. While Stamp eschewed the pulpit, he joined her in this mission.

Like Baby, Stamp relies upon his past as he decides what former slaves need. Where she loses her children and endures brutality, he learns of bondage's costs through dissolved betrothal. He once loved a woman named Vashti, and while he honored their relationship with abstinence, his slave-master bedded her. After this betrayal, he changed his name from "Joshua" to Stamp Paid, suggesting that this slight settled whatever he owed the white man (233). Stamp's renaming stresses defiance; however, his actions among Cincinnati's black folks are empathetic. Nurturing a fragile collective, he and Baby patiently encourage communion as an antidote to servitude's depravity. Their efforts flourished for many years, but in 1855 their affection morphed from grace to offense.

Twenty days after Sethe escaped Sweet Home and arrived in Cincinnati, Stamp picked two buckets of blackberries. His gesture required a twelve-mile roundtrip to a secret riverbank, and within his "labor," Baby detected "his love." To honor that love, she baked pies, an act that somehow grew into roast turkeys, strawberry shrug, and "a feast for ninety people" (136). Such fellowship could have been edifying. As a celebration of one and all who fled enslavement, the party could have bolstered spirits. Baby felt that instead its "excess" aroused repulsion (138). Analyzing this sentiment, James Hans argues that in attempting to kindle life in a community still learning what freedom means, Baby and Stamp

23. Jean Daniels argues that Baby Suggs, through her preaching, inserts "an Africanist narrative" into *Beloved* (1). Lorie Fulton makes a similar point when she notes, "Baby's chosen place of worship brings to mind the sacred groves of African religion" (192). While Daniels contends that Baby neutralizes "white supremacist patriarchy," Fulton sees her as a part of Morrison's desire to "alter the ecofeminist belief that the domination of women directly connects to the devastation of the natural environment" (1, 190). These interpretations diverge, yet they unite in concluding that combating the lingering effects of enslavement is Baby Suggs's true calling.

"embarrass" their neighbors with their "extravagance" (*Golden* 237).[24] The extra that Hans refers to is material (the food, the setting, and the time) and emotional (the happiness, the open expression, and the audacity). If most slaves had to love "small and in secret" because sanity made investing anything more "risky," then here in their neighborhood were other black people "used-to-be-slave[s]" flamboyantly expressing their caring (221, 45). The harvest from this exuberance sprouted the next day when Schoolteacher's visit to claim his property and Sethe's murder of her daughter Beloved occurred in rapid succession. Morrison's intertwining of these events shows the precariousness of Baby and Stamp's efforts and the hazards of personality.

Schoolteacher's appearance challenges the interventions of black Cincinnati's elders, yet at the same moment, it dramatizes the different theories of selfhood within the community. If Baby Suggs's "great heart" and Stamp's nervy caring suggest an identity grounded in collective awakening, then Sethe, reflecting her mother's lessons, chooses stylized violence as her route to individuality (87). This collision between communal and individual notions of personality seemingly affirms white authority. After all, Schoolteacher has the right to reclaim his property because of the Fugitive Slave Act—a white legislative remedy intent on controlling black bodies. While Morrison's portrayal stresses both the formal and the numinous dimensions of white power, it also suggests that a key part of that power's vitality is black discord. This lack of unity surfaces not as mere resistance to consensus rather as absence of generosity. Engaging the daily sacrifices that slavery demanded, Baby and Stamp survived by offering black folks the benefit of the doubt, a margin to operate between a moral ideal and their actual circumstances. The withdrawal of that margin meant a more profound succumbing to dehumanizing white assumptions. While Morrison's interactions with prize-granting bodies lacked the same stakes, her convictions about black attitudes in the face of white literary judgments revealed important continuities.

Like all of the Black Archivists, Morrison's prizewinning occurred against the backdrop of the culture wars.[25] These pitched debates about

---

24. Hans connects Baby's audacity to a "heresy" that she preaches, namely that blacks should not defer life on earth in favor of a heavenly reward (*Golden* 236). As black liberation theology suggests, this tension could be understood as a conflict between black and white styles of Christianity.

25. For a gloss of the culture wars, black studies, and black literature, see Henry Louis Gates, Jr.'s *Loose Canons: Notes on the Culture Wars* (1992) and Donna J. Gough's dissertation, "Ideas Have Consequences: Conservative Philanthropy, Black Studies and the Evolution and Enduring Legacy of the Academic Culture Wars, 1945–2005" (2007). A broader perspective on the stakes of late

America's defining values deeply affected her perspective, and in a way her editing career responded to this philosophical wrangling. Although she once described her job at Random House as merely one of the things she did to make a living, her editing activities actually reflected a lofty ambition. Betty Jean Parker suggested that by 1979, Morrison had "for some time been deliberately encouraging and cultivating a certain kind of Black work" (60). When one considers Morrison's hand in publishing Gayl Jones, Toni Cade Bambara, James Alan McPherson, and Leon Forrest, the deepest implications of what Parker meant by "a certain kind of Black work" emerge. Morrison registered literature's possibilities for giving black culture its swagger, and she used her career as well as those of her peers and forebears to redeem such options. By coercing a confrontation between fiercely talented black writers and the decision-makers at Random House, she insisted that white tastes and economic expediency condition but need not determine black literary ethics. Her convictions about promoting these sorts of charged evaluative situations attracted her to prizewinning, but like Baby and Stamp, she favored a united front over singular genius as the best hope for black success. Her elders taught her intricate lessons about this preference.

Gwendolyn Brooks's 1950 Pulitzer Prize for poetry distinguished her as the first black writer to win a major American literary award. Clustered with Ellison's 1953 National Book Award and Alice Childress's 1956 Obie Award, her achievement signaled powerful possibilities for both racial and gender equality. Though recognition from America's white prize-granting establishment allied Brooks, Ellison, and Childress, their attitudes about black creative fellowship and white aesthetic standards divided them. When he was approached about signing a letter in support of Morrison, Ellison declined, stating that public agitation about her lack of prizes might be "well-intentioned," but it was "pretty annoy[ing]," since to him selecting awards is "a matter of luck . . . Look how long Hemingway and Faulkner had to wait to get their just awards."[26] He notes that individually Morrison can "compete with the best writers anywhere," yet he sees no value in further endorsing her talent (Mitgang B5). In dramatic contrast, Brooks and Childress not only cultivated deep bonds with a wide range of younger black writers but also explicitly

---

twentieth-century cultural wrangling can be found in John Ehrman's *The Eighties: America in the Age of Reagan* (2005) and Sean Wilentz's *The Age of Reagan: A History, 1974–2008* (2008).

26. Ellison, if the clippings in his "Toni Morrison" folder are any indication, followed her career with great interest. That folder is among the Ralph Ellison Papers held by the Manuscript Division of the Library of Congress.

promoted them by pressing editors on their behalf, plugging them in interviews, and writing recommendation letters for fellowships and job applications.[27] These different models of leveraging honor struck Morrison as a crucial impasse for the future of African American literature. With respect to the novel specifically, she felt that until the fullest legacies of collective black excellence were acknowledged, the trite objections of white literary tastemakers would continue to breed insecurity in black writers. The way forward for Sethe and Paul D's romance reflects Morrison's speculations on an effective response to such stigmas.

Sethe and Paul D crave a togetherness that can displace Garner and Schoolteacher's nullification of their every attempt to define themselves. Although the couple's longing affirms Baby and Stamp's communal ethos, each of them embraces sequestering at a crucial moment. Sethe locks herself in a moral gambit, convinced that her salvation hinges on Beloved's forgiveness. Embarking on a spiritual reckoning, Paul D takes refuge in a church cellar and ponders both Sethe's ostensible animalism and his actual infidelity.[28] Each suspends the benefit of the doubt and scrutinizes black behavior through the Manichean lens of white puritanical ethics. While their stocktaking is meant as ritual purification, it evades the discipline of fellowship and thus misses the profound instructions of human failings. Stamp's reassessment of Baby's legacy prefigures Sethe and Paul D's second reunion.

Amid the misery from Schoolteacher's arrival, Sethe's murderous reaction, and black Cincinnati's collective pouting, Baby renounces her ministry claiming that preaching the Word was just "one other thing" white folks "took away from" her (178). Stamp objects to her abdication, insisting that she allows mere shame to give the enemy a victory in the war over black humanity.[29] Looking back at his 1856 perspective

27. For accounts of Gwendolyn Brooks's commitment to younger writers, see Haki R. Madhubuti's edited collection *Say That The River Turns: The Impact of Gwendolyn Brooks* (1987), D. H. Melhem's *Gwendolyn Brooks: Poetry and the Heroic Voice* (1987), and George Kent's *Gwendolyn Brooks: A Life* (1990). Elizabeth Brown-Guillory discusses Alice Childress's impact on her career in "Alice Childress: A Pioneering Spirit" (1987), while Beatrix Taumann asserts that Childress "has been clearing paths for other African American women playwrights to follow for the last 50 years" (53).

28. Beloved, when she first appeared, struck Paul D as like him—illiterate and "drifting from ruin" (52). This connection impels him toward generosity, yet his affair with her bespeaks exploitation and thwarted agency, two concepts that link his deeds to Sethe's. Laura Doyle argues that when "Beloved precipitates Paul D's" unfaithfulness, she "forces [the] anxiety over the distinction between human and animal to a crisis" (221). This anxiety colors Paul D's meditations, reminding him of how life stifles intent and blasting the "flakes of rust . . . away from . . . the tobacco tin" that masqueraded as his heart (*Beloved* 117). In this development, Beloved sowed the seeds of his departure from and return to Sethe's love.

29. John Duvall believes "that although Baby Suggs is gone, her religion of the maternal body

from 1874, he discovers that he misperceived fellowship. His demands that Baby ignore catastrophe are both callous and flattering. Honoring her ministry's power, they at the same time withhold empathy—a withholding that poses great risks both to their friendship and to Cincinnati's black community. Stamp views his and Baby's rescue efforts as akin to functions of nature; she was "the mountain to his sky" (170). While that imagery bespeaks divine sanction and organic partnership, it ignores pain's accumulated perforations of her spirit.[30] Such stinted generosity bothers him. Living even during Reconstruction among a "people of broken necks, of fire-cooked blood and black girls who had lost their ribbons," Stamp believed that former slaves should never mistake tidy piety for deliverance from "the deeper more tangled jungle" that whites sought to cultivate "inside" them (181, 198). He momentarily succumbs to self-righteousness, but the example of his determination to "get right" with Baby amplifies Sethe and Paul D's fate (181).

Sethe says that before Paul D showed up at 124, "words whispered in the keeping room had kept her going." Those words, admonitions from a long-dead Baby Suggs, were to put down "her heavy knives of defense against misery, regret, gall and hurt" and renounce the "war" of atoning for the past (86). If these instructions originated in Baby's ministry, then her final edicts reflected an admission that "God puzzled her" and that "she was too ashamed of him to say so" (177). This confession led her to bed and away from the business of recasting legacies of black suffering. While both of Baby's approaches involve letting go, the latter carries tints of defeat while the former bespeaks liveliness. Paul D, when he returns to 124 for the second time, finds Sethe in the keeping room tottering between these two convictions. By recalling her from solitary weariness, he completed the compassion that Stamp had originated and reminded her that receiving your self "in all the right order" after being smashed to "pieces" can be serene collaboration (272–73).

They Want Affects

Black life in late nineteenth-century America differs considerably from post–civil rights era existence. Despite these distinctions, Morrison aligns

---

animates the community's movement toward redemption." This view of "the afterlife that Baby Suggs's words achieve" reinforces Stamp's misperception of her resignation (130).

30. Although she does not dwell on the tension between Stamp and Baby Suggs, Kristin Boudreau offers a thorough discussion of "physical and emotional suffering" (451).

her professional odyssey with Sethe and Paul D's burgeoning romance. Her connection to this couple shows how white definitions enduringly shape black identity, and one example of this dynamic is the controversy surrounding *Beloved*'s place in awards deliberations. James English holds that during the 1987–88 literary prize season, the elaborate maneuvering on behalf of *Beloved* revealed "broad shifts within the whole system of cultural gift-exchange" (240). Explaining these shifts, he argues that Morrison and her supporters, in the days leading up to the selection committee's decision, simultaneously critiqued the Pulitzer Prize "as a thoroughly social, economic, and (racist) political instrument" and invested it "with real, potentially decisive power in determining long-term literary valuation." He concludes, "The scandalized rhetoric that has surrounded Morrison's Pulitzer derives from the residual but still forceful imperative . . . that the artist, one way or another . . . help to maintain a discernible degree of separation between the scale of aesthetic value and that of public acclaim" (240–41). Because Morrison allowed the gap between art and prize to close, English believes that she "capitulated too fully to the awards mania" (237). His perspective while informative undervalues how Morrison's involvement in arguments about aesthetics and acclaim centers on white attitudes regarding black cultural performance.[31]

Julian Moynahan, a white man and the chair of the three-member fiction jury for the 1988 Pulitzer Prize, explained that after he and his peers read the more than one hundred books that had been nominated, "there was one towering book, a book that was so much better and important than any other . . . *Beloved*." Despite Moynahan's endorsement, a "protest letter" that appeared on January 24, 1988, affected not only public reaction to Morrison's receipt of the Pulitzer but also assessments of her career (Anonymous, "Story" 36).[32] This letter, apparently the

31. The black novelist Gloria Naylor was a judge on the 1987 National Book Award committee that chose Larry Heinemann's *Paco's Story* (1986) over *Beloved*. Even in light and perhaps because of her presence, the controlling frame for those awards deliberations were white standards versus black performance. I analyze the importance of Naylor's judgeship at greater length in chapter 4.

32. Starting as early as January 9, 1988, Wesley Brown and other black writers solicited signatures for an ad that would run in the *New York Times*. This ad lamented the fact that Morrison had not received the "keystones to the canon of American literature: the National Book Award and the Pulitzer Prize" and hailed her advancement of "the moral and artistic standards by which we must measure the daring and the love of our national imagination and our collective intelligence as a people" (Anonymous "Black"). Her peers among the Black Archivists—Ernest Gaines, Alice Walker, and John Edgar Wideman—joined several critics and writers in signing the document. Bemoaning the awards system promotion of such lobbying, Walter Goodman concluded tellingly: "In the long run—and literature is supposed to be a long-run endeavor—[Morrison's] books are

brainchild of poet June Jordan, bewailed the unwillingness of America's prize-granting bodies to reward *Beloved*'s genius. While signatories such as John Edgar Wideman identified the letter as a "tribute" rather than an attempt at "tyrannizing the standards and notions of literary quality," onlookers insisted that Morrison and her supporters violated the spirit if not the letter of the rules (McDowell, "48 Writers" C15). In part, this may have been because Morrison had shown up, only months earlier, at the National Book Awards banquet with an entourage and then implied that she had been slighted when she did not win (English 237). Episodes like these reflected her investment in "redemption" that stemmed from prizes (Anonymous, "Morrison" 14). While such commitments betrayed vanity, they also marked the complicated collision between black expression and white expectation.[33] A detail regarding her composition of *Beloved* proves illustrative.

Morrison's editor for all of her novels from *Sula* to *Beloved* was Robert Gottlieb, a white man who was legendary in New York publishing circles.[34] Though his expertise inspired her belief that a white reader could "grasp a [black] cultural thought or experience," his participation in her artistry also signaled the nuances of interracial encounters related to literature (J. Harris 7). Like Moynahan, Gottlieb revealed that white observers could impartially engage black literary swagger. Their aptitude, however, could not cancel conspicuous prejudices.[35] With *Beloved,* Morrison exploited these tensions within mainstream perceptions and offered a novel that treated slavery, a charged metaphor of America's self-

---

what count, and they will be judged by readers at some distance from today's battles and rivalries who will not remember which awards she received or failed to receive. They may not even know her color" (C26).

33. Toni Morrison in 1976 confessed that she takes writing "very very seriously"; thus, she adhered to basic principles: "I don't lie. I don't mislead. I don't cater to the whole media thing." Though she announced this retreat from "media madness," by roughly a decade later, Morrison's situation involved elaborate negotiations of art, audience, and celebrity (J. Harris 9). Loren Glass in *Authors Inc.: Literary Celebrity in the Modern United States, 1880–1980* (2004) explores the ways in which "celebrity . . . is crucial to [the] understanding of literary authorship in the twentieth century" (2–3). Though Glass's study does not engage Morrison, it does hint at the milieu in which she and her prizewinning black peers carved out their artistic identities.

34. When Gottlieb left Random House in 1987 to take the helm at the *New Yorker,* Morrison rued her loss of a "dispassionate" "third eye" that had had a "superlative" effect on her work (Schappell 68). After his stint at the magazine, Gottlieb resumed his work as Morrison's editor in the late 1990s, working on her novels *Love* (2003) and *A Mercy* (2008). Gottlieb, to whom Morrison dedicated *A Mercy,* represented the apex of her edifying encounters with the New York publishing culture.

35. Tying black prizewinning to affirmative action debates, Martha Bayles's article "Special Effects, Special Pleading" (1988) impugns Morrison's competition for the 1988 Pulitzer Prize. Her candor revealed an opposition that was sometimes obscured as Morrison's reputation grew.

splitting. In doing this, her links to Sethe and Paul D are illustrative. This couples' relationship suggests that liberty inheres in acknowledging white authority's precise capacity to destroy their identities. Such acknowledgment edifies because it is the preamble to accepting the concern that allows them to form healthy black selves. Like Sethe and Paul D, Morrison confronted her connection with white power. By entering the opera that was American prize deliberation, she especially in the aftermath of *Beloved* was simultaneously feted and discredited, an artist split in two. Her renewed convictions that institutionalizing black literature might enhance post–civil rights liberty softened this schism,[36] but Morrison remained convinced that *Beloved*'s prize misadventures dramatized mainstream America's limited patience with black self-determination.[37] If Morrison's exposure to white expectations centered on prize-granting bodies, then Alice Walker and Charles Johnson encounter curbs on swagger in the genial spaces of relationships with mentors.

36. At the same moment that *Beloved* was published, several important critics of African American literature were advancing through the academy. I explore this development's impact on colleges and universities in this study's conclusion.

37. Where some would see sober case making (i.e., "literary lobbying") as par for the course, something that "goes on all the time," the incorporation of race launches the enterprise over the bounds of good taste (Goodman C26). Similarly, creative technique individuates artists marking them as fresh and resourceful, yet when material such as slavery laces the style, readers grow "numb" beneath the "cumulative and oft-repeated miseries, with new miseries and new dimensions of miseries added in each telling and retelling long after the point has been made" (Iannone, "Toni" 63).

Authorized Mentors

To Africa and Back in *The Color Purple* and *Middle Passage*

All of the Black Archivists endure the scrutiny of awards committees, but most explore white influences on black art via other themes. Alice Walker and Charles Johnson offer such explorations in *The Color Purple*'s and *Middle Passage*'s accounts of mentorship. Like many African Americans who attended college in the 1960s, these writers' most significant relationships with white mentors took place on campuses.[1] These relationships were defined by warm conversations, thoughtful criticism, and staunch advocacy, but despite the benefits, each novelist reached an impasse because white assumptions conflicted with autonomous artistry. During a decade that sternly tested American democracy's link with black life, Walker and Johnson's exposure to white mentors epitomized the anxieties of interracial collaboration. Both in college and later, the novelists addressed these anxieties by engaging Africa.

Walker and Johnson matriculated when the independence movements that gripped countries such as Ghana, Uganda, and Kenya were in

---

1. Walker went to Sarah Lawrence in 1964, and Johnson enrolled at Southern Illinois University in 1966. Both had interacted with white teachers before their respective enrollments. Walker's stint at Spelman College (1961–63) was enlivened by interactions with Howard Zinn, a firebrand radical and head of the college's history and social sciences department. Johnson received similar support when he took a correspondence course in high school from illustrator Lawrence Lariar. He also regularly praised the white teachers in the integrated public schools of his hometown, Evanston, Illinois. See Walker's "Saying Goodbye to My Friend Howard Zinn" (2010) and Johnson's "I Call Myself An Artist" (1990) and "The Real Faith and the Good Thing" (2011).

full swing. If African decolonization shaped their outlooks on the motherland, then debates about black cultural formation also influenced their
thinking.[2] Unlike Ralph Ellison, who in 1960 declared that Africa held
"no special emotional attachment" for him, Walker and Johnson made
the continent central to their portrayals of black identity (Isaacs 60).[3]
They were aware of African political and cultural realities; nonetheless, in
their literature, they rejected mimetic representations of the continent.[4]
Starting in the mid-1960s and the late 1970s, respectively, Walker and
Johnson crafted literature that alluded to but did not document African
societies. They mostly treated the African world as a malleable literary
idea, an approach that reflected each author's beliefs about imagination
and freedom. Refined after integration, these beliefs are clearest in their
fiction's use of orphans.

The respective protagonists of *The Color Purple* and *Middle Passage,* Celie and Rutherford, both lose their parents. Although this literal
orphaning is significant, each character experiences a cultural confusion
that also suggests orphanhood. Celie lives in the Jim Crow South, and
the first fifteen years of her life bring rape and impregnation by her stepfather, the spiriting away of her children, and the imposition of a menacing silence. While these circumstances define her intraracial quandaries,
her relationship with God reveals bouts with white power. Rutherford
shares Celie's perplexity about race and morality. Notwithstanding the
fact that his slave-master freed him, he still struggles to find his identity.
His material circumstances influence his struggling, but his fight is truly
about spiritual as opposed to economic liberation. Like Celie, he wrestles
with white definitions of values. In depictions of mentors, *The Color Purple* and *Middle Passage* show how this wrestling influences black selfhood.

Celie and Rutherford respond to cultural orphaning by deauthorizing white mentors. Though such flouting can be exhilarating, defi-

2. Wilson J. Moses suggests that conflicting views about black cultural formation fermented
through the civil rights movement and the Black Power era, and by the early 1970s, they flared
with renewed vigor in arguments about affirmative action and black studies departments. For
more on these debates, see Moses's *Afrotopia: The Roots of African American Popular History* (1998)
and Ron Eyerman's *Slavery and the Formation of African American Identity* (2002).

3. Ronald Segal documents the scattering of black folks from Africa in *The Black Diaspora*
(1996). For a sense of the Black Diaspora's morphing into transatlantic studies, see Paul Gilroy's
The Black Atlantic: Modernity and Double Consciousness (1993) and Brent Hayes Edwards's *The Practice of Diaspora: Literature, Translation, and the Rise of Black Internationalism* (2003).

4. Evelyn White believes that Alice Walker, "like many black Americans who first visited
Africa in the 1960s . . . had been inspired by the independence movement that had swept across
the continent" (110). Though Charles Johnson does not absorb his curiosity from the same well,
his awareness of Africa's history emerges in his fiction, his literary criticism *Being and Race: Black
Writing Since 1970* (1988), and his work on the PBS documentary *Africans in America* (1999).

ance alone does not produce individuality. Independent selfhood requires replacing a faulty compass with a sound one, and in *The Color Purple* and *Middle Passage,* this replacement entails acquiring a broader perception of black existence. By depicting trips to Africa, Walker and Johnson examine how these broadened perceptions impact cultural confusion. Their examinations discount neat resolutions. Concentrating on self-assertion, the novelists imply that American blacks will improvise rather than discover whole the curriculums that shape their identities. These improvisations, for Celie and Rutherford, stress sibling interactions and surrogate guardians; additionally, standard parent-child nurturing gets revised. Because of these revisions, black selfhood attains a telling interdependence. This interdependence becomes an intriguing subtext of Walker's and Johnson's relationships with white mentors and one another.

Focusing on two climactic eras in black American history, Jim Crow and slavery, Walker and Johnson juxtapose the dilemmas of those epochs with their own post–civil rights quandaries. These quandaries involved trying to balance integration era encounters with white authority and the sense of a coherent black self. Africa becomes a bedeviling mediator in this search for coherence. By looking at how *The Color Purple* and *Middle Passage* reflect their authors' experiences with white mentors, this chapter argues that these novels' African plots muse on what resources can challenge white prescription in the development of black art.[5] These musings convince Walker and Johnson that renovated moral vision is the key to managing white expectations. Through such renovations, two very different writers acknowledge the ethics of swagger.

Faithful Guidance

Celie addresses roughly half of the letters that comprise *The Color Purple* to God. Although these letters could be read as prayers in which she records "the text of her life," some scholars contend that the God who

5. For Alice Walker and Charles Johnson, portraying Africa marked intriguing expansions of prior musings. Walker had commenced her meditations with *Once* (1968), her first poetry collection. Although *Once* marked Walker's first published depiction of Africa, she wrote an unpublished story, "The Suicide of an American Girl," which Jane Cooper praised as "a complex, extremely prescient piece that explored the tensions between Africans and blacks in the U.S." (White 105). In *The Sorcerer's Apprentice* (1986), stories from which were composed in the late 1970s and early 1980s, Johnson sketched "the Allmuseri, the fictional African tribe of wizards who" became "the central symbol of [his] aesthetic" (Nash 7–8). Nash's conclusions about the Allmuseri's significance echo the observations of Ashraf Rushdy. See the latter's "The Phenomenology of the Allmuseri: Charles Johnson and the Subject of the Narrative of Slavery" (1992).

is her "epistolary confidant" tyrannizes her (Gates, *Signifying* 245; Juneja 83). The tyranny stems from God's association with "the white folks' white bible" (*Color* 194). Because Celie initially pictures God as a bare-foot, "graybearded," "old" "white" man, many critics have followed her friend Shug Avery's lead and charged that deity with "the nullification of [her] subjectivity" (*Color* 194, Cutter 148).[6] These charges accurately reflect how Christianity has been contorted by white supremacy, yet they ignore the complex black reactions to those contortions. By portraying Celie's faith, Walker remedies this oversight.

Faith, "the substance of things hoped for, the evidence of things not seen," seemingly affirms passivity, but in Celie's life, it prompts an asser-tive act, her attempt to engineer her sister Nettie's deliverance (King James Bible, Hebrews 11:1). Before she leaves home, Celie accepts her stepfather's sexual advances and lets "Nettie remain unscathed" (Wilentz 67). Further, when her new husband Mr. __ kicks Nettie out because she repels him, Celie performs another protective gesture.[7] She directs her sister toward Corrine, the woman who took in her daughter Olivia. Although Shug is often and rightly identified as an "efficacious spiritual guide" who leads Celie toward "wisdom," the latter's journey toward self-actualization begins before Shug appears (Wall 142). Her efforts on Net-tie's behalf signal an active tangling with the submission counseled by "a white Christian God" (Juneja 83). While Celie at first only inches toward independence, her ultimate response to white guidance stems from these seeds sown as she nurtured kinship bonds. The profundity of her response is evident in how she links her orphanhood to the fate of her children.

Celie's feelings toward her children, Olivia and Adam, contradict the sexual abuse through which they were conceived. When her stepfa-ther's serial raping of her caused pregnancies, she—like some women in

6. Shug's objection to Celie's deity notes his sexist attributes, but her remark that "[God] ain't a picture show" also addresses the issue of doing versus watching (195). This issue acquires considerable significance when placed in the dynamics of mentorship. If conceptions of God as a confidant and a confessor stress spiritual development as a result of passive reassurance, then this image is contrasted by a notion of God as an active deliverer. Shug's comment takes up this tension and chides Celie for, among other things, the passivity of her faith. Hinting at a more active pos-sibility, she observes, "The thing I believe. God is inside you and inside everybody else. You come into the world with God. But only them that search for it inside find it" (195). This remark implies two different models of instruction: submission to prescription and searching for revelation. While the former model is associated with white fundamentalist accounts of God, the latter recalls the mysticism of Howard Thurman. Critics have noted that Shug aggressively critiques Celie's cor-rosive perception of what God "look like," but equally important, in the mentorship paradigm, she focuses Celie on how God inspires humans to act (195).

7. Glossing Celie's nuptials, Linda Abbandonato claims, "When Celie marries Mr. __, this man with no name becomes part of the system of male oppression, joining God the Patriarch and Pa in an unholy trinity of power that displaces her identity" (1110–11).

Beloved—could have decided that the offspring of depravity were worthless.[8] She instead embraced motherhood, and even after her babies were immediately taken from her, she remembered them.[9] This remembrance prodded her toward actions that changed her life. By sending Nettie to Corrine, Celie not only sought better circumstances for her sister but also expressed a maternal longing for an improbable substitution. Her hope blossoms into Nettie's surrogate mothering of Olivia and Adam. While this blossoming could be deemed fantastic or like a "fairy tale," Richard Iton has argued that in black life, the fantastic contains insurgent dimensions (Berlant 29). He contends that fantasy or a vision that looks "beyond the already existing" challenges "conventional notions" of "the civil society." While Iton stresses how blacks use imagination to refute "the state as the sole frame for subject formation," Walker portrays the Jim Crow South with scant reference to chronology, a technique that emphasizes nebulous white power instead of specific governmental impositions (17). Celie's actions reflect the feminist mantra that "the personal is political," yet Walker's blending of faith, imagination, and a desperate bid for deliverance connect *The Color Purple* to 1960s debates about black authorship.[10] By studying Walker's educations, one sees how this novel's depictions of white mentors relate to such debates.

Helen Merrell Lynd, her academic advisor,[11] helped Walker when she transferred from Spelman—a historically black college for women

8. In *Beloved,* women like Sethe's mother and her friend Ella throw their rape-conceived children into the sea or refuse to nurse them. Celie's attitude contrasts theirs, mirroring that of some recent African rape survivors. Although the race of the rapist may play a role in these situations, the differences are still striking. By juxtaposing her character's status as a brutalized black American with that of other women in the Diaspora, Walker particularizes suffering even as she insists upon the benefits of communion. For a recent treatment of these realities, see Jonathan Torgovnik's *Intended Consequences: Rwandan Children Born of Rape* (2009).

9. Cheryl Wall argues that "the parallels in the plots" that *The Color Purple* "develops for Celie and Shug—particularly those that situate them as mothers of lost children—reinforce" their identification with one another (148). Although these women bond intensely, their attitudes toward their lost children are not the same. Celie asks Shug whether she misses the "three babies" that she has had with Mr. __, and Shug replies, "Naw . . . I don't miss nothing" (50). This statement could be attributed to Shug's pique that Celie has taken her place in Mr. __'s life, but drafts of *The Color Purple* suggest that Walker purposefully accentuated Celie and Shug's divergent maternal sensibilities. The drafts of *The Color Purple* are housed in the Manuscript, Archives, and Rare Book Library at Emory University.

10. See Carol Hanisch's "The Personal is Political" (1969) for an early exploration of this aspect of feminism. With "A Black Feminist Statement" (1977), the Combahee River Collective directly addressed how the personal and the political intertwined for black women.

11. Helen Merrell Lynd is the mother of Staughton Lynd, one of the Spelman professors who encouraged Alice Walker. While Walker appreciated her largesse, she felt that accepting her help had emotional costs. She stated, "Helen—as wonderful and generous as she was—condescended to me . . . Whenever I saw [her] I was nervous . . . because I never sufficiently outgrew my sense of being . . . the one who would not have made it without [her] help" ("Letter to Muriel Rukeyser" 19 May 1975).

located in Georgia—to Sarah Lawrence—an elite women's college outside of New York City—but her most vital relationship was with Muriel
Rukeyser. On a campus where Walker felt alienated by the wealth and
entitlement, Rukeyser created a spot for her where literature ruled
supreme.[12] She awakened a young Walker to the fact that "poetry, done
well, is always about the truth" and that this truth is "subversive" (White
109). While these insights resonated with the undergraduate, her interactions with Rukeyser were complicated.[13] Walker's 1965 correspondence
with her mentor outlined this complication, but ten years later, a full picture surfaced.[14]

In 1975, Walker boasted a "plum" editorship at *Ms.* magazine and
a poetry collection that had been shortlisted for the National Book
Award.[15] Rukeyser, according to Walker's biographer Evelyn White,
envied these accomplishments because she "had never imagined that
her own literary light might be outshone by the impoverished black
woman from Georgia whom she had 'taken under her wing'" (271).
When Walker produced a forlorn portrait of Zora Neale Hurston during
a television interview, Rukeyser saw a chance to set the record straight.
She wrote to her protégé, "Zora was helped, at Barnard," and this help

12. About Sarah Lawrence, Evelyn White writes, "Although Alice felt affirmed as a creative
writer . . . she initially was taken aback by the tremendous wealth of her new classmates . . . The
majority of Alice's classmates were 'of the manor born.' Their family names graced banks, prestigious museums, and international corporations. Still, as young white women for whom privilege
came as a birthright, they found license, in the 1960s, to rebel against their ruling class status by
playing out the 'rags-to-riches' role—in reverse. For Alice, who'd been raised in paper-thin shacks
without electricity or indoor plumbing, the apparent enchantment of her classmates with 'deprivation' was a constant source of bewilderment" (101).

13. Both Gerri Bates, the writer of *Alice Walker: A Critical Companion (2005)*, and Evelyn C.
White, author of the biography *Alice Walker: A Life (2004)*, identify Rukeyser as an indefatigable
promoter of Walker's career. Rukeyser's good friend Grace Paley said of the relationship between
the two: "There was no question but that Alice Walker was [Rukeyser's] prized student" (White
110), and on Walker's side, her enduring admiration for Rukeyser is clear in her intimation that
"[Muriel] . . . taught me that it was possible to be passionate about writing and to live in the world
on my own terms" (White 109).

14. Despite having known her for only a few months, Walker, after she had an abortion in
1965, wrote to Rukeyser. Her letter was mostly a mea culpa regarding some "slick and desperate
fabrications" she made in a moment of crisis, but what is striking in this document is the buffer that she erected in the face of heartwarming yet disconcerting generosity ("Letter to Muriel
Rukeyser" n.d.). This buffer may date from her childhood when white surveillance inevitably led
to a feeling of not being "worthy or valuable" (White 69). Though southern prejudice differs from
northern condescension, Walker felt that both attitudes meant that her emotions somehow differed
from those of the whites that she encountered.

15. Begun in 1971, *Ms.* magazine emerged as an influential venue for promoting American
feminism. About the publication's history and impact, see Mary Thom's *Inside Ms.: 25 Years of
the Magazine and the Feminist Movement* (1997) and Amy Erdman Farrell's *Yours in Sisterhood: Ms.
Magazine and the Promise of Popular Feminism* (1998). Walker's second book of verse, *Revolutionary
Petunias and Other Poems* (1974), was shortlisted for the 1974 National Book Award.

came from "white women." Rounding out her chiding, she added that
Walker had been "helped at Sarah Lawrence in comparable ways" ("Letter to Alice Walker"). Her mentee replied keenly: "Have you ever considered how like a beggar I felt . . . when all of you were 'helping' me?
How it felt to . . . have to depend on people who had no concept of
poverty that they did not get from visits to it . . . The distance between
us all was too great; an economic and historical distance that I seem
unable . . . to forget or ignore." Regarding Hurston, Walker contended,
"When I spoke of . . . Zora being 'helped' or not 'helped' *I mean by
her own people* . . . White people have helped and our literary history is
full of Van Vechten and Nancy Cunard, but it is not full of black people
who helped each other. When I first noticed this I felt myself shrink-
ing" ("Letter to Muriel Rukeyser" 19 May 1975). Walker's 1975 essay "In
Search of Zora Neale Hurston" is often cited as a catalyst for the revived
interest in Hurston's career, but her colloquy with Rukeyser implies an
intricate backstory. If the essay could be cast as Walker's attempt to make
Hurston a black foremother who balanced the white mentors in her
life,[16] then Rukeyser's letter suggests that her white female advocates
rued such efforts.[17] The missives between mentor and mentee did not
settle this matter; however, they influenced both the form and the content of Walker's prizewinning novel.

The epistolary structure of *The Color Purple* no doubt reflects Walker's attempt "to suggest that a reading audience can, like the audience
of an orally transmitted text, significantly alter" the way that a story is
told (Awkward 145–46). Focusing on God as Celie's addressee, Michael

16. Describing her early life, Alice Walker once observed, "Whenever white people came
around, everybody turned to ice; that was the effect they had on black people" (White 69).
Though the emotional distance described here derives from prejudice, Walker's attitude toward
the whites at Sarah Lawrence evinced a similar remoteness. She suggested this in her description
of "a white girl" that she met while picketing a jail: "We tried to keep in touch—but, because I
had never had very much (not even a house that didn't leak), I was always conscious of the need
to be secure. Because she came from an eleven-room house in the suburbs of Philadelphia and, I
assume, never had worried about material security, our deepest feelings began to miss each other"
(O'Brien 196). This sense of missing each other spurs Walker's racial reserve.

17. The fact of white female mentors who superintended Walker's education both in general and especially as a writer receives voluminous endorsement in all of her speeches, essays, and
books. Notwithstanding her ability to nurture these interactions, her attitude toward Rukeyser
and, to a lesser extent, Helen Lynd reflects the convoluted calculus that can attend those friendships. Gerri Bates explains that "independence and self-sufficiency" were "two important survival
skills for Walker." In talking about Walker's ultimate outlook on Zora Neale Hurston, Bates
states, "Walker concluded that Hurston was too dependent on others, thus her slump into financial ruin.
Hurston, Walker thought, had too little knowledge of survival and too few survival skills" (9). As
Walker's relationships with Lynd and Rukeyser evolve, her tenacious insistence on independence
and racial awareness begins to run headlong into their craving for white liberal affirmation.

Awkward concludes that "Walker constructs a text whose first letters suggest *failures* of communication" because He turns out to be an unengaged reader (148). Awkward's analysis fits readings of Celie that stress her belated empowerment and impotent faith, yet it overlooks how "desperate hope" nourishes fantastic vision (W. Miller, "Broadening" 67). Equally important, it neglects Walker's correspondence with Rukeyser as an influence on her depiction of Celie.

Celie's plight connects to post–civil rights black novelists generally and her author specifically. While her relationship with God seemingly features stasis, her faith reveals an active negotiation in both her writing and her actions. This negotiation centers on her development of a radical imagination. Just as Walker cannot erase the liberal entitlement that leads Rukeyser to confuse generosity with creative supervision,[18] Celie cannot undo the mainstream thinking that conflates a Christian deity with Santa Claus. Walker discovers that despite such frustrations, black identity hinges upon moral vigilance. When Celie apologizes to her daughter-in-law Sofia for telling her stepson Harpo to beat her, she says that she feels "shame" and that "the Lord he done whip [her] a little bit too" (40). Whipping helps her express a guilty conscience, but the diction also casts God as attentive and engaged. Linking this portrait of God to her remorse, Celie implies that His prodding plays a role in shifting her consciousness. Such shifting links morality to imagination, and Walker believes that the black art after segregation must patrol that intersection. *The Color Purple*'s Africa plot shows the perils of this patrolling.

Although it occurs thousands of miles from her sister's rural Georgia home, Nettie's African sojourn links with Celie's dilemmas. Her trip prompts questions about God that echo her sister's, and because the voyage is missionary, it puts this black struggle with white authority in a larger context.[19] While the internationalism and the serendipity of Nettie's odyssey seem implausible, Walker cultivates these dimensions precisely because she wants to dramatize the imagination in Jim Crow black life.[20] Celie has no idea that Nettie will be accepted into Corrine's house,

18. Lawrence Jackson, in *The Indignant Generation,* chronicles how Rukeyser's generation of white liberals often viewed their generosity and their concern as license to supervise black creativity.

19. *The Color Purple*'s missionary theme alternately inspires critics to chide Walker for incompletely engaging the ways that "the capitalist infiltration of Africa" formed the basis of "world racism against blacks" and to praise her for embedding "a post-colonial perspective on the action" (Berlant 35; Selzer, "Race" 68). Although debates about her depictions of Christianity and capitalism illuminate Celie's epiphany, these analyses obscure Nettie's travels from Pa's house to the motherland and her serendipitous chaperoning of her niece and nephew's parallel journeys.

20. Trudier Harris complains that the focus on Africa is "really extraneous to the central

and she certainly did not envision her sister as an African missionary. Despite her limited vision, she knows that placing Nettie in Corrine's house is her only chance to affect her children's fates. Nettie then provokes a shift in *The Color Purple*'s focus, yet this shift extends Walker's portrayal of Celie. By emphasizing Nettie's experiences as a missionary, a witness of colonialism, and a returning Diaspora African, the novelist stresses the protean dimensions of African American cultural orphanhood. The circumstances of the segregated South directly reflect grander realities that condition one's life even when one is ignorant of them. If this invisible conditioning exists, then freedom will demand more textured reactions. These reactions are explored in Nettie's second contribution to illuminating Celie's life, her nurturing of Olivia and Adam.

Olivia and Adam are archetypes of African American orphaning. They do not know their biological parents, and although their early years contain "love, Christian charity and awareness of God," their upbringings also reveal flux (133). Samuel and Corrine, their adoptive parents, work for the American and African Missionary Society. While the children begin their lives in small-town Georgia, they are taken from the South to New York to Senegal through Monrovia and on to Olinka, "[Alice] Walker's invented African nation" (Kuhne 69).[21] Their circuit to Africa could be seen as a sort of black "Grand Tour" since Adam and Olivia's visits to Harlem, Liberia, and the African interior provide potent counter-narratives to Western cultural dominance.[22] Despite such exposure, the pride that would make Senegal vibrate in an African American "soul" is balanced by knowledge of the hidden wounds within black societies (143). Nettie notes such paradoxes and insures that Olivia and Adam engage them. Recognizing that black Diasporic consciousness will not fix African American identity, she places nuance alongside nostalgia. Her efforts not only frame her niece and nephew's education among the Olinka but also their full understanding of their histories.

---

concerns of the novel" ("On" 157). Arguing that *The Color Purple* manifests "an indifference to historical contingencies," Melissa Walker believes that since "none of the [stateside] public events of [Celie's] time" registers in her mind or in "the novel," the protagonist "cannot even imagine that the world outside could affect her" (62, 63).

21. Kuhne notes that "Olinka . . . is much more than a village or a tribe; it is an invented West African nation with an Atlantic coast and considerable inland territory. And, like many actual African nations, Olinka is composed of several ethnic groups . . . Olinka has suffered from colonialism, and like many contemporary African nations, Olinka is ruled by a corrupt leader who has little regard for his people" (69). While Kuhne's catalog sees Walker's Olinka as credible, Cheryl Wall talks about the "problematic" aspects of Walker's invention (156).

22. For a look at black American returns to Africa, see James T. Campbell's *Middle Passages: African American Journeys to Africa, 1787–2005* (2006) and Kevin Gaines's *African Americans in Ghana: Black Expatriates and the Civil Rights Movement* (2006).

Adam's and Olivia's Olinkan experiences are ambiguous. Although this ambiguity surfaces in physical realities, it shows more vividly in their mental outlooks. Their schooling provides one example. Olivia chafes under Olinka's limited notions of femininity. The villagers "don't believe in educating girls," and her best friend's father, after forbidding his daughter Tashi from visiting Olivia, admonishes, "Your Olivia can visit [Tashi], and learn what women are for" (162). If this scenario pairs with Pa's pulling Celie out of school to exemplify "the universality of the oppression of women," then Adam's situation reveals another form of stifling (Kuhne 71). Adam has a "special aptitude for figures," but because Olinka lacks teachers, his skills cannot develop (164). His situation connects to the country's colonizers. Since the rubber company's engineers fixate on numbers, math skill evokes white authority. Adam's frustrated ability signals not only his arrested development but also Olinka's succumbing to European industrial power. Though Olivia and Adam see the village's deficits, they also enjoy its benefits. Each one's relationship with Tashi captures these merits.

Olivia and Tashi promote the feminine fellowship that flourishes in Celie's Georgia life. Just as Shug, Sophia, and Mary Agnes—Harpo's second wife—grant one another space for self-definition amid racist, sexist, and economic threats, Olivia and Tashi make room for expressing black womanhood despite Olinkan society's strictures.[23] Tashi's imaginings become especially charged as she strives to preserve Olinka culture in the wake of colonization. Pursuing this task, she has tribal marks cut on her face and plans to have her society's "female initiation ceremony" (239). Tashi's plight contrasts Celie's; nonetheless, Walker connects these characters as black females who confront white mentorship. Through this connection, the author not only unites moral striving in Jim Crow America and colonial Africa but also implies imagination's role in the success or failure of such striving. Celie's relationship with God changes when she evaluates the consequences of her imagination. While this evaluation involves getting "man off your eyeball" or revising white, patriarchal constructions of truth, it extends to testing and refining your vision of a moral self (*Color* 197). This process concludes not only with indignation but also revelatory possibility. Though Celie's actions on

---

23. *The Color Purple*'s depictions of blues singing and quilting attest the power of female friendship, and critics have robustly engaged this idea. On the blues and "sister bonding," see Cheryl Wall (141) and Michael Awkward (149–51). Catherine E. Lewis takes up the "sense of sorority" and sewing (167), as does Martha Cutter's "Philomela Speaks: Alice Walker's Revisioning of Rape Archetypes in *The Color Purple*" (2000).

behalf of Nettie and her children prove imagination can impact black orphanhood, Tashi's revolt, replete with radical solidarity, mistakes dogma for direction. Her relationship with Adam moves her physically and spiritually closer to Celie.

Adam and Tashi's marriage subjects Jim Crow American and colonial African disorientation to love's guidance. Nettie tries to heal Adam by filling in the gaps of his self-knowledge, and she reveals to both him and Olivia that Celie is their mother. Despite this disclosure, Adam shares with Tashi an unsettled identity. She addresses hers by taking up with the mbele, or "forest people," a kind of resistance movement that battles the white colonial forces (228).[24] Traveling to London, he supports his father's attempt to get the administrators of the African and American Missionary Society to intervene in Olinka. These reactions emphasize adjusting white behavior as a solution to black conundrums. As Celie's experiences with God showed, the focus on adjusting distorted white perceptions often disables imagination. Adam and Tashi arrive at a similar finding, and their commitment to each other belies the certainty of gender oppression and suggests the good in Diasporic exchange, two intraracial concerns. Although their empathy bridges cultural chasms, its costs highlight another dimension of moral imagination. Adam, when he finds Tashi among the mbeles, discovers that she is insecure about her facial scars and fears that he will leave her for a light-skinned, Americanized woman. Getting scars identical to hers, he rends his face to mark his heeding of the Biblical command to "rend your heart" (Joel 2:13). This tearing becomes the viable basis of black solidarity, and *The Color Purple* reflects a resolution of Walker's mid-1970s white mentorship crisis.

Walker matured artistically because of white mentors; nonetheless, she—at times—experienced their encouragement as condescension. If her 1975 letter to Rukeyser expressed her peeve at this dilemma, then the Sisterhood suggested one solution. Organized in 1977, the Sisterhood, a "non-profit" group designed "to unify black women artists," boasted members such as Margo Jefferson, Audre Lorde, Paule Marshall, and Toni Morrison.[25] Walker's hosting of this group's meetings continued a search

24. Linda Selzer states, "The mbeles are particularly significant because they comprise a remnant group defined not by traditional village bloodlines but by their common experience of racial oppression and their shared commitment to active resistance" ("Race" 78). Given this alliance, it is quite apt that Tashi would seek them out as she worked through her identity.

25. Although The Sisterhood consisted of women authors, its meetings often included general attempts to promote publication opportunities for "young black poets and writers." These attempts entailed lobbying *Essence, Ebony,* and *Ms.;* supporting fledgling publications like *First World;* and developing alternative publishing ventures like "Kizzy Enterprises" (Minutes of "The Sisterhood").

for moorings that had begun after she transferred from Spelman to Sarah Lawrence.[26] With *The Color Purple,* she shifted her preoccupations from white injury toward black moral renovation and discovered a cultural grounding. This development—as evidenced by the scathing critiques of Africa in *Possessing the Secret of Joy* (1992) and *Warrior Marks: Female Genital Mutilation and the Sexual Blinding of Women* (1993)—does not signal an embrace of black utopias; rather, it marks her deepest investment in spiritual resources. With this inward turn, Walker challenges Western literary individualism with an empathetic selfhood that retains the burden of communion. Here, she prefigures the vision that she gives to Celie. By the end of *The Color Purple,* Celie's tenacious faith literally summons all of the major actors in her life into an unlikely family. This summoning completes her fantastic imagination, and its results herald "personal transformations" as the vanguard of "social transformations" (Wall 160). While this personality seems either naïve self-indulgence or disguised conservatism, its beliefs were presaged by the ethics of swagger. *Middle Passage* is informed by a similar portent; however, Charles Johnson's route to the expression differs.

Foster Care

Celie snaps to moral attention because of Olivia, Adam, and Nettie. If Rutherford at the outset of *Middle Passage* lacks both offspring and fraternal love, his mind, like hers, does reflect an unresolved collision between black reality and white values. The segregated South stylized her predicament; slavery contextualizes his. Though he lives as a recently emancipated black New Orleanian, he was born in Makanda, Illinois, and raised by Reverend Peleg Chandler. Chandler, like *Beloved*'s Garner, lacks the brutality of other literary slave-owners, but despite the fact that he taught Rutherford and his brother Jackson "more than some

26. Walker's 1965 trip to Africa did not confirm the rhapsodic portraits that black nationalists were painting, yet it did intensify her exposure to African artists leading her in 1973 to ask: "Where is the book, by an American black person . . . that equals Elechi Amadi's *The Concubine* . . . a book that exposes the *subconscious* of a people, because the people's dreams, imaginations, rituals, legends . . . are known to be important, are known to contain the accumulated collective reality of the people themselves" (O'Brien 202). Although enrolled at Sarah Lawrence when she went to the motherland, Walker insisted that Constance Nabwire, her Ugandan roommate at Spelman, inspired her journey by teaching her "to care deeply about Africans and African women." She elaborated, "I went to Uganda trying to understand how Constance had been created and produced by this country which before Idi Amin was very beautiful, very tranquil and green" (A. Goodman). For more on Constance Nabwire, see White (73–74).

white men . . . knew" and then freed them, he still vexed Rutherford by insisting that he "become a credit to [his] Race" (8, 9). By substituting a preacher for God, *Middle Passage* takes the racial dimensions of *The Color Purple*'s theological portrayals and adds class commentary. Chandler's "credit to the race" rhetoric evoked a long tradition of white paternalism, and his focus on "respectability" bespoke bourgeois social values that Rutherford associated with "a kind of living death" (4). While his mindset is equal parts antimaterialist and hedonist, Rutherford also captures circa 1830 the wary interplay of blacks and democracy. Chandler à la Norton in *Invisible Man* implies that black exemplarity will speed access to mainstream society. Rejecting the premise and the process, Rutherford embraces a debauchery that echoes his father's. His attitude—given his enslavement—seems defensible, but his brother Jackson, who shares the same tutelage, raises questions about Rutherford's outlook.

While explaining his migration to New Orleans, Rutherford states that like many of the other slaves under Chandler's ownership, he fled the plantation when the owner freed him. His brother by contrast remained in Makanda, "more deeply bound to our master than any of us dreamed."[27] If sycophancy is one explanation for Jackson's behavior, then his determination to "serve his people by humbly being there when they needed him" invites other interpretations (113). His commitment to service could be read as a testament to Chandler's meticulous theological instructions. Just as Rutherford places his brother in the moral league of "a black saint like the South American priest Martin de Porres," Chandler states that in his selflessness, Jackson has been "an inspiration" to him (3, 118).[28] Far from rubber-stamping Chandler's mentoring, though, Jackson detects that the deeper tension in democracy is an individualist ethos that places personal pleasure above empathy. His life then is like Ruth-

27. Celestin Walby contends that Charles Johnson "models his characters in *Middle Passage* on Osiris, Horus, Seth" from Egyptian mythology. For Walby, Jackson represents Horus, the "falcon-god" who "sacrifices himself for the sake of the community," while Rutherford embodies Seth "Horus's worldly alter-ego" who rules "over the sensuous and purely physical" (661, 660). Walby's analysis not only suggests that African cosmologies form part of the intellectual crucible that Johnson concocts but also reinforces the tension between Johnson's decision to eschew the reality of Africa in favor of a personal myth of the continent.

28. Pianist Mary Lou Williams, a devout Catholic, premiered her composition "Black Christ of the Andes (Hymn in Honor of St. Martin de Porres)" in 1962. Gayle Murchison analyzes this premiere against the backdrop of "the civil rights movement, the Second Vatican Council, and Williams's return to jazz" (591). Although Johnson makes no reference to Williams in interviews, her connection of St. Martin de Porres to the fight for racial equality, the evolution of religious thought, and black artistic life makes Rutherford's quip about Jackson even richer. For more on Williams's composition, see Murchison's "Mary Lou Williams's Hymn *Black Christ of the Andes (St. Martin de Porres)*: Vatican II, Civil Rights, and Jazz as Sacred Music" (2002).

erford's one of active dialogue with Chandler's beliefs. The differences in
the brothers' styles reflect different reasons for their convictions.

Rutherford's Big Easy existence includes whoring and gambling. In
fact he is first drawn to New Orleans because it is "tailored to [his] taste
for the excessive, exotic fringes of life" (1). While he casts these appetites
as antibourgeois, his motives are multifaceted. Chandler, when Rutherford is still a child, notes "stickiness" within his fingers and "a tendency
to tell preposterous lies for the hell of it." Though his master sought in
vain to turn him to "Old Testament virtues," Rutherford adopted social
critiques that synced with his indulgences (3). This tendency emerges
most vividly in his theories about stealing: "Theft, if the truth be told,
was the closest thing I knew to transcendence. Even better, it broke
the power of the propertied class, which pleased me" (47). Rutherford's
remark betrays an opposition to class ascendancy and reification. Despite
these putatively lofty bases for his outlook, there is in Rutherford also a
tendency to romanticize his predicament. He observes, "The Reverend's
[Chandler] prophecy that I would grow up to be a picklock was wiser
than he knew, for was I not, as a Negro in the New World, *born* to be a
thief? Or, put less harshly, inheritor of two millennia of things I had not
myself made?" (47). As William Nash has pointed out, this musing evokes
black victimization and shows Johnson's desire to engage late twentieth-
century debates about black identity politics.[29] In addition though, it begs
a question tied to Johnson and his mentor John Gardner's debates about
art: what defines moral identity?

Johnson's relationship with Gardner commenced at the Southern Illinois University in Carbondale, a white campus lacking the drama that
Walker confronted at Sarah Lawrence. While SIU was a fairly benign
environment by 1972, the year the two met, their interactions still evinced
volatility. Johnson, looking back on their days together, deemed Gardner the best "teacher of the craft of writing in our time" ("World").[30]
Because he was a "skills . . . junkie," he felt that Gardner's admonitions
about "form as a meditation" were crucial to his grasp of writing's significance (Byrd, *I Call* 12; Watterson). These lessons about hard work and

29. Nash argues that Rutherford's "victimization mentality" leads him to "negative actions"
(145). By presenting this connection, Johnson, in Nash's view, continues a critique of "the heritage
of victimization" that runs through his entire oeuvre (45).

30. Johnson's claim about Gardner's teaching prowess appears in a blog, E-Channel. Conceived by his buddy Ethelbert Miller, this yearlong project allowed two black male artists space to
range over numerous topics. Johnson's friendships with Miller and August Wilson provide a fascinating complement to his experiences with white mentors. See his essay "Night Hawks" (2009)
for more on his interactions with Wilson.

technique united the two men, but when Johnson's creativity evolved, their exchanges revealed tensions.[31]

Gardner felt that great writing derived its power from classic Judeo-Christian verities. Because his "moralistic certainty about . . . art" reflected such Eurocentricism, his aesthetics dismissed certain creative experiments (Little 131). Johnson initially took his mentor's "word on literature as law," but by 1982, Gardner encountered fresh innovations in his pupil's work (Byrd, *I Call* 23). Incorporating the "meta-fictional" devices that Gardner had elsewhere criticized, Johnson also used Buddhism more conspicuously (C. Johnson, *Oxherding* xvii). These changes did not precipitate a falling out; however, they did show the inevitable stretching that accompanies an erstwhile student's growth. While Johnson and Gardner's disagreement reveals the generic conflict between a teacher and an apprentice, it also demonstrates the precise challenges that accompany a white mentor who seeks to shepherd an independent black artist. Johnson detected within Martin Luther King, Jr.'s study of Gandhi and Clarence Major's formal daring alternate paths for his own writing. While his interest in morality remained, his sense of the moral self defied Gardner's truths. *Middle Passage,* through the life of a man emancipated thirty-five years before slavery ends, allegorizes this defiance. Revisiting both *Beloved* and *The Color Purple*'s musings on freedom, Johnson's novel announces a black moral transcendence that affirms democratic pluralism. It does so starting with a slaver bound for Africa.

Rutherford's departure for the motherland lacks the salvific dimensions of Nettie's embarkation. In fact, his presence aboard the slave ship *The Republic* is directly connected to his sybaritic habits. He has amassed gambling debts, and when his creditor Papa Zeringue bargains with his girlfriend Isadora, Rutherford finds himself caught between certain maiming and imminent matrimony. Escaping the consequences of his debauchery, he unknowingly heads toward Senegambia. The closer that the ship gets to the motherland, the more intensely he, the sole black crewman, deals with questions of betrayal. These questions initially center on his relationship with the ship's captain, Ebenezer Falcon.

If Chandler exemplifies white mentorship on land, then Falcon supervises Rutherford's seaside apprenticeship. Falcon, as others have pointed

---

31. Regarding Johnson's divergences from Gardner, see Jonathan Little's *Charles Johnson's Spiritual Imagination* (1997), especially the section "Anxiety of Influence: Johnson and John Gardner" (127–35). Little's insights helped refine my linkage of *Middle Passage*'s characterizations and mentoring.

out, embodies an American tradition of oversimplifying duality.[32] In his discussions of merit, he offers Rutherford a template for white expectation and black behavior that is a conservative complement to Chandler's liberal one. He tells Rutherford, "I believe in *excellence* . . . Eighty percent of the crews on other ships . . . are *incompetent,* and all because everyone's ready to lower the standards of excellence to make up for slavery, or discrimination" (31–32). Falcon suggests that mediocrity rather than race and oppression determine the debased status of blacks. Aside from offering a chiding commentary on the affirmative action debates, this portrayal also shows the dangers of submitting to white constructions of black realities. A fuller sense of that danger surfaces in Falcon's attitudes toward the Allmuseri, the fictitious African tribe whose members form *The Republic's* cargo.[33]

Slavery's central transaction changes a human being into property, and that absurd transformation becomes the baseline from which the institution is judged. While *Middle Passage* makes Rutherford's antiestablishment posture a rebuke of such absurdity, Falcon's ambitions vis-à-vis the Allmuseri reveal the former slave's glib rage as an insufficiently rigorous response. Falcon wants to take the Allmuseri God and insert the deity into a system governed by "exchange value" (Selzer, *Charles* 190). Beyond producing a triumph of white Western power, this gesture signals blackness as a metaphysical vacuum. Falcon seeks to affirm the Hegelian edict that Africa and Africans are "no historical part of the world" (99).[34] Against this backdrop, Rutherford searches for solutions other than a conning indignation and a "bitter obsession with racial difference" (Nash 132).[35] His dilemma indicates the range of white expectations and the

32. William Nash claims that Falcon has "white supremacist convictions" that lead him to view "racial separation" as a natural adjunct to his dualistic vision (134). Embellishing that notion, Linda Selzer contends that the captain evokes a "rapacious nationalism" that prompts him "to police the borders of ethnic difference" (*Charles* 178, 181).

33. Ashraf Rushdy notes that the "Allmuseri are a tribe on the West Coast of Africa" which exists "only as a fictional product of Charles Johnson's fertile imagination" (Byrd, *I Call* 369, 370).

34. Hegel's contentions gain him a pride of place in almost all catalogues of anti-black thought; however, in the 1960s, British historian Hugh Trevor-Roper infamously reprised Hegel's sentiments when he observed, "Nowadays, undergraduates demand that they should be taught African History. Perhaps in the future there will be some African History to teach. But at the present there is none; there is only the history of Europeans in Africa. The rest is darkness, and darkness is not a subject of history" (9).

35. Nash is not the only critic who notes that Rutherford must shed his belief that "racially related suffering" entitles him to special privileges (133). For other voices supporting this position, see Philip Page's *Reclaiming Community in Contemporary African American Fiction* (1999), Linda Selzer's *Charles Johnson in Context* (2009), and Jonathan Little's *Charles Johnson's Spiritual Imagination* (1997).

flawed views "of what black literature . . . should be" and thus were part of "a universe silent to its sense" ("John" 623).[44] Caught between these realities, Johnson refined his aesthetic that fused Buddhism, American democracy, and black cultural experience. This refinement proved a powerful response to black cultural orphaning, and since *Middle Passage* won the National Book Award, "the only national prize [Johnson] ever wanted," it seemed triumphant (Ross).[45] In a telling paradox, his achievement exposed him anew to white literary expectations. Alice Walker, who wanted nothing to do with awards, joined him.[46] With their experiences, serious questions about art and authorization surfaced.

Co-opted Independence

Carol Iannone's "Literature by Quota" (1991) remains one of the few published pieces to ever link *The Color Purple* and *Middle Passage*. Evoking Walker and Johnson's accomplishments as evidence that late twentieth-century American prize grantors are more interested in "act[s] of repara-

44. Drawing on Charles Johnson's *Turning the Wheel: Essays on Buddhism and Writing* (2003) and the research of John Whalen-Bridge and Gary Storhoff, Marc Connor and William Nash conclude that Johnson's 1982 return to "sitting meditation" allowed him to see "engaged Buddhism" as useful for blacks "facing the systematic racism woven firmly into the fabric of American life" (xxviii, xxx). Though Johnson's *moksha* is unassailable, his spiritual development bespeaks both a generic penchant for refinement and a specific awareness that in black communities, his religion, writing, and philosophy are at times dismissed as substitutions of enlightenment for action. Johnson takes such dismissals seriously perhaps because of his father. See Watterson and Byrd (*I Call* 3–16) for more on their relationship.

45. In a 2010 interview with Michael Ross, Johnson explained: "The only national prize I ever wanted was the National Book Award because [Ralph] Ellison got it." Jonathan Little notes that when "Johnson won the National Book Award for *Middle Passage* in 1990, his acceptance speech was an opportunity to lavish praise on Ralph Ellison, whose aesthetic precedent and vision had long inspired" him (135). Though Little's statement conveys generous homage, Linda Selzer comprehensively grasps Johnson's affinity for Ellisonian ideologies: "The 1990 [NBA] award ceremony cemented Johnson's identification with the cosmopolitan wing of black intellectualism" (*Charles* 173). Johnson's alliance ultimately becomes his reply to questions about his art's cultural authenticity. Just as Ellison scorned those who lectured him on just how much whiteness his black creativity could include, Johnson saw in his work and his awards justification for his intellectual eclecticism. This chapter's conclusion suggests that his outlook was not shared by all of mainstream America.

46. Evelyn C. White observes, "[Alice Walker] did not and would not have lobbied Harcourt to submit *The Color Purple* to the Pulitzer jury . . . Nor had she sought the novel's nomination for the 1983 American Book Award in fiction, which it had also won the previous week. With regard to prizes, Alice was satisfied that she'd served, with openness and admiration, as a medium for her characters. That she'd rendered the lives of Shug, Celie, and Mr. __ with authenticity and compassion was all the reward she needed" (358). Where Morrison could and did make prizewinning an integral facet of her negotiations with white expectations, Walker rejected the awards metric even as she racked up envy-inspiring plaudits.

tion" than "the ethic of excellence and merit," the essay collapses these novels' explorations of white mentors and black apprentices into the more incendiary interracial narrative of affirmative action (51, 50). Iannone's motives for vilifying Walker and Johnson have been analyzed, but her remarks hint at how these writers' prizewinning books carry prophetic commentary on white expectations and the ethics of swagger.[47] *The Color Purple* and *Middle Passage* use two venerated forms in Western writing, the epistolary novel and the seafaring adventure respectively.[48] Employing these putatively white structures, they test the conventions of sentimental fiction and democratic pluralist allegory to see if they can be tailored to fit African American experience. Both books conclude that through a revised individualism, blacks can renovate their moral visions and create room for themselves amid the nation's gracious plenty. By perpetuating the "gross and dangerous oversimplification" that white supremacy monopolizes the judgment of merit and hence the parameters of American-ness, Iannone vivifies the tides against which Celie and Rutherford swam (Miles). Her efforts also suggest the after-the-prize complexity of the Black Archivists' negotiations.

Although Walker and Johnson began their lives amid rich black cultures, each writer advanced professionally with the aid of white mentors. Muriel Rukeyser set in motion events that led to the publication of Walker's first book.[49] John Gardner placed a chapter of Johnson's first novel in the journal *Fiction Midwest*.[50] Though both black authors were grateful for this help, their lives and their fiction dramatized the difficulty of balancing independent artistry and white expectations. Advancement,

47. For accounts of Iannone's agenda, see James English's *The Economy of Prestige* and Jack Miles's "The 'Dictatorship of Mediocrity'" (1991).

48. This chapter discusses *The Color Purple*'s epistolary aspects above. For more on Johnson's interest in American seafaring literature, see William Nash (146–50).

49. Rukeyser sent Walker's manuscript to Monica McCall, her literary agent. When McCall forwarded the book to Hiram Haydn, an editor at Harcourt, he accepted it and launched Walker's career. For a concise account of this episode, see Haydn's 1974 memoir *Words and Faces*. Haydn's role in promoting fledgling writers has been noted, but his specific contributions to black writers ranging from Paule Marshall to David Bradley is a leitmotif of this study.

50. Johnson had finished six unpublished novels, but by 1972 when he began working on his seventh, he concluded that he needed better instruction. While "working on *Faith [and the Good Thing]*," Johnson learned that one of his six apprenticeship novels had been accepted for publication. Though he "want[ed] to get published," his consultations with John Gardner convinced him that the book "wasn't" representative of his "philosophical vision." He explained, "[This novel] was very much in the style of James Baldwin, which is why I believe the publisher liked it . . . Gardner's influence helped me understand all of what is at stake when you write . . . Knowing him ratcheted up my concern with craft . . . and literary aesthetics" (Watterson). For an account of Gardner's role in Johnson's "first 'serious' literary publication," see Johnson's essay "John Gardner as Mentor" (622).

in the 1960s and 1970s, became easier with influential white friends. This truth undergirded Walker's editorial position at *Ms.* magazine and Johnson's writer-in-residence post at the University of Washington. If mainstream mentors could open doors, they also offered reminders that the power distribution between white teacher and black student was not equal. This inequality pertains in all mentoring relationships, but for black writers in post–civil rights America, the insecurities reached back a long way.

From the earliest days of African American writing, white mentors produced ambivalent effects. They authenticated black writing for a skeptical white public, and at the same time, they often tried to frame black art for a mainstream readership's consumption.[51] Walker and Johnson had carefully studied the black literary tradition and knew the history of these interactions. Although each correspondingly wrote *The Color Purple* and *Middle Passage* as a seasoned novelist, both saw the growing uneasiness regarding black artistic autonomy and used their own experiences with white expectations to ponder this phenomenon. One effect of their pondering was a kind of communion. The second part of this study will take up this communion more expansively, but here, the alterations that blacks and democracy demand of one another proves illustrative. Iannone suggests that such alteration may not be possible, but Ernest Gaines's *A Lesson Before Dying* shows that she is part of a "conflict of interpretations" which signals that change is already underway (C. Johnson, *Being* 20). Foraging among the "ruins of modernity," he sets the margins of such changes (R. Miller, *On* 1).

51. See chapter 1 of Robert Stepto's *From Behind the Veil: A Study of Afro-American Narrative* (1979) for an account of white authentication and black authorship. The enduring anxieties created by white mentors are evidenced not only in the eighteenth and nineteenth centuries, but also in the twentieth. For an overview of how sponsors like Charlotte Osgood Mason, Carl Van Vechten, and Nancy Cunard influenced the Harlem Renaissance, see Cary Wintz's *Black Culture and the Harlem Renaissance* (1996). Regarding Edwin Embree and the Rosenwald Fund, see Lawrence Jackson's *The Indignant Generation* and Alfred Perkins's *Edwin Rogers Embree: The Julius Rosenwald Fund, Foundation Philanthropy, and American Race Relations* (2011). Tom Wolfe's *Radical Chic & Mau-Mauing the Flak Catchers* (1970) updates the survey through the Black Power era.

3
three

A Lesson Before Dying
as Style Guide

Literary prizes and mentors reveal the diverse ways that white expectations challenge an ethics of swagger. Where the former exemplifies impersonal intrusion, the latter features intimate coercions. Thus, white authority conditions black writing both publicly and privately. If the Black Archivists confronted this conditioning through prize-granting and mentorship, then conflicts about style also affected their works. These conflicts were significant because they centered on creative innovation. Although Walker's experiments with the epistolary novel and Johnson's manipulation of the seafaring tale touched upon these issues, Ernest Gaines's revisions of classic literary strategies engaged them more directly. His style seemingly reflected an embrace of white aesthetics, yet in crucial ways his techniques and themes troubled the assumptions behind mainstream approaches. As his career progressed, the pitch of that troubling heightened.

Citing Ernest Hemingway, James Joyce, and William Faulkner, critics often ally Gaines with white influences. They are largely following his lead. In addition to the white modernists above, Gaines also mentions his artistic debts to Greek tragedians such as Sophocles and Russian masters—namely Turgenev, Tolstoy, and Chekhov. His writing, based on such statements, could be read as a product of white stylists and black topics. Gaines, a native of Louisiana, appreciates cultural hybridity. He recognizes the complex hierarchies created by creoles, whites, blacks, and even the gradations produced by skin tones. While such sensitivity offers a cosmopolitan outlook, he still notes racism as an organizing principle in southern society. This consciousness of racial reality produces a tension in his oeuvre, and especially in his later books, Gaines presents knotty musings about white influences and black style. In *A Lesson Before Dying,* these musings emerge luminously.

Examining *Lesson's* accounts of black male interaction, this chapter argues that Gaines's depictions should be understood as both social commentary and stylistic referendum. His novel's wrongful conviction plot refines the modernist trope of grace and at the same moment engages black men's dehumanizing encounters with the American justice system. By blending these purposes, Gaines not only indicts New Criticism's inveighing against politicized fiction but also dramatizes the tension between form and experience in the representation of black life. His conclusions regarding that tension are evident in how he uses the observer-hero narrative, a mainstay of white canonical texts, to probe the relationship between his two central characters, black males who are separated by class and temperament. Through these strategies, Gaines enters late twentieth-century debates about literary sophistication that are dominated by white judgments. His entrance raises questions about merit, race, and democracy.

Setting Style

Ernest Gaines sets his 1993 masterpiece *A Lesson Before Dying* in 1940s Louisiana, and the novel's attention to, among other things, separate but equal schools, humiliating retail experiences, and fatal encounters with law enforcement mark it as a meditation on a segregated southern world.[1] Given *Lesson's* preoccupation with marquee themes of African American protest literature,[2] one could be excused for calling it a vintage text.

---

1. John Lowe suggests that Ernest Gaines "had originally intended to set" *A Lesson Before Dying* "in 1988" (306). This abandoned plan has many interesting implications, but I want to emphasize Gaines's deliberate choice of a pre-integration environment. For more on this issue, see Gaines's essay, "Writing *A Lesson Before Dying*" (2005).

2. Protest literature centrally engages Anglo-America's inhumanity to its domestic black population. Claudia Tate says this about the protest tradition: "We . . . generally expect" black writers "to contest racist perspectives and the resulting oppression. Consequently, we require these texts and especially those of canonical status to foreground the injustice of black protagonists' persistent and contested encounters with the material and the psychological effects of a racially exploitative distribution of social goods, services, and power. We might call this the manifest text of black literary discourse" (*Psychoanalysis* 3–4). For more on protest literature, see Noel Schrauf-

Although its mise-en-scène and pastoral lyricism seem incongruous in the often experimental and sometimes arcane world of the Black Archivists, Gaines's book engages matters of black art and white influence that directly recall *Beloved, The Color Purple,* and *Middle Passage.* Toni Morrison, Alice Walker, and Charles Johnson inspect aesthetic conundrums using transnational phenomena such as slavery and missionary activity, but Gaines focuses on the Jim Crow South. In the 1990s, with the success of a film such as *Driving Miss Daisy* (1989), this focus might have marked him as somewhat hip. Gaines's South, though, eschews trendy racial mutuality. Charting the rifts that Dixie caused and the spiritual renovation that it could host, his accounts of alienated African American males revise white modernism's technique fetish and infuses its conception of grace with black southern tints.

Lesson focuses on Grant Wiggins, a thirty-something schoolteacher, and Jefferson, a twenty-one-year-old field hand. These two were initially united for the latter's formal education, and they are reunited when he is sentenced to die for a murder that he did not commit. Reflecting how the American justice system dehumanizes black men, *Lesson's* portrait of wrongful conviction evokes novels such as Mentis Carrerre's *Man in the Cane* (1956), Nathaniel Hook's *Town on Trial* (1959), and Harper Lee's *To Kill a Mockingbird* (1960).[3] Despite sharing earlier texts' interest in black male experiences of trials and incarceration, Gaines's novel revises their emphases. *Lesson* rejects the interracial plot that casts the white lawyer as the savior of the black accused.[4] By replacing the lawyer-client pairing with a teacher-convict one,[5] the book curtails white control of dignity. In the place of mainstream liberalism, it offers the difficult proposition of black male empathy. *Lesson's* chief negotiations appear to be male-

---

nagel's *From Apology to Protest: The Black American Novel* (1973) and *Pamphlets of Protest: An Anthology of Early African American Protest Literature, 1790–1860* (2001).

3. Carlyle V. Thompson discusses Jefferson's case in "From a Hog to a Black Man: Black Male Subjectivity and Ritualistic Lynching in Ernest J. Gaines's *A Lesson Before Dying*" (281–82). For more on black masculinity and incarceration, see Keith Byerman (45, 47). Gaines discusses the inspirations for Jefferson's situation in (*Mozart* 53–54).

4. This plot emerges in several black civil rights novels, including Richard Wright's *Native Son,* Mentis Carrerre's *Man in the Cane (1956),* Nathaniel Hooks's *Town on Trial (1959),* and William Bosworth's *The Long Journey* (1956). It resurfaces in feature films such as *A Time to Kill* (1996), *Amistad* (1997), *Hurricane* (1999), and the television show *Raising the Bar* (2008).

5. Concerned about this scenario's verisimilitude, Gaines "wrote a letter to the warden at Angola, the state prison . . . in Louisiana" trying to determine whether "it would be possible for someone not kin to the condemned man who was not a minister of religion or his legal advisor to visit him on death row" (*Mozart* 52). When that appeal received no answer, he queried an ex-sheriff who informed him that decisions like that "would be entirely up to the discretion" of local law enforcement officials (*Mozart* 55).

dominated; nevertheless, Gaines's inclusion of guardians such as Tante Lou and Miss Emma and Grant's love interest, Vivian Baptiste, implies that black women influentially admonish black men as they strive to fulfill their potential. Responding to signature novels within the twentieth-century literary canon, these representations suggest that segregated Louisiana—replete with sharecroppers, one-room schoolhouses, and a tenacious racial hierarchy—holds keys to Reagan era black masculinity.[6] The first step in acquiring such keys is appreciating the life rhythms of a "very old place."[7]

Nearly all critics of Gaines's work have remarked upon his abiding interest in rural Louisiana. Though it is tempting to group him with other master evokers of Dixie, Mary Ellen Doyle warns that his "parish is not the same in terrain, history, or culture as other parts of the South of modern literature . . . nor is his fictional re-creation of it truly comparable in content, style, or tone" (4, 5). Much of this distinction arises from the extremely personal contours of Gaines's landscape. Explaining why, when he was living on the West Coast, he had to "come back to the South again," he confessed, "I can write in San Francisco, but I could not stay [there] and write without coming to Baton Rouge. I must go back to the plantation where I was born and raised. I have to touch, I have to be, you melt into things and you let them melt into you . . . the trees, the rivers, the bayous, the language, the sounds" (Knight 69). This sentiment was offered in 1974, and more than twenty-five years later, he reaffirmed it: "[My] body had gone to California to be educated, but [my] soul was still there in Louisiana . . . It was only that place that I really wanted to write about, from the beginning and even to this day" ("Ernest").

Gaines's affinity for the Louisiana countryside reflects his passionate desire to document the part of his home folks' "history" that "has not been told" (Tarshis 74). Recalling that when he went to California in late 1940s, he "read and read, but . . . did not see [him]self and [his] friends and family and relatives in the stuff " he was reading, Gaines betrayed a goad for his career that anticipated black women writers

---

6. In addition to revising his Black Archivists peers, in particular Alice Walker's *The Color Purple*, Toni Morrison's *Beloved*, and Charles Johnson's *Middle Passage*, Gaines also takes on depictions of the rural South like those offered in Ralph Ellison's *Invisible Man*, Richard Wright's *Uncle Tom's Children* (1938) and *The Long Dream* (1959), and William Melvin Kelley's *A Different Drummer* (1962).

7. Borrowed from Albert Murray's 1971 memoir, the phrase—"South to a very old place"— evokes Dixie's hidden cultural and spiritual repositories. Even as this phrase honors spaces of nurturing, it also carries a hint of exhaustion. This tension between regeneration and fatigue aptly marks Gaines's portrayals of his home region.

such as Morrison, Gayl Jones, Walker, and Gloria Naylor (Fitzgerald and Marchant 8). Like these authors, he turned to his pen because he did not see his life reflected in literature. Thus, every time he recorded southern existence, he paid tribute to ancestors who were silenced. Though commemoration undoubtedly fueled Gaines's creativity, his explorations of blackness via Louisiana plantation culture bespoke futurity in addition to nostalgia. Just as Morrison's Reagan era accounts of slavery registered as a musing on 1980s cultural realities, Gaines's portrayal of segregation created distinct ripples in the 1990s. The writer felt that though his novel "would have been a totally different book had" it been set "in 88 instead of 48," he still saw it "speaking to 88 . . . trying to demonstrate to readers how" the situations of the 1980s and 1990s "came about" (Lowe 309). One of the most interesting late twentieth-century situations involved the rural/urban divide in black life.

The 1990s world in which *Lesson* was published confronted problems related to policing, education, and gender strife that were devastating in black communities. While explanations for these phenomena evoked "postmodern urbanity," Gaines saw these city-centered analyses as inadequate (Dubey, *Signs* 15). The simultaneous growth of the black middle class and of the black poor and imprisoned was a fulfillment of many 1970s prophecies of division; nonetheless, for black men, the roots of this polarization predated both the civil rights movement and the Great Migration.[8] Gaines suggested that notwithstanding urban relocations, late twentieth-century black masculinity entailed a literal or a metaphorical journey South. Put differently, solving the riddle of black male wholeness hinged on a return to the spaces where inequality was spawned. Once the black man arrived, his most poignant withdrawal would be a grace filled with the complex obligations of love.

The segregated South sought to free the black man "from addressing the question of personal responsibility" (Byerman 48). This describes Jefferson when his defense attorney misguidedly compares him to a hog, but in equally pernicious ways, Grant also gets tempted to abdicate his duties. Matthew Antoine, his former teacher, outlined the temptation. When an exuberant Grant visited Antoine after his first semester in college, instead of receiving support, he heard this opinion about his parish and his fate: "You have to go away to know about life. There's no

8. The specter of alienation has haunted black male success narratives at least since Frederick Douglass recorded his experiences learning to read. In *The Future of the Race* (1996), Henry Louis Gates, Jr., and Cornel West suggest that "mounting intraracial disparities" insure that such polarization will not soon diminish (36).

first in outlook or life-style and as embodying in purer or more extreme form qualities which the observer has or sympathizes with in moderation" (93). Buell concentrates exclusively on white American and European texts, but his observations' relevance to *Lesson* is telling.

Gaines's preoccupation with the observer-hero narrative emerges in "the inseparability of [his] two main characters"; however, he moves outside of an abstract juxtaposition of "divergent psychic universes" and makes Jefferson and Grant's relationship a metaphor for his commentary on black masculinity (Buell 94, 104). Like Morrison when she grapples with New Criticism, Gaines's use of the observer-hero narrative shows both a thorough awareness of American and European master tropes and an abiding insistence that black experience retains distinctness.[17]

Thematically, this surfaces in *Lesson*'s reconfiguration of classical narratives of crime such as Charles Dickens's *Bleak House* (1853) and Dostoevsky's *Crime and Punishment* (1866). In those texts, the intellectual's energy is directed toward detection and imprisonment. That is his proper work. Extending traditions evident in a work such as John Edgar Wideman's *Reuben* (1987), Gaines depicts an intellectual bent on redemption. The novelist's depictions of southern grace's impact on Grant and Jefferson's interactions extend and complete his critique.

Gaines, paralleling Ralph Ellison's sentiments in "A Very Stern Discipline" (1967), has long identified Ernest Hemingway's notion "grace under pressure" as a model for his depictions of black life (Rowell 91).[18] In *Lesson*, he adds an interesting inflection to his explorations of this theme. The minister in *Lesson* plays a more flattering role than in any other book by Gaines. In fact, a few observers believe that Rev. Ambrose is one of, if not the most respectable preacher in the novelist's oeuvre.[19]

17. Gaines's concern with narrative emerges throughout his career. In a 1976 interview, he discusses his approaches to writing points of view: "When I start a book in the first person point of view my characters take over very soon and then carry the story themselves. From the omniscient point of view, it is harder for me (for the characters to take over), because it seems that I'm always interrupting them" (Rowell 88). Regarding *Lesson* specifically, see Lowe (299–301) and Gaines's essay "Writing *A Lesson Before Dying*."

18. About Hemingway, Gaines observed, "[His] writings of . . . grace under pressure, his writing about the white characters, made me see my own black people. For example, who has more pressure on him than Jackie Robinson when he was playing baseball . . . or Joe Louis? No man has had more pressure on him than Martin Luther King" (Rowell 91). While Hemingway throws pressurized reality into graphic relief, Gaines notes that the white writer's "black characters" were "very seldom . . . given any kind of sympathetic roles" (Rowell 91). This discrepancy perhaps merely emphasizes the difference between good technique and progressive content, but in *Lesson* the relationship between skill and theme facilitates a musing on cultural particularity and aesthetic fusion.

19. See William Nash's "'You Think A Man Can't Kneel and Stand': Ernest J. Gaines's Reassessment of Religion as Positive Communal Influence in *A Lesson Before Dying*" (2001) for more

Although a positive portrait of the clergy could serve many ends, the author here uses a venerable man of the cloth to explore southern grace. Christianity gives the name grace to the divine sufficiency unleashed in the wake of Jesus's crucifixion and resurrection. Thus, in Protestant theology, grace is tied to unmerited and replete favor. If Dixie's religious heritage makes this perspective on grace resonant, then another rich connotation also circulates. Southern hospitality includes not just rote kindness but also sincere generosity. Distinctions like these demarcate well-mannered gentility and the emotional commitment to another's comfort. Grace then, at its most profound, is not mere cheeriness; rather, it is an acceptance of the unrequested and often unwelcome obligations that impinge upon individual freedom. In *Lesson*, Gaines posits a multivalent southern grace as the catalyst to Jefferson and Grant's successful confrontations with human messiness.[20] By doing so, he customizes redemption and sends reverberations along both white canonical wires and the lines of urban-centered narratives of black misery. Grant is the key to deciphering such vibrations.

When Tante Lou forces Grant to endure entering Henri Pichot's back door and being searched at the jail, her nephew accuses her of "helping them white people to humiliate" him. He explains, "Everything you sent me to school for, you're stripping me of it" (79). Grant's remark reflects plausible indignation. To him, grace and humility do not mark resourcefulness; rather, they are the defense mechanisms of a community so overwhelmed by "bewilderment and disenfranchisement" that it "does not possess the means to sustain resistance in the face of white hostility" (Beavers 139). Thus, the concession that Jefferson's guilt or innocence is pointless becomes for Grant a stinging rebuke of black impotence. When he is talking to Tante Lou and Miss Emma about their request that he make Jefferson a "man," Grant registers his pain with defiant sarcasm: "Jefferson is dead . . . He's dead now. And I can't raise the dead. All I can do is try to keep others from ending up like this" (13, 14). The teacher's statements seem impersonal, but his confession to Vivian proves that his assessment is more profound: "I need to go someplace where I can feel I'm living . . . I don't feel alive here" (29).

---

on negative portrayals of ministers in Gaines's work. About the Reverend Ambrose, Gaines says, "I had [him] start out as the old stereotypical black minister . . . just doing odd jobs . . . But at the end he seems stronger than Grant, in a way" (Lowe 324).

20. Katherine Daley and Carolyn M. Jones argue that *Lesson* "is a story of faith that uses Christian symbols and myths as vehicles for communicating a set of social values" (84). Where they see an antirational "love" impelling Grant and Jefferson to "undergo willingly" what they would "have been forced to undergo in the past," I argue that the love that leads both men to graceful action is tied to careful calculation (113).

Grant's anger, defined by a fusion of naiveté, entitlement, and pride, evokes the idealistic calls for cultural ascendancy voiced by the Black Arts Movement. His judgments reveal a clear anxiety regarding submission; thus, he itches to resolve the collision between helplessness and agency by raging against the machine. Though Grant's fury finds vent in *Lesson,* its efficacy dissipates quickly.[21] Just as BAM's internalization of the European tendency to valorize culture could not translate neatly into American blackness, Grant's swashbuckling aspirations, part Nietzschean übermensch and part silver screen phantasm, collapse. This collapse powers Gaines's meditations on style. If earlier Grant's impulses were toward violence in the service of honor, then with Jefferson, he seeks at least metaphorically an all or nothing prison break. Incremental change strikes him as quiet concession, a sentiment next door to enabling acquiescence. Grant's techniques of freedom are the counterpart to flourish with no substance, and Gaines sees black novels in the late twentieth century as afflicted with soulless virtuosity. If such performances hold no hope for reviving black communities, Gaines suggests that there might be a more viable resource.

Gaines turns Grant, the black intellectual, into a vehicle for his ruminations on "adequate witness" and "proper . . . testimony" (Beavers 141). At the same moment that Grant facilitates this foray into the breach between religious and juridical possibilities for blackness, he also symbolizes the aesthetic options that can solidify the twentieth-century novel. Grant cannot glibly import external prescriptions into the dense peculiarities of his community's existence, and likewise Gaines contends that his narrative's incorporation of cues from Anglo-American and European masters of the idiom must be sublimated to culturally specific experiences. Thus, from his early admiration of Russian writers such as Turgenev to his abiding affinity for technicians such as Joyce, Gaines always balanced white models with black sensibilities. Grant's life seems utterly divorced from such necessities. After all, he lives in a rigidly segregated world. Still, like many characters in novels by the Black Archivists, his capacity to testify stalls because of a foreclosed vision. Grant's interactions with Jefferson's writings become *Lesson*'s corrective lens.

---

21. Grant's rage evokes the rebellious spirit that Gaines encountered at San Francisco State in the 1960s. The novelist recalls, "I was . . . attacked by many of the black militants for having spent my time working on [*The Autobiography of Miss Jane Pittman*] when I should have been out there fighting cops . . . I said, 'listen . . . I'll go back home and I'm going to write the best paragraph that I can write that day; I'll make it so good that it'll be read long after Bull Connor . . . and the cops" are "dead" and "gone" (Lowe 317). This commitment to a testimony that lasts beyond suffering becomes Grant and Jefferson's biggest accomplishment.

Incarcerated Heroes

Tante Lou, Miss Emma, and Vivian all offered Grant enlivened imagination as the antidote to apathy, but Jefferson's diary with its misspell-
ings, improper grammar, and tangled syntax becomes the touch-point for
Grant's true emergence into alternate options. Though the diary could
be seen as an appropriation of Faulkner's approach in the opening pages
of *As I Lay Dying* (1930), it also bears traces of Celie's odyssey in *The
Color Purple*. This triangle intimates Gaines's investment in a fusion aesthetic that will bolster black writing, and Grant's reaction to the diary
bears out this optimism. The schoolteacher brings Jefferson a notebook
with the suggestion that maybe the prisoner "could write down [his]
thoughts" (185). Cast then as a performance of literacy and as a docu-
mentation of consciousness, the diary could be seen as Grant's assignment
in humanity for Jefferson. Gaines acknowledges this possibility, yet he
also suggests that the diary is a part of Jefferson beyond Grant's access. He
observes, "I had to get into Jefferson. No matter how much Grant would
ask him questions, he was evasive . . . I needed something to get into Jefferson's mind . . . The diary was there for the reader to see who he was"
(Lowe 300). This mechanism for probing Jefferson's essence becomes a
metaphor of authoritative witness. In his diary, Jefferson hazards a mode
of expression that unapologetically communicates his identity. Through
this depiction, Gaines exposes Grant to the purest possibilities of self-
knowledge, and by extension, he isolates black narrative's swagger.

Jefferson's diary forms an interesting adjunct to his execution. While
Rev. Ambrose's strength emerged because he attended the latter, Grant's
graciousness centers on what he does with the former. Paul Bonin, the
kindly white deputy, arrives at the end of *Lesson,* to tell Grant that Jefferson was "the strongest man in that crowded room" (253). Aside from
offering this perception, Paul has also been tasked to deliver Jefferson's
diary. He shares with the schoolteacher, "I didn't think it was my place
to open the notebook. He asked me to bring it to you, and I brought it
to you. But I would like to know his thoughts sometime—if you don't
mind" (255). Ed Piacentino stresses that Paul's curiosity signals "the
possibility for eventual change and racial harmony in the segregation-
ist South" (83). While such "racial reconciliation" may lurk in the novel's offing, *Lesson's* chief priority at its conclusion—à la *Beloved*—is the
shedding of crippling criteria regarding exemplarity (Piacentino 73).[22]

22. In an earlier draft, Gaines planned to have Paul tell Grant's class how Jefferson died coura-
geously. His agent objected, "You can't have this white guy come through there now" (Lowe 305).

A *LESSON BEFORE DYING* AS STYLE GUIDE   **85**

Grant detects segregated society's belief that "upward mobility alone is the signifier of heroic action," and despite his resistance, he himself starts with the idea that "the heroic ideal is . . . middle-class, financially comfortable" (Beavers 145). When he interacts with Jefferson, Grant must move beyond sociopolitical propaganda and venture into the unruliness of black survival. The schoolteacher by the end of *Lesson* is humbled, admitting that the jailbird Jefferson is "better" than him (193). By accepting such a valuation, Grant takes on a humiliating truth. His tear-filled clutching of Jefferson's diary, the record of the young man's "true self," not only ends *Lesson* but also it frames Gaines's commentary on narrative (Lowe 301).

Describing his anxiety about the stream-of-consciousness style and the dialect in Jefferson's notebook, Gaines writes, "I was a bit concerned about the reader . . . I thought, 'I can't play the Molly Bloom thing and go to sixty pages.' Joyce was writing an experimental novel, and people want to read him for that. But in my case they're going to read . . . the story, as it is" (Lowe 301). Gaines's comment conveys his status as a writer's writer, one who always considers his craft's practical demands. In addition, his remarks include a subtle reminder of the negotiations concealed in masterful expression. Early in his career, Gaines made it clear that while he counted white American and European writers as influences, no black authors, "not . . . Richard Wright or Ellison or Baldwin or anybody like that," figured in his development (Fitzgerald and Marchant 13). He explained why: "In all the creative writing classes I took there were no stories by black writers . . . *Invisible Man* was out but nobody was assigning it . . . You were just beginning to read Baldwin's essays, *Notes of a Native Son* . . . There was very little emphasis upon writing by black writers" (Tooker and Hofheins 110). By the time that he was writing *Lesson,* Gaines retained his conviction that Turgenev, Hemingway, Faulkner, Gogol, and Eudora Welty shaped his sensibility, yet his sparring with the dense lyricism of Morrison's *Beloved* and the pun-laden pedantry of Johnson's *Middle Passage* suggests his awareness of new voices in the debates about artistic fundamentals. Gaines's determination then to write "cleanly, clearly, and truthfully . . . so that anyone might be able to pick it up and read it" speaks to the Black Archivists' aspirations to spurn other folks' "Molly Bloom thing[s]" and embrace a sublime born of ordinary individuals making their way as real people

---

Thus, just as Robert Gottlieb lurks within Toni Morrison's *Beloved,* a white interlocutor haunts Gaines's *Lesson.*

(Rowell 97).[23] With characteristic generosity, he shared his treasures with others.

Ralph Ellison acknowledged black folk culture as a vital influence in creative expression, yet he relied on white modernists such as T. S. Eliot and James Joyce to organize his incorporations. Because of this, at crucial moments, he manifested an incomplete trust in his work's folk values. Lawrence Jackson, Lena M. Hill, Adam Bradley, and Barbara Foley have all commented upon the ways in which Ellison's editing of the Mary Rambo sections of the drafts of *Invisible Man* radically affected the novelist's putative agenda.[24] While Gaines was perhaps unaware of these particular manuscripts, his questioning of Ellison's grasp of southern life surfaces prominently in Tante Lou and Miss Emma.[25] These women oversee Grant's interactions with Jefferson from start to finish. Possessed of onerous demands, they nonetheless instruct him in the dignity of indignity. Tante Lou sacrifices to fund Grant's future; Miss Emma uncomplainingly gives her labor until the debt of her generosity comes due. These examples propel Grant into an understanding of what Robert Hayden called "love's austere and lonely offices" (10). Gaines's portrayal thus sharply critiques *Invisible Man*'s protagonist, who flees Mary Rambo and seeks solace in the Brotherhood.

If *Invisible Man* provided one target for Gaines, then Black Arts Movement texts such as Amiri Baraka's *Dutchman* (1964) and Charles Gordone's *No Place to Be Somebody* (1969) get addressed in Grant's fantasies of epic heroism. Certainly, Joe Louis and Jackie Robinson penetrated the vice-grip that segregation placed on black possibility, and in many ways, characters such as *Dutchman*'s Clay Williams and *No Place*'s Johnny Williams emblematized a black everyman that sought such neat triumph. Grant, the middle-class black male, revealed Gaines's belief that when confronted with cultural agony, ornamental protocols evaporate. These revisions of black feminine and black masculine portraits connect

23. Assessing Gaines's second novel *Of Love and Dust* (1967), John Edgar Wideman wrote, "Eschewing Faulknerian montage and metaphysical rhetoric is consistent with Gaines's description of his writing as characterized by the 'simplest terms'" ("Of Love" 82). Thus, Gaines even then was refining his attitude toward white modernist exemplars.

24. For discussions of the Mary scene in both draft and published forms, see Lawrence Jackson's *Ralph Ellison*, Michael Hill and Lena Hill's *Ralph Ellison's Invisible Man: A Reference Guide (2008)*, Adam Bradley's *Ralph Ellison in Progress: From Invisible Man to Three Days Before the Shooting* (2010), and Barbara Foley's *Wrestling With the Left*.

25. Gaines's most explicit statement regarding Ellison and southern culture occurs in a 1994 interview. Gaines observes: "I don't think that [Ellison] really knew the Southern land—the swamps, the bayous, the fields, picking cotton. I think because of that, he just overplayed his hand sometimes" (Lowe 312).

to a theory of artistic practice, a theory that subordinates white modernist conventions to a faith in black folk expression. Gaines thus calls the
twentieth-century African American novelist back home.[26] Ironically, the
mainstream critical establishment remained mute to the call.

Verdicts on Black Eloquence

Lesson's responses to white aesthetic expectations may indicate Gaines's
peeve with the chronic oversimplification of his art. Listening to yet
another commentator call him a quaint yet grave chronicler of agrarian
demise, he might have declared that enough is enough and started com-
posing a novel that rebutted their pabulum. Such a response would be
understandable, but Gaines's disposition makes this gesture unlikely.[27] As
was the case when he lost the Pulitzer Prize to his mentor Wallace Stegner, he would probably greet ostensible snubbing with a dismissive wave
of his hand. Gaines might deem it inappropriate to upbraid critics of his
work; however, he by contrast felt compelled—as Ronald Reagan's second presidential term ended—to take up his ongoing meditations about
the rural/urban divide in African American experience. These meditations were fateful work, akin to the ruminations on cultural erasure that
had initially led him to pick up a pen. As had been the case in the 1950s,
his thoughts alerted him to an absence and prompted him toward filling
it.

By the late 1980s, a curious combination of demographic shifts, mar-
keting manipulation, and political debate conspired to make public black
identity a predominantly urban phenomenon. This development profoundly affected African American music and fashion, and in literature, it
prompted a crisis because "claims to racial representation could no longer be objectively grounded on organic models of community" (Dubey,
Signs 5). While Gaines acknowledged how income disparities, incarceration, and gaps in education splintered black lives, he resisted assertions

26. On "Back Home," a cut from Gill Scott-Heron and Brian Jackson's *Winter in America*
(1974), the Great Migration's unfulfilled promises dishearten the song's speaker. Still, if the metropolis's streets leave him "lost and searching for one warm friendly smile," then the remedy is a
return to Dixie, where he has "got him some people" who "love" him (Scott-Heron and Jackson).
Using these conventions, Heron and Jackson evoke what bell hooks calls a "beloved black community," one that survives exodus and terror to preserve African American culture (*Yearning* 36).

27. Gaines's staid outlook on prizes can be discerned from his 1994 remark about his Mac-
Arthur Foundation Genius Grant. He stated, "I knew people who had won the MacArthur, but I
never thought I'd win . . . I assumed they [the awards] were political" (Laney 293).

that folk values, the source of black survival since slavery, had been over-whelmed by the postmodern city. Gaines's resistance, brilliantly mani-fested in *Lesson,* seemed outmoded and naïve in sociopolitical terms, but by manifesting suspicions regarding classic and avant-garde strategies of literary representation, it presciently predicted the subtlety of white expectations.[28] His eloquent warning had an ambivalent afterlife.

White expectations bedevil the Black Archivists' pursuit of swagger in dynamic ways. At one moment, white authority assumes a New Critical guise and invalidates political content. Two decades later, white aesthetic fashion veers toward postmodernism, championing stream-of-conscious-ness narratives and suspicions about the author's role. Gaines saw this as a shell game and, returning to the orienting verities of black southern life, advocated an aesthetic authorized by grace. The 24-person selec-tion committee for the National Book Critics Circle Award rewarded his efforts and gave him its fiction award. On one level, his NBCCA could be seen as an instance of white affirmation. No black writer had won that prize since Toni Morrison in 1977, and as Jack Miles, former presi-dent of the National Book Critics Circle, explained, the NBCC's exten-sive polling and its larger judging board mean that this award "represents the literary establishment far more closely than any other body in this country" ("Dictatorship"). While such prestige was not to be sneezed at, Gaines's illustrations of how black art could effectively engage white aes-thetic traditions were incompletely registered. His swagger was trumped by post-structuralism's hankering after experimental aesthetics, a hanker-ing gratified by some of his Black Archivists peers.[29]

Although Gaines's retooling of modernism and the observer-hero narrative were ingenuous, his techniques showed indirectness. This

28. Gaines's responses to wrongful conviction and black middle-class impotence featured humility as potentially edifying. In a moment coursing with a "marvelous new militancy," his prescriptions seemed anachronistic (Hansen 87). For evidence of both popular and bourgeois re-bellion, see, respectively, Public Enemy's classic album *It Takes A Nation of Millions* (1988) and the April 1990 *Ebony* cover story, "Success is the Best Revenge," about Vanessa Williams, the former Miss America whose crown had been stripped. This article focused on Williams's marriage, her booming record career, and her family life. This portrait of bourgeois bliss engaged a specific tri-umph over racial prejudice, but the story's title phrase emerged as a generic slogan of affluence as activism. A vivid example of this temperament is a poster—from the early 1990s—that pictured a black man standing in front of a garage where a Lamborghini, a Porsche, a Ferrari, and a Mer-cedes-Benz are parked. Beneath, the caption reads, "Success is the Best Revenge."

29. Gordon Hunter, in a lecture entitled "Prestige and the Case for Contemporary American Realism," argued that in many ways, the late twentieth-century canon of American novels reflect-ed seventy years of tyranny by avant-garde tastemakers. Because of this tyranny, Hutner believes that many literary critics have minimized the importance of accessible narratives. His assessment holds important insights regarding *Lesson.* Professor Hutner delivered his lecture on Thursday, September 17, 2009, at the University of Iowa.

indirectness may constitute a final aspect of white expectations' impact on black swagger. Post–civil rights novelists mostly eschewed incendiary confrontations with white literary authority. When friends of Toni Morrison violated this rule to protest the 1988 National Book Award decision, they were roundly criticized. The factors driving that criticism were complex, but the problem that such criticism revealed was simple. In the late twentieth century, black novelists were uncertain regarding the appropriate form and tone for critiquing white values. Almost any contrarian utterance ran the risk of being dismissed as racial victimizing.

The first part of this study argues that the ethics of swagger forces black novelists to look at how white expectations influence their art. If such looking shows the delicate and difficult process of claiming autonomy, then it also reveals that journeys into the black archives were crucial to creative innovation. My treatments of Morrison's engagement with Alice Childress and Gaines's revisions of Ralph Ellison allude to these journeys. In "Black Traditions," the second part of this book, I will explore how the Black Archivists' profound knowledge of literary history burnished the ethics of swagger. I start by reconsidering a situation that Walker and Johnson illustrated, the work of one Black Archivist prompting a reply from another. Where Walker and Johnson produced a single exchange, Gloria Naylor and Toni Morrison's rebuttals cover a much longer history.

II

Black Traditions

One to Write On

Communion Without Consensus in
The Women of Brewster Place and *Jazz*

The Black Archivists' struggles with white expectations are not about cataloging prejudice; rather, they are meditations on the prospects for democratic pluralism.[1] Just as these meditations focus on white authority, they also explore black traditions. Gloria Naylor and Toni Morrison undertake such explorations in *The Women of Brewster Place* and *Jazz*. Although the Great Migration shapes these novels' plots, both books link that southern exodus to commentary on black fiction.[2] The commentary examines cultural communion. While some critics see a romanticized South and a retreat from cosmopolitanism in works such as *Women* and *Jazz*, their interpretations overlook the intergenerational conflict that keys these texts' action.[3] These conflicts cast the collision between rural

1. Herman Gray captures how mainstream America constantly confuses special pleading and democratic work when it comes to its black citizens. He notes that the nation's "unwillingness, even inability, to see communities of color as more than aggrieved political subjects is evidence of the lingering effects of a post–World War II liberal discourse of national identity" (91).

2. The Great Migration names "the mass movements of Blacks to American cities in the twentieth century" (Pruitt 437). According to Bernadette Pruitt, "scholars since the 1960s have estimated that 7 million African Americans between the years 1915 and 1970 abandoned the rural and urban South for metropolitan and industrial centers across the country" (437). See Isabel Wilkerson's *The Warmth of Other Suns: The Epic Story of America's Great Migration* (2010) for a narrative history of this phenomenon. Focusing on literature, Farah Jasmine Griffin's *"Who Set You Flowin'?": The African American Migration Narrative* (1995) and Lawrence Rodgers's *Canaan Bound: The African American Great Migration Novel* (1997) both analyze relocation plots.

3. W. Lawrence Hogue and Madhu Dubey talk about urban crisis and black southern nostalgia in *Race, Modernity, Postmodernity: A Look at the History and Literatures of Peoples of Color Since the 1960s* (1996) and *Signs and Cities: Black Literary Postmodernism* (2003), respectively.

origins and urban change less as a fall and more as a test. If this collision signals the different responses that elders and youngsters give to the questions implicit in modernity, then it also shows how survival entails paying attention to the link between individual flair and collective discipline. That attention edifies psychologically and literarily. In fact, the ethics of swagger hinges on such scrupulousness. Naylor and Morrison's experiences with black writing reveal why.

While she was an editor at Random House, Morrison researched earlier black authors and promoted promising new ones.[4] Naylor's pursuit of African American literature took her to university libraries, and her efforts turned up similar treasures.[5] Refining recovery instincts that first led them to write, Morrison and Naylor believed that engaging black authors who had been ignored was apt commemoration. Still, they did not unearth the literature merely to lionize it. In prior writings they noticed techniques, themes, and ideas that could enhance late twentieth-century representation. By studying their predecessors, Morrison and Naylor hoped to make blacks more than "leftovers in the imagination of white America" (Williams-Forson). They wanted to balance preservation and critique and advance a notion of growth through interdependence. Avoiding glib unity, they depicted belonging that did not stem from consensus. Their depictions reflected an artistic innovation where black authors used one another to write on.

Women and *Jazz* recalled earlier novels such as Ann Petry's *The Street* (1946), Dorothy West's *The Living is Easy* (1948), Ralph Ellison's *Invisible Man,* and James Baldwin's *Go Tell It on the Mountain* (1953).[6] Although these books routinely celebrated relocation, they also revealed anxieties about such movement's impact on African American "cultural cohe-

4. For an overview of Morrison's editing career, see Cheryl Wall's "Toni Morrison, editor and teacher" in *The Cambridge Companion to Toni Morrison* (2007). Jessica Harris and Dana Williams also engage her support of black writers in "I Will Always Be A Writer" (1976) and *In the Light of Likeness Transformed: The Literary Art of Leon Forrest* (2005).

5. Between 1975, when she started college, and 1981, when she completed her B.A. in English and her first novel, Naylor "read voraciously, discovering a rich history of black writers" (Fowler 14). Her Yale master's thesis in Afro-American Studies (1983) extended her explorations of this "newly discovered . . . literary tradition" (Whitt 7). Because of this training, Henry Louis Gates, Jr., concluded that Naylor was arguably "more immersed in the formal history" of "the African American literary tradition" than anyone could have been "before the late seventies" ("Preface" ix).

6. The themes of black women confronting the city not only recur in literature but also in music. Songs such as The Friends of Distinction's "Willa Faye" (1970) and The Whispers' "Olivia (Lost and Turned Out)" (1975) stand alongside better known cuts such as Stevie Wonder's "Living for the City" (1973), George Benson's "On Broadway" (1978), and Gladys Knight and the Pips' "Midnight Train to Georgia" (1973), conveying the extent to which rural/urban circuits struck black artists in the 1970s.

sion" (Tally 17). These anxieties confirmed that the move from the South to the North was a bedeviling project, one that even by the twenty-first century remained incomplete. Concerned that the Great Migration had buried crucial memories, Naylor and Morrison explored how novels could counteract cultural forgetfulness.[7] Thus, while *Women* and *Jazz* included classic accounts of South-to-North trips, their portrayals also meditated on how urbanization impacted post–civil rights black creativity. Specifically, these books show Naylor and Morrison's desires to not only address the Reagan era's "political fable[s]" but also the "critical fable[s]" that divorce black art from its moorings (Fraser 90).[8] The former was evident in the pathological narratives of black city life that America's political leaders produced beginning in the 1960s.[9] By the 1980s, the latter emerged in critical theories that neglected the fellowship that fed the rise of the black novel. *Women* and *Jazz* revised these fables, stressing the exchanges that made black urban community meaningful.[10] In Naylor and Morrison's correctives of one another, such exchanges feature unity without unanimity. This trait's benefits extend from the pages of their fictions to the writers' professional interactions.

Contemplating Naylor and Morrison's takes on narration, housing, and violence, this chapter considers how *Women* and *Jazz* connect the Great Migration plot to debates about black writing. While these

7. Naylor lamented that in the 1960s, not many books contained "reflections of . . . [her] experience" (Goldstein 4). Because of that absence, she felt that the novel circa 1980 should be retooled to testify on behalf of black females who could not find "a mirror of [their] worth in society" (Naylor, "Conversation" 189). Morrison expanded this idea. Sensing that the moment where music and other "ceremonies . . . sustained [black] culture" had passed, she believed that the novel must now provide "information about how to hang onto what . . . is important and how to give up things that are not" (McCluskey 41).

8. Linking her perceptions to Hortense Spillers's remarks about the American literary canon, Celeste Fraser defines Reagan era political fables by referencing family values and black female poverty. She joins several critics who read black women's literature of the 1970s and 1980s as a reaction against the Conservative Revolution. For examples, see Barbara Christian "Naylor's Geography: Community, Class, and Patriarchy in *The Women of Brewster Place* and *Linden Hills*" (1990); Melissa's Walker's *Down From the Mountaintop: Black Women's Novels in the Wake of the Civil Rights Movement, 1966–1989* (1991); Gloria Wade-Gayles's *No Crystal Stair: Visions of Race and Gender in Black Women's Fiction (1997);* and Claudia Tate's *Black Women Writers at Work* (1984).

9. James Berger's "Ghosts of Liberalism" usefully summarizes how the political narratives of the 1960s registered in African American thinking in the 1980s. See also Ashraf Rushdy's *Neo-Slave Narratives.*

10. Naylor and Morrison complete *Women* and *Jazz* during the sociological revival of the 1960s and 1970s. This moment is pejoratively associated with the Moynihan Report, but it also produced "Black Sociology," a branch of study conducted by black scholars and for black people (Watson 109). For more on this epoch, see Arthur S. Evans's "Role Relations of Black Sociologists With the Black Community: Perceptions of Sociologists" (1983) and Neil J. Smelser's "Sociology: Spanning Two Centuries" (2003). The interventions offered by black sociology register with writers; however, black novelists felt that city life demanded fictional explorations.

novelists note past strategies for depicting the metropolis, they juxtapose alienation and collectivity to ponder culture and consensus. Their juxtapositions present healthy artistry as a posture that questions both the mainstream and the tribe. Recognizing the necessity of such questioning, *Women* and *Jazz* nonetheless suggest that the ground on which black artists stand will be much more stable if they are aware of who stood there before them.

Broken Dreams

Women and *Jazz* use trios of characters to explore the Great Migration. Lacking the ruthless ambition or the work issues emphasized in earlier migration novels, both books sketch black folks that have come north and discovered a puzzling space. These middle-aged individuals often possess wisdom; still, their functions are diffuse, a fact borne out by *Women* and *Jazz*'s narrative structures. In musical terms, the trio provides space for individual voice and for harmonic interplay. *Women* and *Jazz* envision pleasing blends of individuation and harmony; however, they also capture dissonance. With this tension, Naylor and Morrison suggest the gaps in even a shared black experience. Their suggestions relate to notions of community. Everyone in *Women* and *Jazz*'s trios endures the Great Migration firsthand, yet their attitudes tax black collectivity. Probing dashed dreams, escapist vices, and tempered despair, these books chronicle attempts to turn hard knocks into nurturing. A glimpse at *Women*'s major migrants shows the stakes.

Etta Mae Johnson and Mattie Michael—her Rock Vale, Tennessee, running buddy—confirm Naylor's interest in "the redemptive possibilities of female coalescence"; however, Ben's inclusion complicates the significance of the novel's trio (Awkward 98). Aging residents who all descend to the novel's eponymous apartment building, Etta Mae, Mattie, and Ben consider whether a "Southern trace" in their characters can translate into northern endurance (R. Miller, *Literary* 201).[11] Their considerations imply shifting cultural curriculums. Etta Mae departs Dixie

11. Maxine L. Montgomery argues that "the descent motif," which depicts "a protagonist's physical or psychological journey to a place where he or she attains self-knowledge," generally explains Naylor's narrative strategy in *Women* and specifically accounts for the consciousness of Mattie, Ben, and Etta Mae. Though I agree that each member of the trio acquires self-knowledge, the notion that such knowledge equals "anonymity" misses a crucial lesson regarding black humiliation (42–43).

because the region was not ready for her "blooming independence" (26). Tinged with repression, her life seems a Janie-esque battle against limits; thus, her departure could be a renunciation of horizon-pinching matrons.[12] While aspects of this scenario fit her situation, her behaviors defy simple conclusions. Etta Mae ties seduction to security. If sex for her suggests freedom, then it also promises a satisfaction marked by commitment. She finds sexual liberty, but after chasing fulfillment all over the North, she sees sensuality as a hurdle instead of help. In many ways, her sentiments match her pal Mattie's. Mattie was propelled onto a "northbound Greyhound" by an unplanned pregnancy and her father's religious convictions (24). Revising Etta Mae's hype regarding the metropolis, her plight exposes her to squalor in "an unnamed Every-city somewhere in urban America" (Goldstein 3). When Mattie's young son Basil gets bit by a rat, he not only joins a host of black fictional characters who have endured the tenement's perils but also propels his mother into a desperate search for other accommodations.[13] This desperation eventually lands her amid the "expensive mahogany furniture" and the "china bric-a-brac" that filled the home of her benefactor, Miss Eva (32). Where Etta Mae came north looking for independence, Mattie was directionless until Miss Eva delivered somewhere "safe and comfortable" for her and her son (40). Her reckless belief that she could secure this treasure yields to recognition that the city makes such attainments too costly. Ben's odyssey also bears this out.

Arriving "*a year before the Supreme Court decision in* Brown v. Topeka Board of Education," Ben, an alcoholic "*janitor and handyman,*" was Brewster Place's first black resident. He resided "in the basement of 312" and has access to every apartment in the building (3). Although his underground dwelling recalls the protagonist of *Invisible Man* and that character's predecessor, Fred Daniels from Richard Wright's "The Man Who Lived Underground" (1942), Ben also evokes the Super who terrifies Lutie Johnson in *The Street*.[14] Super inspires fear because he trades

12. Margaret Whitt links *Women* and *Their Eyes Were Watching God* through the pairs of Mattie Michael/Butch Fuller and Janie Crawford/Johnny Taylor (22). Though the former couple's conception of a child separates them from the latter, it also shows why Etta Mae, like Janie, flees her restrictive environment.

13. Mattie's experience in a rat-infested apartment ties her to the Thomas family in *Native Son* and to Maud in Gwendolyn Brooks's *Maud Martha* (1953). These connections suggest Naylor's awareness of the black literary tradition and show her engagement with several intertexts, a key strategy for her expressions of black urbanity's dilemmas.

14. Henry Louis Gates, Jr., contends that Gloria Naylor used "Ann Petry's *The Street,* the classic work of black feminist naturalism, as her silent second text" in *The Women of Brewster Place* ("Preface" ix).

in lascivious gazes, but Ben's defining gesture is agonizing confession. His central agony regards why he left the South. While he was share-cropping, Ben noticed that his landlord had taken an unseemly interest in his daughter. He could not muster the courage to confront the white man, so he took to liquor and effectively pimped out his child. Like Mattie, Ben at first viewed the city as shelter from shame, but unlike her, he never experienced its deliverance.

For *Women's* trio of migrants, the novel's unnamed metropolis proves coterminous with the quandaries that sent them scrambling northward. Their Dixie distresses never recede; rather, they tax the rituals that nurtured black survival below the Mason-Dixon line. From Christianity to the blues, no coping behaviors provide a panacea within urban space. These facts threaten to turn Brewster Place, the last stop in several of its inhabitants' free falls, into a graveyard of frustrated folk aspiration. Although the neighborhood's fate lends credence to morbid assessment, Naylor's novel persistently unsettles standard calculations of value.[15] For instance, *Women's* Mattie, Etta Mae, and Ben do not equal success when measured by bourgeois yardsticks, but as occasions for exploring life's lacerations, they produce immense benefits.

Although Mattie never reconciled with her father, her religious faith signaled an attempt to square two dispossessions that framed her life. Her father impelled her toward *Women's* unnamed city when he kicked her out, and her son Basil jumped a bail she secured, thus forcing her move away from the house that Miss Eva left her.[16] If Mattie endured by refining her father's Christianity, then her friend Etta Mae used hustling to shape her existence. From the moment that she judged Rock Vale too small for her tastes, Etta Mae wandered from one spot to another, scrambling to find lovers to sponsor her lifestyle. Her movements bespoke a determination to live pleasurably, yet just as Mattie's agenda prompted a throwback reckoning, Etta Mae's rambling eventually begged the question of what offers true satisfaction. Etta Mae's life contained stops at the fork dividing settling down and loneliness that conjured *The House of Mirth's* Lily Bart. Unlike Lily though, she cherished female fellowship as

15. For an analysis of Brewster Place's death, see Jill Matus's article "Dream, Deferral, and Closure in *The Women of Brewster Place*" (1990).

16. Basil's encounter with law enforcement anticipates Jefferson's situation and the torturous realities that fuel John Edgar Wideman's fictions. His panicky flight before his trial dramatizes the difficult questions regarding American institutions and black male liberty that surfaced in *The Chaneysville Incident* when John Washington's brother Bill was faced with a draft notice.

a port amid emotional storms.[17] The male among *Women*'s elders receives no such solace.

Reminiscent of Pilate and Reba in Morrison's *Song of Solomon*, Ben combines fretting over parenting with alcohol.[18] Those women sold wine in part to fulfill their charge's appetites, but Ben drank to quiet his daughter's incriminating calls. By the time he arrived at Brewster Place, he has not been in her presence for many years; nevertheless, her importuning, a "bell-like voice" that enters his ears and commences a "deadly journey toward his heart," remained a spur to his binges (154). Ben then seems less "an ever-present reminder of the failure of America's economic system" and more an example of enduring misery by "drinkin', the rest of [his] worried days" (Bonetti, "Interview with Gloria" 43; Bogan, "Drinking Blues"). Philip Page describes Mattie as hemmed in by "the implacable harshness of reality," and his contention applies equally to Ben and Etta Mae. Paralyzed by their lack of "transcendent or mythic powers," this trio, for Page, symbolizes Brewster as a site where one "can only dream of better conditions and more viable selves" (*Reclaiming* 163). Page's analysis casts dreams as souvenirs of impotence, but Naylor—evoking Martin Luther King, Jr.'s prophetic vision—emphasizes the rewards of imagination.[19] Facing urban repression, blacks, in Naylor's view, thrive not by controlling physical space but rather by diligently tending emotional obligations.[20] This outlook also conveys the novel's commentary on black literary tradition.

While Mattie, Etta Mae, and Ben possess an impressive collection of soul scars, the trio's purpose is not just documenting woe. Each character's suffering surfaces in *Women,* but Naylor's uses of their suffering reveals her outlook on black cultural consensus. Mattie, Etta Mae, and

17. Maxine L. Montgomery persuasively argues that Mattie Michael allows Etta Mae the freedom of fellowship. When the latter returns depressed from another one-night stand, Mattie "offers the warmth and support" that Etta Mae needs by empathizing via the "common bond" of disappointing "romantic relationships" (45).

18. Ben exists in intriguing literary company. Although his wine-fueled escapades lacked the boisterousness of *Song of Solomon*'s Henry Porter's, they did evoke characters like Frank in *Go Tell It on the Mountain,* who self-medicated to quiet demons.

19. Michael Awkward suggests that such imagination could be compensatory as opposed to revolutionary. He explains, "With respect to its negative consequences, not only does the female flight into imagination represent at times a 'pathetic' attempt to transform a painful experience, but also it serves to compel women to commit plainly injurious acts of self-deception" (113). For more on dreaming in *Women,* see Jill Matus's "Dream, Deferral, and Closure in *The Women of Brewster Place.*"

20. Naylor's focus on empathy as opposed to property may reflect her engagement with Black Nationalist debates about the land question. For an overview of those debates, see Russell Rickford's "'Claiming Earth': The Land Question and Pan Africanist Theory in the 1970s" (2012).

Ben are rarely in the same room with each other, and they never share a conversation together. Notwithstanding this separateness, their afflictions and more importantly their survivals limn a representative range of Great Migration experiences. Their representativeness is qualitative rather than quantitative, and this effect is purposeful. Just as 1950s novelists grew to mistrust the sociological accounts of black life offered in works such as Gunnar Myrdal's *An American Dilemma* (1944), so too did 1970s writers view documents such as the Kerner Commission Report (1968) as informative yet flawed. Their narrative structures strive to address those flaws using a sampling technique, and Naylor's approach in *Women* is illustrative.

Instead of making her trio of black elders comprehensive, Naylor imbues them with singular, yet resonant life stories and sends them, jazz-style through shifting chords of experience. An understanding of their situations depends in part on analyzing earlier characters in black literature. Mattie and Etta Mae recall Elizabeth and Florence in Baldwin's *Go Tell It On Mountain*. Revising his portrait of fallen black womanhood, Naylor removes marriage from her characters' lives and enhances their friendship's ability to blunt urbanity's effects. Her reactions to Baldwin exemplify the value of black literary archives. While her engagement with him refines her art, it also enriches black literature's response to truncated accounts of African American city life. These benefits are not confined to exchanges that cover several decades. As was the case with *Middle Passage* and *The Color Purple,* the Black Archivists sometimes revise one another. Morrison's efforts in *Jazz* are emblematic.

Jazz reprises *Women*'s focus on a trio of migrants by depicting the married couple Joe and Violet Trace and the widowed seamstress Alice Manfred, middle-aged characters that have navigated the city for decades. While Mattie, Etta Mae, and Ben's navigations take place in an anonymous metropolis, Harlem, the setting of *Jazz,* produces mythic resonances.[21] Morrison heightens this impact by setting her book during the 1920s, a moment when cultural excitement exploded.[22] Despite allud-

21. In *Harlem Crossroads: Black Writers and the Photograph in the Twentieth Century* (2007), Sara Blair argues that *Jazz* represents Toni Morrison's "first direct confrontation with the phenomenal precedent" and the "iconic power" of both Harlem and the Harlem Renaissance (256). Blair states that up until *Jazz,* Morrison's portrayal of "the Renaissance" made the movement "a monitory point of departure and a place of no return" (257). These sentiments reinforce a prevailing perspective on Morrison's novels, namely that she willfully marginalizes major historical events in favor of mining more obscure episodes in African American life.

22. For portraits of Harlem during the 1920s, see David Levering Lewis's *When Harlem Was in Vogue* (1981). Ann Douglas's *Terrible Honesty: Mongrel Manhattan in the 1920s* (1995) offers careful and sustained scrutiny of New York City as a whole.

ing to the neighborhood's iconic status, she quite often writes around its brio. The fabled community's coursing energy can be detected, but *Jazz* gives the reader a Harlem pulsing with possibility and undergirded by melancholy. The reasons Joe, Violet, and Alice inhabit the Big Apple bear out this paradoxical simultaneity.

When they met in Vesper County, Virginia, Joe fell out of a tree and almost landed in Violet's lap. This uncanny event began the process whereby she "claimed him" (105).[23] Describing that claiming, Joe confessed that he "had not chosen" marriage to Violet "but was grateful . . . that he didn't have to; that Violet did it for him, helping him escape all the redwings in the county and the ripe silence that accompanied them" (30). "Redwings" and "ripe silence" are images from Joe's fruitless search for his mother. Though he could never locate his lost parent, Violet's laying claim replaced maternal absence and eventually propelled the newlyweds out of Dixie and onto New York City's trains and boulevards. If orphanhood and figurative adoption define Joe's trek, then Violet's migration odyssey carries alternate cravings for family reunions.

Violet knows her mother and father; however, the former's death and the latter's sporadic presence throw her into the care of True Belle, her maternal grandmother. This grandparent child-rearing arrangement recalls black narratives from Hurston' *Their Eyes Were Watching God* to Randall Kenan's *A Visitation of Spirits* (1989); however, where those texts present elders who constrain youthful ambition, *Jazz* presents True Belle as a promoter of adventure.[24] A former slave who had, like Frederick Douglass, left a plantation and lived in Baltimore, True Belle told Violet and her siblings "spellbinding tales" about the city's wonders (102). These

---

23. Claiming here could be romantic or socioeconomic, but the act also carries traces of redemption and prizewinning. These are Violet's cues regarding family. Her maternal grandmother, True Belle, and her father both enter Violet's life using the vocabulary of rescue and reward. After her mother gets dispossessed, True Belle shows up with "ten eagle dollars" and "Baltimore tales for grandchildren she had never seen" (142). Her father, arriving "two weeks after [his wife's] burial," dispensed "ingots of gold for the children, two-dollar pieces for the women and snake oil for the men" (99). These episodes express affection as intermittent and as a perforator of crisis.

24. In African American literature, intense conflict defines guardian/grandchild arrangements. Janie famously charged Nanny with trying to take the horizon and pinch "it in to such a little bit of a thing that she could tie it about her granddaughter's neck tight enough to choke her" (Hurston 85). Likewise, Horace Cross, the protagonist of Randall Kenan's *A Visitation of Spirits* (1989), senses that his grandfather's Christianity included "a biblical intolerance of homosexuality" that not only "alienate[d]" these two family members but also made the older "complicit" in the younger's death (Coleman, *Faithful* 65). These depictions suggest that caregivers risk more than rapport when they impose their worldview on their charge. The cost of communal preservation—figured as maintaining the elder's values—is at least hatred and at worst death.

tales touted Baltimore's "more sophisticated way of living" and introduced Violet to "a beautiful young man" named "Golden Gray" (139). Born to True Belle's white mistress and "a black-skinned nigger," Golden, whom Violet never met, "tore up" her "girlhood" by starring as the love object in her youthful fantasies (143, 97). His centrality to her romantic ideas caused her to question whether Joe had merely been a "substitute" for him (97). This capacity for substitution also registered in her attraction to New York City.

Joe and Violet, as a young married couple, "bust out" of the South "just for the hell of it" (181). Each of them has intricate reasons for such capriciousness, yet at base, they seek "their stronger, riskier selves," the selves "they always believed they were" (33, 35). True Belle's loving portrait of Golden fuels Violet's belief that the city can harbor inspiring affection, and Joe's thankfulness for Violet's soothing of his motherlessness yokes him to faith in the metropolis. Connecting hope and relief to the energy of the urban grid, the Traces then seek to substitute a space for their emotions. They depend on New York City for "somewhat which" they do "not carry," transgressing Ralph Emerson's axiom regarding travel ("Self-Reliance" 149). Their actions bespeak miscalculation of the city's talents, and the final member of *Jazz*'s migrating trio makes a similar misjudgment.

Alice Manfred left Springfield, Massachusetts, when her husband chose life with his mistress over marriage to her. This event stoked a "fear" that had dogged her, but it was not the chief motive behind her relocation to New York City (54). Alice's fear stemmed from stark racial realities rather than mere infidelity; nonetheless, for her, the causes of both events were the same, submission to disorder. From Illinois to Springfield, black communities were menaced by white threats. Alice's solutions to such threats were retreats into homogenous neighborhoods and unassailable dignity. Her remedies proved dicey when her husband preferred a woman that "wore white shoes in winter" to his "elegant" spouse (86, 83). Though New York City might not undo such selections, in 1896, when Alice arrived, it boasted possibilities that suited her reverence of bourgeois respectability. Her assumptions counterpoised racial terror and cosmetic correctives. In juxtaposing these forces, she clarifies *Jazz*'s creative amendments.

Women replaced *The Bluest Eye*'s focus on the "*inter*racial sources" of black female pain with an exploration of such hurting's "*intra*racial" dimensions (Awkward 103).[25] In light of this replacement, Morrison's

25. While *Women* possesses other crucial intertexts, Awkward's claim remains illuminating. In

decision to make *Jazz* an answer to Naylor's artistry is understandable. Her depictions address Naylor's reactions to *The Bluest Eye*, yet *Jazz*'s engagement with Naylor's perceptions of *Beloved* is also illuminating. During the mid-1980s, Naylor and Morrison took part in a long dialogue that *The Southern Review* published. Their conversation has been hailed as the sort of "symbiotic merger" that typifies interactions between black female writers (Awkward 7).[26] Although that discussion prompted warm feelings, by 1987, when Naylor served on the National Book Award panel that did not select *Beloved* as a winner, the writers' symbiosis appeared less certain.[27] *Jazz* subtly answers such uncertainty.

Critiquing the untroubled camaraderie of Mattie and Etta Mae's friendship, Joe and Violet's interactions, while grounded in love, are friction-filled. Morrison complements this adjustment by replacing Ben with Alice. Where he reveals self-destructive coping with interracial affront, she suggests the limited efficacy of elevating such hurt over intraracial pains. Negotiating these competing emphases enhances *Jazz*'s accounts of the Great Migration, and at the same moment, it grants *Women* a shrewd reading from a skilled reader. Thus, the Black Archivists provide support even as they offer critique. This model of interaction becomes crucial for the cohort's artistic advances, and in *Women* and *Jazz,* it drives their portraits of the black community. Considering these novel's commentaries on residence shows their investment in cultural fellowship.

---

addition to *The Bluest Eye,* Naylor's early novels—especially *Linden Hills*—are seen as revisions of other works by Morrison, namely *Song of Solomon*. For more on this idea, see Barbara Christian's "Naylor's Geography: Community, Class and Patriarchy in *The Women of Brewster Place* and *Linden Hills.*"

26. Michael Awkward contends that it is the "sense of bonding, of energetic explorations for and embrasure of black female precursorial figures, which distinguishes the Afro-American women's novels . . . from competitive black male intertextual relations" (7–8). While his claims bear consideration, Naylor and Morrison suggest that black female rewriting is not devoid of competition.

27. Gloria Naylor probably served on the selection committee because she won a National Book Award (First Novel) in 1983. Joined by Richard Eder and the panel's chair Hilma Wolitzer, she evaluated a group of finalists that included Philip Roth, Alice McDermott, Howard Norman, Larry Heinemann, and Morrison. In what Wolitzer described as a "majority vote," Larry Heinemann's *Paco's Story* (1986) was a surprise winner of the prize. Asked about the deliberations, Naylor stated, "If the award was not predictable, that's because literature isn't predictable" (McDowell "Book"). Some publishing officials thought the outcome's capriciousness was healthy. Morrison's supporters saw the decision as a gross miscarriage, and many looked at Naylor as a voice who could have prevented such upheaval. James English observes, "For her part, Naylor's vote may be inferred from the degree to which she was ostracized afterward by the many offended partisans of Morrison. Her planned month-long residency at SUNY Stony Brook, for example, was reportedly canceled by June Jordan, a member of the faculty and a friend of Morrison's who had led the public outcry against the NBA decision" (151).

Houses, Not Coffins

Barbara Christian argued that from 1975 to 1985, there arose in America "a more distinctly visible black middle class than had ever existed before" (121).[28] Exploring this idea, *Women* presented Kiswana Browne, a young activist who grew up in Linden Hills, a tony suburb adjacent to Brewster Place. Kiswana moved to Brewster so that she could be "in day-to-day contact with the problems of [her] people," and her mother who visits her occasionally wonders whether living among the "people" qualifies as a commitment to social progress (84). Kiswana's mother strikes many critics as *Women's* chief expositor of black bourgeois virtues. Though Mrs. Browne is an eloquent apologist, Miss Eva and Mattie enrich the novel's portraits of middle-class aspiration. These women's encounters with the city's ownership/leasing dynamic discount demonization of property owning.

Miss Eva, perhaps the namesake of Eva Peace from Morrison's *Sula,* kept a house where "lemon oil" and "cool, starched linen" held the power to assuage "the spirit" (35, 40).[29] Unlike social climbers whose residences were museums, Miss Eva loved her home's lived-in quality.[30] She adorned it with warm comforts transforming her experiences into hospitality. Despite the likelihood that her house was a bequeathal of husbands whom she had "outlived," morbidity does not reign within its walls (32).[31] Instead, hope swells. Mattie absorbs these doctrines. Her abrupt move from a rat-infested boardinghouse to a "beautiful" dwelling contains an almost Dickensian reversal of fortune (40). While Dickens's characters usually thrive in situations turned by chance, she gets dispos-

28. Christian believed that Naylor's second novel *Linden Hills* most vigorously engaged the "money and power" theory of progress (121).

29. Miss Eva differs from Eva Peace in her decorating tastes, but the two share an occasionally troublesome attraction to men. As Eva Turner states about her husbands, "I like 'em all, but they don't seem to agree with me" (34). Miss Peace, based on her experiences with Boy Boy, would probably agree with that sentiment.

30. Miss Eva's therapeutic finery seemingly evokes the white emulation agendas of fictional characters from *Beetlecreek's* Mary Diggs to *Song of Solomon's* Ruth Foster Dead, but her house frustrates such assessments. The tension between black middle-class life as a sign of comfort and as a refutation of racial inferiority is palpable in fin de siècle America. For analysis, see David Levering Lewis and Deborah Willis's *A Small Nation of People: W.E.B. DuBois & African American Portraits of Progress* (2003) and Michael Bieze's *Booker T. Washington and the Art of Self-Representation* (2008).

31. The five marriages that preceded her old age lurk as uncertain contributors to Miss Eva's possession of her own home. Describing one of her marriages, she states that she and her husband "joined the vaudeville circuit and went on stage" (34). While she does not identify her role in the act, the mere fact of a stage career suggests freedom. This attitude partakes of Shug Avery's bold revisions, yet Miss Eva's nurturing instincts separate her from Walker's character.

sessed and lands at Brewster Place.[32] Her plight could be understood via *Women*'s "descent" motif. According to Maxine Montgomery, Mattie cannot attain a "sense of wholeness" until she abandons the "outward trappings that signal middle-class success" (42). Montgomery's theory links Mattie's situation to Mrs. Browne's implying that just as the latter advances socioeconomically by being what her daughter terms "a white man's nigger," there is something in Mattie's pursuit of home ownership that smacks of racial self-hatred (*Women* 85). Though Mattie descends from a sharp-tongued, proud clan, her ambitions, like those of *A Raisin in the Sun*'s Lena Younger, arise less from copying white folks than from a desire to have the outcomes in her life match her labor. Mattie resurrects Miss Eva's and other black Americans' desire to possess a secure home.[33] Her challenges reflect the ambivalence of *Women*'s setting.[34]

Mattie's experiences straddle two myths of the city. On the one hand, her arrival as an unmarried, unskilled, expectant mother means that she must endure exorbitant rents and low-wage employment. Urban life in this scenario involves getting exploited. On the other hand, the metropolis is a promised land.[35] In this scenario, the city delivers an individual from peril. Mattie's movements from the boardinghouse to Miss Eva's and finally to Brewster Place show a fluidity that critiques determinist narratives of black fate. Though her shifts imply agency, this appearance is misleading. Mattie no more chooses to be delivered by Miss Eva than she desires to lose a home that had "a lifetime of work laying in the bricks" (53). By presenting these unpredictable developments, Naylor challenges

32. Consider, for example, the fates of characters such as the eponymous protagonist of *Oliver Twist* (1838) and Esther Woodhouse in *Bleak House* (1853).

33. For discussions of black home ownership, see Andrew Wiese's *Places of Their Own: African American Suburbanization in the Twentieth Century* (2005), Beryl Satter's *Family Properties: How the Struggle Over Race and Real Estate Transformed Chicago and Urban America* (2010), and David M. P. Freund's *Colored Property: State Policy and White Racial Politics* (2010).

34. Several studies in the 1930s and the 1940s analyzed the Great Migration and its impact on black housing. Herbert Hoover's Committee on Negro Housing (CNH) undertook the most formal efforts. Founded in 1928 and including members such as Nannie Helen Burroughs, Charles S. Johnson, Moses McKissick, and Daisy Lampkin, the CNH produced a report *Negro Housing* (1932) that recommended "the construction of low-income housing, the elimination of restrictive covenants, and the end to discriminatory actions on the part of real estate agents and private lenders" (Whitaker 161). See Skip G. Gates's "Of Negroes Old and New" (1974) and Gilbert Osofsky's *Harlem: The Making of a Ghetto* (1966).

35. Lawrence Rodgers evokes Canaan, the Biblical Promised Land, as the marker of the southern migrant's envisioning of his northward journey as deliverance. While this sublime metaphor offers immense hope, Rodgers suggests that many migrants such as the protagonist of Ralph Ellison's *Invisible Man* mistakenly enter the city as seekers of Canaan only to discover that they are "nameless Adam[s]" who have been tricked into abandoning "their roots" (2). Naylor's life and her fiction document a middle way between these two attitudes regarding migration.

quantitative analyses of city life and reveals the elided exchanges that tex-
ture black existence.[36] Mattie's return to renting suggests why scripts of
pathology demand this rebuttal.

Brewster Place is "four double housing units" pressed into a dead end
street (1). Although it seems a step up from the boardinghouse that Mattie fled decades earlier, the apartment building reveals the same "decay"
that produces division in so many black communities (4). Thus, just as
Petry's *The Street* and William Fisher's *The Waiters* (1953) portray rental
properties defined by irredeemable wornness, *Women* also emphasizes
the creeping disrepair of Brewster's buildings. This physical malfunction
complements an emotional one. Although thin walls and curious eyes put
inhabitants close to one another, no intimacy develops.[37] When Sophie,
one of Brewster's residents, looks through a window and sees the les-
bian couple Lorraine and Theresa making out, she bewails their "nasty
ways" and complains that the two "ain't wanted here" (145). This scene
illustrates how "spectatorship and surveillance" can disintegrate fellowship (Hicks 21).[38] While Sophie's objections purport moral authority, her
sentiments reflect "failures of vision" and a commitment to "voyeuristic
modes of knowing" (Hicks 21; Dubey, *Signs* 99). Mattie's experiences
challenge such knowledge, attesting other possibilities for urban sight.

Several scholars note that the inhabitants of Brewster Place form "a
community of transients" (Christian 114). Emphasizing the fragility of
the neighborhood, Philip Page asserts that the tenants are alienated both
from "white society" and frequently from each other (*Reclaiming* 162).
Sophie's complaints show such alienation, and Mattie's latter day arrival
confirms the itinerancy of the buildings' residents. Nonetheless, community hinges less upon duration of interaction and more upon shared consciousness. This idea about neighborhood emerges forcefully in the black

36. Literature's capacity to depict black experiences often devolves into questions of narrative mode. Although naturalism, realism, modernism, and postmodernism describe some options
for storytelling, the Black Archivists complicate cultural identity by exploring what literature can
express about survival.

37. The debilitating effects of proximity can be seen in Gwendolyn Brooks's *Maud Martha*
and Lorraine Hansberry's *A Raisin in the Sun*. Sharing bathrooms and blackouts could promote
solidarity, but in both of these works, city dwellers want to flee their surroundings. Frank London
Brown's *Trumbull Park* (1959) also presents this reality. When a young girl falls to her death, Louis
"Buggy" Martin, Brown's protagonist, determines that hazarding the racism of a suburb is preferable to staying in his high-rise. Though Brown's novel focuses on a man, *The Street, Maud Martha,*
and *A Raisin in the Sun* depict black women whose hopes are frustrated by leasing.

38. Heather Hicks argues that the "dynamics of spectatorship and surveillance . . . animate the
racist social formation of Harlem." Although she focuses on Ann Petry's *The Street*, Hicks's attention to "vision and failures of vision" clarify Naylor and Morrison's explorations of how looking
relates to community (21). For more on vision and urbanity, see Madhu Dubey's *Signs and Cities,*
especially chapter 3, "Urban Writing as Voyeurism: Literature in the Age of Spectacle."

nationalism of Kiswana and her boyfriend Abshu, but Mattie's Christian ethics lead to the most reliable day-to-day practice of togetherness.
When Sophie questions Theresa and Lorraine's relationship, Mattie calls
her a "busybody" (140). She still wonders whether lesbianism is "quite
right"; however, because of her experiences as an unmarried mother,
Mattie knows that calloused judgment splits affection (141). Her actions
ally her with Lorraine, an alliance that intensifies because each has been
banished by her father.

Neither Lorraine nor Mattie shares her history with one another.
Despite this silence, their interaction reveals the possibilities and the limits of shared consciousness for Brewster Place's residents. When Sophie
upsets her, Lorraine does not turn to Mattie; rather, she seeks solace from
Ben. Her revelations of her dad's angry reaction to her lesbianism meet
with his regrets about his daughter's plight creating a momentary surrogacy. In his "damp underground rooms," Ben can be a consoling father,
and Lorraine can be a forgiving daughter (147). The haste and the setting of their meeting hint at peremptory connection. Despite the allure
of their role-playing, her murder of him implies its insufficiency. Mattie's
"ricocheting . . . screams" form the first testimony to the tragedy (173).
Beyond mourning loss of life, her screams identify sincere commemoration as one option for urban community.[39] Mattie's pursuit of this option
re-frames the importance of property.

Urbanity limits Mattie's ability to preserve family, much less a neighborhood. Oscillating between renting and owning, she discovers that
security stems from temperament as well as circumstance. This security
does not preclude catastrophe nor does it promote unanimity; instead, it
subjects pain to communion and produces intimacy. Mattie, like *A Lesson Before Dying*'s Jefferson, discovers the tutelage of suffering. Although
her studies cannot transform reality, they do align with spirituals and
the blues, folk traditions of organizing loss.[40] Combining these traditions

39. In *Passed On: African American Mourning Stories* (2003), Karla Holloway asserts, "Black
folk—whose indomitable and full presence articulates the best of this country's spirit, intelligence, and politics—bridge [grief's] cultural haunting with hope, grace, and resilience" (3). Mattie's screams preamble her affirmation of Holloway's assertion. They are a brief interregnum that
sutures recognition of wasteful loss to the slow recuperation of lament.

40. Maulana Karenga, in "Black Art: Mute Matter Given Force and Function" (1968), argues
that "the blues are invalid" because they teach black folks "to submit to . . . resignation" (1976).
This disdain for resignation, which gets echoed by Larry Neal and Amiri Baraka, makes martyr-
dom and Hollywood heroism the sole options for dignified black existence. Ernest Gaines opposes
this thesis, and Morrison and Naylor suggest that the sinews that can redeem black urbanity will
not arrive in a blaze, rather more likely a shadow. For Baraka and Neal's outlooks, see "The Revolutionary Theatre" (1969) and "The Black Arts Movement" (1968), respectively.

generates an antidote to materialism and manners, faulty bases of solidarity. Mattie echoes the hopes of *The Bluest Eye*'s Geraldine, a striver who ascends by shedding black life's "funkiness" (Morrison, *Bluest* 83). While Mattie's plight judges Geraldine's tactics, she retains the latter's neighborhood model of unity. In *Jazz,* Morrison suggests that communal consciousness demands interactions beyond your block.

Unlike Miss Eva, Alice Manfred's loss of her husband does not translate into home ownership. Although she lacks property, her bourgeois aims surface as she selects her apartments. She moved from "Eleventh Avenue" to "Third Avenue" to "Park Avenue" trying to find an enclave where taste could protect her from racial prejudice (54). In addition to threats from white folks, she also noticed an assault on her elegance by black "juke joint, barrel hooch, tonk house, music" (59).[41] Her responsibility for raising her niece Dorcas makes policing the effects of this music crucial. *Jazz*'s aunt-niece caregiver dynamic evokes *Go Tell It on the Mountain,* in which Elizabeth Grimes is taken from her pimp father by a maternal aunt. Dorcas's dad owns a pool hall, but he and his wife are not morally maligned. Rather, as victims of the race riots in East St. Louis, their deaths mark the stakes of Alice's desire to cordon off a city's influences. Her intentions recall Mattie's failed efforts even as her approach revises the elder woman's.

Reprising Mattie's mistaken faith that physical space will protect her and her son, Alice believes that "on Clifton Place" where there was "a leafy sixty-foot tree every hundred feet," menace would yield to impeccable landscaping (56). Neat hedgerows were sentinels outside her apartment, and inside, she "outlawed" "high-heeled shoes with the graceful straps," "the vampy hats closed on the head," "makeup of any kind," and "especially the coats slung low in the back and not buttoned, but clutched, like a bathrobe or a towel" (55). Against these fashions, she mounted a strictness that judged Mattie's indulgence. Basil, Mattie's son, was spoiled; Dorcas received love as bound breasts, censured hips, and

41. Freeda French from John Edgar Wideman's *Sent For You Yesterday* precedes Alice as a disapprover of secular music's penetration into black urban neighborhoods, and I treat her more expansively in chapter 6. If that resonance is intriguing, then the way that Dorcas and Alice signify on *Women*'s Etta Mae suggests the resourcefulness of Morrison's creative critiques of Naylor. While *Women* does not extensively portray music or musicians, it shows Etta Mae returning to Brewster Place carrying a stack of albums and includes snatches of lyrics from Billie Holliday to church songs in Etta's chapter to show that she is—to some extent—mothered by music. Dorcas's reprisal of Etta's temperament, and Alice's response to that attitude, show Morrison's determination to re-inscribe aspects of the transgenerational conflict that *Women* elides. Reflecting the recuperative possibilities of a fuller exploration of tension, Morrison presents a model of communing with deep implications for black literary history.

covered legs. No matter how diligently expressed, such strictures proved inadequate to the city's challenges. The reasons for inadequacy centered on misperceptions of the metropolis' appeal.

Madhu Dubey asserts that *Jazz* presents a "rigidly gridded struc-ture of the city" that exemplifies "easy semiotic readability as well as the socially repressive effects of urban spatial form" (*Signs* 109). Though Alice's negotiation of the grid affirms Dubey's outlook, her inability to contain Dorcas suggests some hidden meanings that defy her understand-ing. These concealments ostensibly originate in the city itself. Thus, the narrator, "the voice of the City," intimates that the metropolis is "smart at . . . sending secret messages disguised as public signs" (Rodrigues 748; *Jazz* 64). This description seemingly alludes to the city's chummy cover-ing over of adulteries and other indiscretions; however, it also refers to self-deception. Alice is known as a woman whose quiet judgment chas-tened indecorous acts. Her rectitude succeeded as a public sign, but this dignity veiled a never-before vented appetite "for blood" (86). Learning this truth means leaving behind the carefully gridded city and entering the unmapped territories of the human spirit. Joe and Violet usher her through this terrain.

The distance between Clifton Place, where Alice lives, and Lenox Avenue, the location of Joe and Violet's lodgings, covers nearly thirteen miles. If this physical gap seems substantial, consider also these char-acters' radically different personalities. Where Alice shares tea with the Miller sisters, prim neighbors whose favorite topic is New York City's many "signs of Imminent Demise," Violet straightens the hair of pros-titutes, and Joe beds a teenage girl (56). These stark distinctions imply separation, but these characters' fates are closely intertwined. Alice explains her strictness toward Dorcas by alluding to her own girlhood, in which "hysteria . . . violence" and the "damnation of pregnancy without marriageability" often caused black folks to make their young women "prisoner[s] of war" (76, 77). Though this history clarifies her behavior, her breakthrough occurs when she shares the consciousness of "mean" women like Violet and lovesick adulterers like Joe (4). Her shared con-sciousness does not entail approval of the Traces, yet it does require moving the couple's situation from gossip to concern. By smashing the silence that separated her from them, Alice discovers within Joe and Vio-let vestiges of her own tamped down anger and fear. Just as her emotions moved her about the city, generating misguided faith in exclusivity, the Traces also cut a path albeit from the South to the North that sees set-ting as destiny.

Before they reside in New York City, Joe and Violet farm in Virginia. This thirteen-year stretch, from 1893 to 1906, not only solidifies their marriage but also connects them in intriguing ways to Alice, Mattie, and Ben. Where renting apartments exposes Alice and Mattie to estrangement, exploitation, and despair, Joe and Violet begin their lives together by experiencing tenant farming, a rural renting with some dangers akin to its urban cousin. Tenant farming was one of the "roots of . . . black poverty," and Ben's dilemma verified its emotional tolls (Mandle v). Despite these perils, it emerged as a site of bonding for Joe and Violet. The couple worked some of "the worst land in the county" for two years (126). After their debt ballooned to eight hundred dollars, he cobbled together profits from milling while she tended their rental. Five years of labor cleared their ledger. Framing their relationship to property, the Traces' accomplishment reinforces the limits of physical space's impact on identity. This truth surfaces in Dixie but Morrison lets it travel.

While socioeconomic accounts accurately capture some realities of practices such as tenant farming, their snapshots are rarely comprehensive. Joe and Violet confound these foreshortened narratives. Even as the couple confronts hardships, their spirits register resolve rather than defeat. This resilience goads their adventurous trek to New York City and suggests their ideas about black community. Where *A Lesson Before Dying* presents Tante Lou's belief that serving your people required physical presence, *Jazz* elevates shared consciousness to an equal footing. Joe's infidelity and Violet's stalking show that such sharing is no panacea; nonetheless, communion replaces bourgeois bases for collectivity. Revising property pursuits so that empathy as opposed to exclusivity reigns, *Jazz* portrays its elders' journeys toward sincere devotion and their inchoate attempts to divert younger generations away from an ethics of pleasure. These wildly diverse efforts signal *Jazz* and *Women*'s engagement with twentieth-century creative quandaries.

African American novelists, especially between 1945 and 1970, struggle with artistic liberty in the context of white prescriptions. Reminiscent of Mattie and Alice facing American myths about property, these writers too often disparaged black resources. *Women* and *Jazz* use their elders' disillusionments regarding real estate and community to suggest that ignoring cultural affinity can cause innovation to stagnate. This becomes a crucial message for prizewinning black novelists as they sort their literary traditions. Although black archives do not nullify white aesthetic expectations, they do orient artists in cosmopolitan spaces that strive to get them lost. Like *Women* and *Jazz*'s cities, such spaces could be symbolic (i.e., an apartment building's fragmentation) or literal (i.e., New York's grid). The key when navigating these spaces is grounding one's responses in empathy. The portrayals of violence in *Women* and *Jazz* clarify the merits of this approach.

Violent Reconciliations

In *Violence and the Black Imagination* (1993), Ronald Takaki observed that too often, analysts generalized group behaviors without sufficiently accounting for personality.[42] He concluded that by examining "blacks . . . as individuals" who "uniquely experienced . . . often chaotic and always terrible social realities," a researcher could glean cultural attitudes about "violence and rebellion" (12, 13). Even though Takaki focused on the nineteenth-century psyche, his insights apply to *Women* and *Jazz*. Morrison and Naylor wrote these two novels during a moment when policies such as mandatory sentencing, antigang policing, and three-strikes statutes were beginning to dominate public discussions about violence.[43] Sensing within these conversations the totalizing tendencies that Takaki rued, the novelists responded by placing vicious acts in the center of their plots. Each woman explores black on black violence, and though *Women* and *Jazz* are set in the 1960s and 1920s respectively, these novels dialogue with post–civil rights realities. These dialogues not only address social constructions of aggression but also the representation of blackness. Naylor make her novel's structure central to this engagement.

Women, for Michael Awkward, "demonstrate[s] that the narratively disconnected texts of individual protagonists can be forged into a unified whole" (98). Though his observation clarifies how the book combines varied accounts of black womanhood, it skims over why the tension between disconnection and unity exists. Naylor's narrative structure symbolizes the hazards of collectivity, and her treatment of violence shows why such dangers matter. C.C. Baker, a young resident of Brewster Place,

---

42. *Violence in the Black Imagination*'s publication history interconnects interestingly with those of *The Women of Brewster Place* and *Jazz*. Takaki's book was initially printed in 1978, three years before Naylor finished *Women*. In 1993, a year after *Jazz*'s publication, an expanded edition of *Violence in the Black Imagination* appeared. This edition included a preface where Takaki suggested that the 1992 Rodney King incident showed how America's racial tensions mounted during the Reagan era. *Women* and *Jazz* address these realities in their probing of violence.

43. Regarding race and law enforcement, see Michelle Alexander's *The New Jim Crow: Mass Incarceration in the Age of Colorblindness* (2010).

heads a crew that rapes Lorraine, and Ben tries to aid her after the attack. Instead of welcoming him, she responds by grasping a brick, "splitting his forehead and . . . rendering his brains just a bit more useless than hers" (173).[44] This murder narrowly precedes her death. If Ben's and Lorraine's corpses delineate threats of escapism and hatred, then their senseless passing also tests Brewster Place's posture toward a "world tumbl[ing] down around" it (141). The blended fate of an elder and a young woman invest this testing with powerful significance. Although C.C. and his pals do not endorse Alice Manfred's elitist strategies, their sexist attempts to control the neighborhood reflect a similar investment in hierarchies of belonging. C.C.'s criteria stem from intimidation, and his violent repression threatens to become Brewster's binding agent. While Lorraine lacks such spitefulness, her brutality carries unmistakable judgment. Life, for her, when laced with inconsolable misery demands the deliverance of death.[45] Facing this uncertain harvest, Kiswana tries to redeem calamity with idealism.

Kiswana's dream of a Brewster Place tenant's association captures the enthusiasm and the sincerity of 1960s activism.[46] Her grassroots commitment, though it vexes her mother, is inspiring.[47] Despite her inspiration, she discovers that unity requires more than just positive energy. Lorraine expresses the challenges: "That was the problem with so many black people—they just sat back and complained . . . Grabbing an atti-

44. Lorraine's gesture holds several possible meanings. It could be seen as retaliatory. Aware of his alcoholism, she perhaps views his inability to stop her rape as a byproduct of drunken disregard and thus a betrayal of the father-daughter surrogacy that emerged in their earliest meeting. Alternately, her act could be deemed a merciful release. If her meetings with Ben have introduced her to his spiritual lacerations, then she may feel that confronting her ravaging may add another octave to the tinkling "crystal bells" that already reverberate across his conscience (149). Believing that such a sound might be too burdensome, she may have opted—in a kind of mercy killing—to silence the havoc in Ben's head.

45. Lorraine's act in some ways recalls Eva Peace's decision to set her son Plum on fire. While she knows that he will die, Eva also believes that because of his drug addiction, he is already succumbing to lifelessness.

46. Barbara Christian observes, "In the geographical world Naylor is creating, Brewster Place and Linden Hills coexist, and persons from each place have attitudes about the other. So touched by the revolutionary fervor of the 1960s, Melanie Browne of Linden Hills changes her name to Kiswana and goes down to live with 'the people'" (108). In this regard, Kiswana recalls Beneatha in *A Raisin in the Sun* and the title character of the Friends of Distinction's song "Willa Faye."

47. In addition to optimism, black activism also bred disenchantment. Nelson George argues that black nationalist characterizations like the ones found in Toni Cade Bambara's *The Salt Eaters* (1980) tap "into the collective exhaustion of the generation that fought furiously for black advancement but" then found "itself confronting an unfinished agenda and middle age" (16). Though Naylor writes in the context of that exhaustion, she chooses in *Women* to focus on the cusp of such frustration. A decade later, John Edgar Wideman would offer a full-blown radical burnout in *Philadelphia Fire*.

tude and thinking that you were better than these people just because a lot of them were poor and uneducated wouldn't help either" (141–42). Attempting to bridge the gaps in schooling and finances that separate her from many Brewster residents, Kiswana promotes informed, collective action. Her prescriptions—rent strikes, Shakespeare in the park, and the block party—represent one form of black unity. Joined by her boyfriend Abshu, she seeks a Marxist-inflected empowerment.[48] Though her agenda stresses pride, it underestimates the empathy and the trust that must precede such remedies. Like the Brotherhood in *Invisible Man,* Kiswana's brand of rescue neglects too much of the human equation. If romantic radicalism cannot stop the tenant's association from foundering, then Naylor suggests that elderly perspective could aid in addressing urban disarray.

Mattie administers emotional salves throughout *Women,* and, like the matriarch in Bill Wither's 1971 hit "Grandma's Hands," she specializes in comfort without judgment.[49] Her experiences of exile and abandonment allow her to midwife folks through distress. In particular, she does not shrink from the transgenerational dilemmas that threaten Brewster Place's future. When Sophie's homophobia discomfits Lorraine, Mattie speaks up. Following Ben's and Lorraine's deaths, she remains committed to Kiswana's block party, a fundraiser meant to promote harmony. Mattie's efforts though consistent seem ineffectual. She cannot stem intolerance's murderous consequences, and her participation in the block party is marred by confusion between dream and reality. While these results inspire pessimism, Mattie's example replaces an activist agenda with fellowship rituals. Tragedy, in many shapes and sizes, embroiders urban existence, yet kindness and care undergird a healing concern. While that emotional investment cannot staunch pain, it fosters possibilities that might otherwise be obscured. This potential for imagination forms a connective tissue within *Women's* black community. In *Jazz,* Morrison revises the source and the shape of such connection.

48. Abshu's production of Shakespeare's *A Midsummer Night's Dream* reflects a tendency to use colorblind casting to transform the consciousness of black communities. By producing western canonical works, black actors and actresses—according to this performance philosophy—proved their skill and ennobled their ostensibly black patrons. As Naylor's depiction shows, this approach to art proved popular, controversial, and largely ineffectual. For more on colorblind casting, see Ayanna Thompson's *Colorblind Shakespeare: New Perspectives on Race and Performance* (2006). I take up John Edgar Wideman's treatment of this issue in chapter 6.

49. Margaret Whitt asserts that Mattie Michael functions "as matriarch, surrogate mother, and mentor" (17). Mattie anticipates such figures in the fiction of John Edgar Wideman, Toni Morrison, and Ernest Gaines. She also intriguingly inflects the anxieties about white mentorship that Alice Walker and Charles Johnson manifest.

Jazz explores disaffected lovers, a theme that Morrison has treated repeatedly.[50] By presenting Joe and Violet's strained marriage, the novel hints at the impulses that lead one to mistake excitement for satisfaction. Joe's relationship with Dorcas carries that misperception. He casts her as the listener to whom he could unburden himself. In place of the "inside nothing" caused by his mother's abandonment, he gained succor, the ear of a girl who understood him better than folks "his own age" (37). This emotional connection appears an essential part of Joe and Dorcas's relationship, and it colors their coupling: "They try not to shout, but can't help it. Sometimes he covers her mouth with the palm of his hand . . . and if he can, if he thinks of it in time, he bites the pillow to stop his own yell" (39). The couple's passion seems spontaneous and convincing, but just as Alice deals with self-deception Joe struggles to decipher his lust. On the one hand, Dorcas is to him "the reason Adam ate the apple and its core" (133). Alternately, she represents capriciousness, the type of young girl who would throw him over for a womanizing young rooster. Joe and Dorcas's affair becomes a crucial catalyst. They deliver both the Trace and the Manfred households from the tyranny of the urban grid, yet the city remains a space where "blood will have blood" (*Macbeth* III, iv, 123). Just as epiphany in *Beloved* costs a human life, enlightenment in *Jazz* begins with a dead body.

Dorcas thrills to the trickiness of the city. She is, like Joe and Violet, a claimed orphan, yet her temperament betrays a compensatory volatility. Holding to the memories of her lost parents, she cries in Joe's arms and puts her loss beside his so convincingly that he announces that she is a revelation as eventful as original sin. He says that because of her, he will, like Adam, carry the "taste of the first apple in the world in his mouth for the rest of his life" (133). Despite such devotion, she manifests hardness and begins a relationship with a man whose diffidence toward her shames Joe's gifts of Cleopatra cosmetics and the cuticle-clipping manicures she performed for him. In Dorcas's volatility, Morrison not only offers an allegory of New York City but also a caution regarding human character. Dorcas's death extends these connections.

---

50. Morrison's interest in cooled affection surfaces as early as *The Bluest Eye* where Cholly and Pauline's most tender moments precede their move to Lorain, Ohio. Likewise in *Sula*, Eva and Boy-Boy begin amid tangerine dreams and end in hateful estrangement. The same could be said of Nel and Jude, a pair whose love always seems more expedient than passionate, but their severance carries electricity. Extending the line, Son and Jadine in *Tar Baby* join Macon Dead II and Ruth in *Song of Solomon* to create a passel of Morrisonian characters that have loved and lost. These returns, I believe, constitute a professional taking stock—an activity that is quite significant both in the aftermath of the controversies surrounding *Beloved* and in anticipation of the Nobel Prize, an honor that Morrison could not have known was coming.

Joe Trace conflates his southern upbringing and his urban disorientation when he takes his gun and goes "hunting" for his mistress.[51] Though
he claims that her gender precludes any desire to "hurt" her, his anger
along with her vanity prove fatal. Joe tracks Dorcas to a house party,
and to his surprise, he finds her there with a younger man whose type
she had ridiculed as lazy and inattentive. This development pushes Joe,
a hunter's hunter, beyond his training and induces him to give vent to a
"broken heart" (133). Though his shot wounds Dorcas, her best friend
Felice tells Joe and Violet later that the reason she died was because she
would not go get medical treatment. Her last words, according to Felice
were, "There's only one apple . . . Just one. Tell Joe" (213). While it is
tempting to read this remark as further evidence of Dorcas's conceited-
ness, such an interpretation overlooks her legitimate communion with
Joe. In a callous city, Dorcas provides an emotional space into which
Joe can fit his emptiness. Her complexity joins with his hunger, and the
result is an unruly comfort, one unraveling expectations and convictions
across several households. Joe's interactions with Violet and his implicit
ones with Alice show how tragedy insists upon community.

The Trace and Manfred households are thirteen miles apart, but the
keener separation is caused by "*the impunity* of the man" that slept with
and shot a "defenseless girl" (73). Twenty years after a hopeful departure
from the South, Joe and Violet are "barely speaking to each other" (36).
Similarly, Alice Manfred had mulled the "brutalizing men" and "brutal
women" who had invaded her "house," and like Baby Suggs, she had
"withdrawn in her grief and shame" (74). The divisions among these
three characters metaphorically represent major rents in late twentieth-
century black existence. By candidly confronting these sites of humiliation, Morrison suggests that healing requires both desperate affection and
mortifying commitment. She rejects an ethics of cool and the luxury of
dignity; rather, the novelist places her characters outside of propriety in
a space of raw frankness. They sacrifice respectability in the service of
fellowship.

Like Sethe and Paul D, infidelity separates Joe and Violet, but this
betrayal recalls them to the appetites that first joined them. Running
from motherlessness and fantasies of Golden Grey, they indeed wonder

51. Joe's hunting signals Morrison's return to a trope that she had explored in *Song of Solomon*. There, Guitar Bains is another hunter who shelves his gun in the confines of the city. If Guitar's anecdote about shooting a doe metaphorically registers the shame associated with wounding
a female, then Joe's fatal shooting of Dorcas suggests the dangers that regional baggage poses in the
metropolis. Joe Trace also offers Morrison's reaction to David Bradley's *The Chaneysville Incident*
and Gloria Naylor's *Mama Day* (1988), other novels about woodcraft.

whether they have substituted one another for these earlier fixations, yet through the season with Dorcas, the couple discovers the truth of what they share, a dedication to intimacy. Ironically, Alice's reminder to Violet lubricates the discovery. When Violet arrived at Dorcas's funeral and tried to deface the girl's corpse, she not only aroused wonderment about her sanity but also reinforced for Alice the perversity of black powerlessness. The grieving aunt stated that she would have had both Joe and Violet locked up if "everything she knew about Negro life had made it even possible to consider" voluntarily calling the police (74). Capping Alice's realization that "reraising" of Dorcas had been unsuccessful, Violet's performance at the funeral formed a gulf between these two women (60). Still, when Violet sought her out, Alice—who initially insisted that she didn't "have a thing to say to" Violet—concluded that she did want to say a few words about "loss" (75, 87). These words led the women to meditations on "real thing[s]," and in that moment of bluntness, Alice told Violet: "You got anything left to you to love, anything at all, do it . . . Nobody's asking you to take it. I'm sayin make it" (113). Alice's admonition not only anticipates the pain of forgiveness, but also shows that you will never escape the cuts to your spirit. Despite or perhaps because of such wounds, love spawns unity.

Women and Jazz present violence as a prelude to reconciliation within black communities. Although Lorraine, Ben, and Dorcas all recall Invisible Man's Tod Clifton as folks whose deaths are linked to urban chaos, Naylor and Morrison eschew the underground retreat that Ellison grants his protagonist. They force their characters toward socialization. Their decisions suggest a deeper faith in black communion, but even in their portrayals, telling differences emerge. The block party that concludes Women culminates in the dismantling of the wall that separates Brewster Place from the rest of the city. While this action seemingly signals optimism, it masks a lingering polarization. Theresa, Lorraine's partner, initially tries to leaves Brewster Place as the neighborhood's women destroy the wall. When a cabbie speeds off with her suitcase, she joins the female throng and lobs bricks into the avenue. Theresa's actions burnish the community's cohesion, but tied to her flight, her deeds bespeak catharsis rather than empathy. This eruptive release contrasts sincere consciousness sharing, and such contrasts generate sustainability concerns. When fellowship follows from shame, can it last? Jazz takes up this question by focusing on eccentricity.

Joe and Violet are both tied to peculiar aspects of Dorcas's death. From shooting her to slicing her, this couple epitomizes quirky or "spooky"

you don't get published" (Blake and Miller 38). Morrison and Bradley's remarks suggest how market expectations condition literary liberty, and in *Song* and *Chaneysville,* these suggestions inform portrayals of freedom, labor, and love. These portrayals initially center on fin-de-siècle choices. By focusing on the post-bellum strivings of Milk's and John's ancestors, Morrison and Bradley render post–*Brown v. Board* black selfhood as a direct inheritance of late nineteenth-century decisions. Their portraits of black identity resemble the determinative strategies of naturalism, and in many ways, Milk's and John's forebears attempt to imbue their choices with fate-making energy. Despite their dynastic desires, their bequeathals are tangled. *Song* explores such tangling.

The prestige of the Dead clan has its roots in entrepreneurship. Though it is tempting to connect this impulse to bourgeois aspiration, the novel frustrates simplistic conclusions. It does so here through the differences between Macon Dead II and his sister Pilate. Although Milk's father Macon operates a real estate practice, his exploitative methods and ruthless temperament mark him as a slumlord. He shares his business philosophy with his son: "Let me tell you right now the one important thing you'll ever need to know: Own things. And let the things you own own other things. Then you'll own yourself and other people too" (55). If Macon's reasoning shows an alarming dehumanization, then his sister offers a powerful foil.[6] Pilate's most treasured possessions are an earring, a sack of rocks, and a geography book, yet she still needed a way to provide food and shelter for her daughter and her granddaughter, so "winemaking" and "cooking whisky" became her livelihood (150). Her bootlegging violated prohibition laws. While the illegality of her efforts distinguished them from Macon's real estate ventures, both sister and brother rejected working for someone else. Their choices reprise their father's example.

After the end of slavery, Pilate and Macon's father Jake acquired a 150-acre farm, Lincoln's Heaven. Pilate viewed this property as a spot where security "taught her a preferable kind of behavior" (150). Though Macon initially accepted the land's tranquil influences, his father's death transformed his convictions. Pilate and Macon saw Jake's "sixteen year" journey to "get [his] farm to where it was paying" as a Reconstruction era success story. When some white men "tricked" their father into signing something and then "told him that they owned his property," Jake

---

6. Susan Willis concludes that for "Milkman's father, all human relationships have become fetishized by their being made equivalent to money." (97).

began a five-night vigil that ended with him getting shot (53). His murder signaled the limits of black access to America's constitutional rights.[7] Only a few years before *Plessy v. Ferguson* minted the nation's commitment to "separate but equal," Jake strove to activate promises related to life, liberty, and the pursuit of happiness. His fate becomes an enigmatic riddle that Pilate and Macon struggle to solve, and each child's solution involves decisions about love.[8]

Macon's real estate ambitions are born at the intersection of his father's hustling and white power's confiscations. Instead of questioning this gap between blacks and national values, he makes wealth an antidote for indignity and forges family as weaponry. His marriage to a woman from a storied background shows his outlook. Ruth Foster, Macon's wife, was the daughter of one of the first blacks to practice medicine in the Michigan town where *Song* is set. Although Macon and Ruth wedded because they ostensibly "agreed on what was important," the basis of that agreement seemed more about status than emotional fulfillment (70). Ruth proudly asserted her identity as her "daddy's daughter" (67). Since she luxuriated in the fashion and fellowship that Dr. Foster's stature secured, her allegiance appeared a byproduct of his rank. She no doubt enjoyed the fact that the Foster family was "the second . . . in the city to have a two-horse carriage," but the crux of her devotion to her father was his unconditional love for her (197). When she sought this same love from Macon, she discovered that their marriage reflected profound discrepancy. He thought that his wealth would produce enduring satisfaction, and she felt that her elegance would burnish his dynasty. Each of them discovered too late that their superficial appetites concealed more elemental cravings. Because they could not share these cravings with one another, their marriage existed as a barren adornment. Macon's sister rejected such arrangements.

Pilate abjures marriage, and her choice not only repudiates the institution's capacity for distorting love but also reflects her general distrust

7. In "What America Would Be Like Without Blacks" (1970), Ralph Ellison compares the boldness necessary to see American culture clearly to the attitude of "Western pioneers confronting the unknown prairie." Ellison's imagery evokes his Oklahoma frontier upbringing and the optimism that inspires former slaves such as Jake to redeem the nation's promises. Morrison's portrayal examines the aftermath of such boldness, exploring how dashed hope circulates in subsequent generations. For more on black citizenship in the nineteenth century, see Ivy G. Wilson's *Specters of Democracy: Blackness and the Aesthetics of Politics in the Antebellum U.S.* (2011).

8. In the 1976 essay, "A Slow Walk of Trees (as Grandmother Would Say), Hopeless (as Grandfather Would Say)," Toni Morrison described her grandfather John Solomon Willis who "lost all eighty-eight acres of his Indian mother's inheritance to legal predators who built their fortunes on the likes of him" (*What* 3). Morrison's grandfather not only inspires her portrayal of Jake/Macon Dead but also perhaps indicates the Solomon to whom her novel's title refers.

of white strategies for organizing black sentiments. In her view, the alliances forged by Ruth and Macon may have their basis in a legitimate if misguided desire to expand black freedom; however, the legacy of Jake's death for her is a deep suspicion that white structures will never work for blacks the way they do for their creators. This outlook leads to an illustrative conjoining in Pilate's life. Where her brother separates the space of work and marriage, Pilate acknowledges no such division. For her, work is, like love, another instrument of pleasure that she should share with her family. This immediacy can be dangerous; however, it subjects conventional scripts of progress to careful scrutiny. In itself, such examination syncs with Pilate's spirit. Combined with her brother and her sister-in-law's views, it fleshes out her nephew's conundrum.

Milk symbolizes the post–*Brown v. Board* search for a coherent black selfhood. Although his identity should be shaped by "personal and collective history," he finds that perversions, elisions, and ignorance mar his progress (Mobley 41). His father headlines this inhibition, but his mother and to a lesser extent his aunt are also complicit. Through their impediments, Milk sees the value and the limits of their respective visions. Macon, Ruth, and Pilate improvised a conditional independence within segregated America. While their efforts sufficed under Jim Crow, expectations shifted with the advent of integration. Milk inherited great expectations, but like African Americans in general, he did not instantly comprehend equality. This confusion reflected both inexperience and his family's silences. Attempting to balance labor and love, a crucial task in black life after segregation, his weaknesses were crippling. *Chaneysville*'s John could empathize.

Where Milk's father achieves status via real estate, John's dad Moses Washington acquired land and a considerable fortune selling moonshine. This enterprise provided him and his family a comfortable life; however, his interest in the profession was less monetary and more ideological. Born in 1890, Moses grew up in Philadelphia, where his father Lamen was a wealthy undertaker.[9] Lamen gave Moses a superb education; however, he actively dissuaded his son's interest in his family's past. Convinced that black liberty at the turn of the twentieth century lay in business acumen and strategic coalitions, he saw no value in dredging up

9. As a mortician, Lamen not only directly evoked Tyree Tucker in Richard Wright's *The Long Dream* but also participated in an industry where segregation was encouraged by the earliest black professional organizations. For more on black undertakers, see Robert Boyd's "Black Undertakers in Northern Cities during the Great Migration: The Rise of an Entrepreneurial Occupation" (1998) and Suzanne Smith's "To Serve the Living: The Public and Civic Identity of African American Funeral Directors" (2008).

unpleasant histories.[10] His priorities promised safety, but they also evaded
America's vexing racial legacies. Moses was not inclined toward such evasion, and following in the footsteps of Lamen's father C.K., he pursued
a life of illicit liquor sales and risky exploits. Framing a central tension
in *Chaneysville,* Moses and Lamen's disagreement also raises a key question related to the Black Archivists: is success in America predicated on
emphasizing or ignoring the racial past? The question for this father-son
duo involved transgenerational debates; yet, just as Macon looked for
Ruth's help, Moses implemented his freedom plans by taking a wife from
the black elite.

Yvette Stanton, Moses's spouse, came from a family that had been
free almost sixty years before the Emancipation Proclamation. Her father,
Professor Stanton, taught at Howard University. Though these facts
marked her as a fortunate child, her priorities were complex. She told
her son John, "Don't ever forget, that white people are the ones that
say what happens to you. Maybe it isn't right, but that's just exactly the
way it is. And so long as you're going to their school . . . you have to
be quiet, and careful, and respectful. Because you've got your head in
the lion's mouth" (119).[11] Yvette preaches respectful submission to white
authority, yet her attitude bespeaks cagey emulation rather than overt
self-hatred. When asked about her marriage, she felt unsure whether her
husband had given her love: "Moses didn't love the way most people
would think a man should love," but she knew that the couple had been
"allies . . . We didn't want the same things, but what we each wanted was
close enough" (308). Their shared desire fuels their son's redemption of
integration's possibilities even as he denies the fusion. In John's friendship with Jack Crawley, the basis of such denials becomes obvious.

Unlike Milk, who lives until his thirties in the same house with both
of his parents, John loses Moses when he is ten years old. His father's
death creates a vacuum, and to fill that void, Moses, before he dies,
recruits his best friend Jack. If Pilate epitomizes antiestablishment thinking in *Song,* then Jack exists as her counterpart in *Chaneysville.* He not
only reprises her unmarried state but also echoes her suspicions about
white society. With this echoing, Jack completes a tutelage that Moses

10. Discussing Lamen, Ashraf Rushdy writes, "[He] rejected a knowledge of his familial
past . . . and invested . . . in his Europeanist beliefs" (*Remembering* 94). Silla Boyce, in Paule Marshall's *Brown Girl, Brownstones* (1959), precedes Lamen as a black individual who sacrifices her past
for capitalistic stability in America.

11. Philip J. Egan offers the most thorough account of John's relationship with his mother
in "Unraveling Misogyny and Forging the Self: Mother, Lover, and Storyteller in *The Chaneysville
Incident*" (1997).

started during John's infancy. Yvette states that when John was a baby, his father loved to watch him tear apart toys. Once he found a doll that John could not destroy; he laughed while his son cried, a combination that maddened her. She explained, "The sound the two of you made, him laughing and you crying. I couldn't stand it" (196). Moses, with the dolls, was preparing John for the day when he would challenge America's white Western ethos,[12] and although Jack's stratagems originated in different rituals, they had the same aims. These goals produced conflict between John's mentor and his mother.

Reminiscent of Lamen, Yvette tried to funnel her son toward bourgeois assimilation. Moses objected to these gestures while he was alive, but after he died, she felt certain that the field had been won. Through Jack's efforts, she saw John getting infected with his father's habits. His hunting and drinking may have aroused her ire, but more than either of these, his determination to tear apart his family's history truly frightened her. Having watched Moses disappear into his attic filled with books, records, and a folio, Yvette believed that studying this archive equated to spending his life "going crazy" (196). She rightly sensed that insanity could follow John's exposure to the truth; nonetheless, her belief that freedom could be attained without engaging such truth isolates a serious concern in post–civil rights black identity. This concern returns to the intersection of labor and love and invests this linkage with practicality and fantasy.

Moses, Yvette, and Jack are like Macon, Ruth, and Pilate, preoccupied with harvesting the freedom that their ancestors sowed. Although joined by the desire for a harvest, these elders contrast in their estimates of how such work should be done. *Chaneysville*'s trio in particular discounts affection's place in the job. Because of this discounting, they often stress pragmatism to the neglect of imagination. John's pursuit of his family's past has often been analyzed as a tension between reason and fancy. On the surface, this tension looks like a contrast of work and procrastination. America's slow racial progress adjusts this perception. The span from Lamen's nineteenth-century striving after liberty to his grandson's

---

12. In late twentieth-century African American literature, destroying dolls repeatedly symbolizes the confronting of white expectations. For example, Claudia McTeer in Toni Morrison's *The Bluest Eye* "destroyed white baby dolls" (22). Where the racial implications of Claudia's act were explicit, John is being trained even as an infant to encounter the world as a creation that he must resourcefully deconstruct. The popularity of representing such deconstruction via a doll may reflect Kenneth Clark's sociological studies in the 1940s. For discussions of Clarke's doll tests, see Saul Feinman's "Trends in Racial Self-Image of Black Children: Psychological Consequences of a Social Movement" (1979).

twentieth-century resumption of that work suggests that freedom, even for middle-class blacks, involves deferral. If these delays in part reflect an incomplete grasp of democracy's possibilities, then they also suggest intricate suppressions that originate in both white expectations and black traditions. John faces these suppressions, and as he researches them, he not only recalls Milk but also the Black Archivists. Through this conflation, Morrison and Bradley's commentary on post–civil rights black literature crystallizes.

Milk is a scion, and John holds a PhD. Despite these attributes, both men still "lacked coherence" (Morrison, *Song* 69). Their plights exemplify a post–*Brown v. Board* black middle class whose accomplishments do not create stable identities. While members of this group suspect that cultural ignorance handicaps them, mainstream success distracts from the ache of lost histories. This success soothes them temporarily, but they wonder whether their pasts hold better options for selfhood. In *Song* and *Chaneysville,* this wonderment ties Milk and John to post–civil rights novelists who espy the black literary tradition. These writers weigh whether integration proffered a facile pluralism that overlaid more nuanced sites of memory.[13] Persuaded that such evaluations were worthy, Morrison and Bradley leveraged their knowledge of the mainstream publishing industry to advance the effort.

While editing books for Random House from the 1960s to the 1980s, Morrison derived "*huge* joy" from helping other black writers navigate the space between "white established publishers" and the development of their "art form[s]" (Stepto 29). Bradley worked at J. P. Lippincott during a shorter window from 1974–76; nevertheless, in that interim, he learned how to "deal with the political nonsense" that dogged works by blacks (Bradley, "Novelist" 29). Because of their jobs as editors, Morrison and Bradley not only augmented black literary archives but also meditated on creative work, assimilation, and pleasure. These meditations informed Milk and John's attempts to fashion identities that were "open to experimentation" yet cognizant of their forebear's sacrifices (Bakerman 35). At crucial points in each man's life, these efforts entail relocating.

---

13. In her 1987 essay "The Site of Memory," Toni Morrison suggests that while authors of nineteenth-century slave narratives had to veer their writings away from representing too much of the interior of black life. She believed that as a late twentieth-century novelist, her job was to "rip the veil drawn over 'proceedings too terrible to relate'" (*What* 71). Thus, although going back to the site of memory paid homage to earlier black cultural experiences, the trip also served as a corrective, a provision of new perceptions for a new day.

Archival Sites

Milk was born on February 19, 1931, and for his whole life, he dwells in a city roughly an hour away from Fairfield, Michigan. During 1963, he embarks on his first trip to his paternal family's home space. The circumstances surrounding this trip are zany. Convinced that his sister has kept some gold that they glimpsed after Jake died, Macon commissions Milk and his friend Guitar to rob her. This robbery miscarries; nonetheless, Macon remains convinced that a treasure exists. Sending Milk from Michigan to Virginia, he hopes to secure the loot. John's travels lack such distance but are equally dramatic. From his birth in 1948 until 1966, he lives on the Hill, the black section of his Western Pennsylvania hometown. When he leaves to attend college, he separates from his mentor, his mother, and his brother Bill. Because of Bill's death in the Vietnam War and his mother's hand in that event, John's departure stretches to more than a decade. Thus, his 1979 return acquires poignancy.

When Milk and John exchange urban towns for ancestral homelands, they not only enact a rejuvenating ritual of past great migrants but also predict the demographic shifts that will take place by the end of the twentieth century.[14] The timing of their movements is significant. While Milk travels in 1963, John visits in 1979. These dates frame a transition from the civil rights movement to the start of urban blight. On one level, this span marks a shift from the South to the North as ground zero for discussing black social ills. This shift critiques liberal attempts to corral American prejudice in a single region, and it insists that viewing black history holistically corrects such myopia. In another corrective, Milk and John's trips put a major modernist trope against the backdrop of black existence. *Song*'s and *Chaneysville*'s depictions of the hunt clarify Morrison and Bradley's outlook on artistic innovation. By examining Milk's search for his paternal heredity, the outlines of her perception take shape.

Song's original hunting expedition involves detective work. While this situation emphasizes Milk's confusion, it also makes disorientation a basis for self-discovery. Milk ostensibly arrives in Virginia to track down some gold. After a few days, he concludes that his family's saga constitutes a better legacy. This conclusion not only contrasts the greed that sent him southward but also deflates his ennui. However, before he can fully embrace the chase, he must see what a familial past represents. His

---

14. For more on the reverse Great Migration, see William H. Frey's "The New Great Migration: Black Americans' Return to the South, 1965–2000" (2004), Ta-Nehisi Coates's "Reversing the Great Migration" (2011), and Conor Dougherty's "South Draws U.S. Blacks" (2011).

grandfather promotes this vision. To Macon and Pilate, Jake reveals black orientation in America. Each child perceives him as an anchor, but each senses his hold uniquely. Remembering his father, Macon noted how "something wild ran through him" when "he saw the man he loved and admired fall off the fence" and lie "twitching in the dirt" (50–51). His affection rapidly succumbed to ambition, and Jake lived forever as a monument to lost dignity. Although his sister also witnessed this scene, she reacted differently. Pilate insists that she did not "see [her father] die" (140). Sustained by his traversing of the material and the spiritual worlds, she counts Jake as a lifelong "mentor" who counsels a "deep concern for and about human relationships" (150, 149).[15]

Milk's confrontation with his father's and aunt's perspectives colors his journey through the South and defines his investigative work as the pursuit of a moral compass. Though Macon and Pilate have decided what the Dead past means to them, he scrambles to fit events to his identity. As he collects information, he recognizes that he cannot make sense of his clan's southern details. His liberation from that bafflement occurs when he participates in a literal hunt. Critics have correctly identified the sexist dimensions of *Song*'s male bonding ritual, and it is certainly defined by phallic power, ribald competition, and, at the end, whoring. These distorting effects are difficult to overlook, yet Milk's epiphany here is the recognition of his impotence. He cannot discover his prey; he mishandles his weapon and in a crowning blow becomes utterly lost in the woods. These markers of defeat should disqualify him from any insight, but in this debilitated state, he hears the voice that allows him to construct Jake as the son of Solomon and Ryna. This detail clears the way for his personal claiming of his great-grandparents and for his accurate deciphering of Jake for both Macon and Pilate. Given his father and aunt's tough experiences with tenderness, it is telling that Milk's insights arise from studying love.

Milk's great-grandfather Solomon inspired awe as the man who literally flew away from bondage. Legends tout his actions; however, his decision also contains less flattering resonances. Marianne Hirsch writes, "Solomon's . . . flight, a heroic return to Africa, offers his descendants a mythic form of transcendence with which to identify, an admirable and

---

15. Preceding *Beloved* by more than a decade, Pilate and Jake's interactions show Morrison's engagement with African cosmology. La Vinia Jennings's *Toni Morrison and the Idea of Africa* (2008) offers the most expansive account of Morrison's attention to African cosmology. Her readings of Pilate in the context of Bandoki and Banganga, witches and healers, are especially insightful. Ashraf Rushdy also offers intriguing observations in *Remembering Generations*.

legendary rejection of his slave condition, a revolutionary rebellion. But his flight can also be seen as an act of paternal irresponsibility and abandonment" (77).[16] Milk's grappling with this ambiguous freedom displays his deeper appreciation of messy humanity. Such appreciation arrives courtesy of his great-grandmother.[17] Solomon's rejection of slavery took courage and inventiveness, yet it drove Ryna, the mother of his children, "out of her mind" (324). When he committed to his world-beating gesture, she was left behind companionless.[18] Ryna's Gulch, a landmark in rural Virginia, captures her mindset. Encountering the area's sounds during his hunt, Milk asks about them and is told: "Folks say a woman name Ryna is cryin in there. That's how it got the name" (274). By empathizing with Ryna, "the black lady still crying in the gulch," Milk not only adds branches to his family tree but also discovers the burden of those who are left in love's wake (304). This belated discovery adjusts his outlook on self-definition and alerts him to love's place in the work of liberty. Through his interactions with Sweet, the early impact of these adjustments appears.

Milk's sister Lena suggests that since his birth, "everything in [the Dead household had] stopped for him" (215). Although her remarks predate his southern sojourn, they capture how his atrophied caring linked with his inheritance. He addresses this situation in part via a prostitute. After the humiliation of the hunt, he is sent to Sweet, a woman who as her name implies offers pure pleasure. Her profession exists in euphemism, but the fifty dollars that Milk gives her implies much. Despite such crudity, their trysting "constitutes a significant moment in his maturation" (Leak 113). Jeffrey Leak admits that Sweet helps Milk express "reciprocal" intimacy, but he warns that their coupling conveys a desperate attempt by rural black men to control "pussy" and "dick," two

16. Joseph Skerrett argues that by being able and then choosing to fly away, Solomon begins the process of "denying the finality of death through the continuity of art" (201). If African cosmology informs Morrison's characterizations, then the myth of Icarus and airplanes also illuminate Milk's attraction to flight. See Robert Hayden's "O Daedalus, Fly Away Home" (1943), Richard Wright's *Native Son* and *The Long Dream,* and Ralph Ellison's "Flying Home" (1944) for prior explorations of the black male fixation on flight.

17. Describing black women in *Song of Solomon,* Trudier Harris observes, "The success of Milkman's journey depends in large part on the string of female bodies, figuratively and literally, that he leaves along his path. The women form a long line of mothering and nurturing that culminates in Milkman's renewed sense of himself; they become sacrifices on the altar of his possibilities" (*Fiction* 107).

18. Solomon's flight evokes freedom and abandonment, two evocations that are reflected in the larger black literary tradition. See Percival Everett's *Suder* (1980), August Wilson's *Fences* (1983), and Sterling Brown's "Long Gone" (1929) for depictions that explore black manhood and ambivalent notions of leaving.

things that they cling to as manageable markers of "black masculinity" (112, 113). While Leak's warning deserves heeding, his overall assessment downplays what Morrison presents (113). Milk, in making love to Sweet, detects not just the possibility of climax but also and more importantly the sublimity of sharing. With that simple detection, his lineal pursuits come full circle.

Whether the target is information or live game, Milk's hunting failures closely connect to getting lost. This lostness, from childhood, carries an unpleasant vulnerability, yet during his southern swing, such disorientation defines his life. In one sense, his state reflects the immensity of his family's legacy. Daily epiphanies send him spiraling, and succumbing to the motion, Milk cannot find himself. Although this idea allies him with the songwriter who "once was lost," his situation more closely recalls Jesus's suggestion that "whoever wants to save his life will lose it" (Luke 9:24). Milk's bourgeois upbringing sprouts inanities. While these markers suffice to pass the time, he suspects their inadequacy. As he moves about the South, he senses that his middle-class life foregoes empathy. This neglect of generosity emerges as the hole within his clan's soul, and once he finds himself with it, he concludes that lostness proves the best remedy. If John has too much training to copy Milk's dilemma literally, he nevertheless notes that tracking in the spaces of the spirit confounds even veteran hunters.

Chaneysville's chapter titles mimic the index cards of the professional historian; therefore, from the outset, John's investigative work, while analogous to Milk's, bears traces of the expert. Although his bachelors and doctorate in history suit him for intellectual foraging, in 1979, when he returns to the Hill, his readiness for a physical hunt remains uncertain. The numerous texts that fill his family's history suggest that logic may be what he needs to corner his quarry, but a detail regarding his father's moonshining hints at complication. Moses valued the time that brewing liquor gave him to figure things out. That figuring, as his attic library confirms, sometimes took the form of reading and note taking, but just as often, it involved outdoor activities such as calculating on his feet and constructing maps in his mind. This tension between John and Moses's hunting strategies first emerges when the former is fifteen and home sick from high school. During that illness, John discovers his father's archive and begins chasing after his paternal ancestors. He then enjoyed Old Jack's tutelage in woodcraft and thus was confident of his skills. When he rejoins the pursuit over fifteen years later, ailment again haunts his efforts, and this time, John has not been in the woods for more than ten years.

John returns to the Hill because a sickly Jack asks for him; thus, his trip gets framed as a caretaker's journey. Once he arrives though, his mentor positions him anew as a student. John's earliest meeting with Jack occurs after Moses's funeral when he visits the older man's cabin and learns via toddies and storytelling about his father's life. As the two reunite in 1979, their bonding resumes this familiar pattern. Jack's health arouses John's concern, and in the younger man's mind, the threatening weather and the Spartan conditions make escape an urgent matter. Jack prioritizes a selfless need for deathbed instruction. When Moses, his best friend, told him to teach John how to be a man, Jack took the charge as an obligation and a labor of love. Thus, for him, the necessity of squeezing out one more lesson trumps the unlikely comfort of hospitalization.[19] John's schooling does not prepare him for this sort of reasoning, but Jack's mindset recalls an earlier moment burnishing his point.

After Jack had been arguing with teenage John about whether physics or spirits produced the noises that he heard on the wind, he tells his young charge a story about the runaway slaves whose plight gives Bradley's novel its name.[20] He says, "I ain't never heard 'em that often—maybe five, six times in ma whole life . . . I only ever heard 'em when I was on the trail a somethin' else, an' I'd be listenin' for whatever I was after, jest settin' there lettin' the sound come to me, an' then I'd hear 'em" (63). Mocking John's belief that Western rationalism could unlock the mysteries of black identity, Jack counsels receptiveness as a key tool in tracking down one's history. A young John resists this counsel preferring an existence where "African American and European American epistemologies" exist in "bipolar opposition" (Kubitschek 762). By 1979 when he confronts a dying Jack, he still embraces a "rationalistic . . . sense of himself," but he starts to appreciate how black "communal literacy" plays a part in his life (Byerman 129; Kubitschek 762). Ironically, his maternal grandfather spurs him toward Jack's model of hunting with the head and the heart.

When John was a boy, he despised Yvette's father, Professor Stanton,

19. Analyzing *Chaneysville*'s portraits of mortality, Ashraf Rushdy concludes: "Bradley takes a Western idea of death as a rupture signifying the unalterability of the past and accents it with an African belief system in which death is part of a continuum from being born to becoming an ancestor. In that model, dying and death itself are part of a process of gaining knowledge about the past . . . But that African belief also holds that dying is never done, never completely and wholly in the past" (*Remembering* 98).

20. In 1969, David Bradley's mother Harriett was commissioned to chronicle the lives of Bedford County, Pennsylvania's black inhabitants. During her research, she discovered the legend that sits at the center of *The Chaneysville Incident*. For more on her role in the novel's genesis, see Blake and Miller (25–26).

because he would not allow John to read the books in his private collection. Stanton's archive included first editions and autographed copies by black writers, works that no library in Western Pennsylvania and few in the world could boast; however, his insistence that John could not "comprehend" the texts alerts his grandson to the failings of fetishistic archiving (129).[21] Moses says that John checks out books that he is not supposed to and will reread them five or six times to figure out their meaning. By invalidating his grandson's tenacity, the Professor disables or at least defers historical excavation. He understandably wants to preserve his collection so that its treasures can be appreciated by posterity, but his preservationist zeal alienates the very boy by whom the legacy would be most deeply appreciated. Stanton's mindset and the black bourgeois conformity that it betrays inspire John's determination to become a part of the scholarly fraternity. At a key moment, its tendency to turn black cultural experience into a museum rather than a dynamic happening sparks liberating intellectual experimentation. This experimentation successfully hybridizes John's notion of hunting.

Because Jack has painstakingly taught him the discipline, John's humiliation as he is hunting does not stem from ignorance; rather, it issues from his alienating practice of the enterprise. Solitude seems integral to the hunt, but key scenes from *Chaneysville* suggest camaraderie as normative and needful. Jack and Moses embroider their friendship with zigzagging hunting expeditions throughout the county. Along with their cut buddy Uncle Josh White, this duo gained fame not only for being "ornery" but also for an unbreakable, woods-welded fellowship (78). Their togetherness never diminished their individuality, and it provided life-saving support during crises. If John received such delicate care through Jack's loving instructions, then he may have misapprehended the tender offices because they were surrounded by a distracting misogyny. It is possible that as John lounged in his Philadelphia apartment, he acknowledged Jack's gifts to him, but without question he notes these treasures while he tends a frail old man who is embarrassed by being bathed and fed by someone whom he helped raise. In these interludes of convalescence, John fully comprehends how human contact becomes an indispensable weapon. This comprehension points him toward a clearer conception of his family's past. His clarity mirrors that of the Black Archivists.

---

21. John Washington's antipathy toward the Professor inspires sympathy; yet, it also evinces a bratty sense of entitlement. While he, a precocious boy, had "read and reread every book the County library had to offer," he still was a youth subject to accidents, forgetfulness, and an incomplete sense of a rare book collections' worth (129).

Morrison's and Bradley's engagement of hunting evokes mainstream American modernists such as Ernest Hemingway and William Faulkner. Although these writers' ideas about masculinity inflect *Song's* and *Chaneysville's* portraits of Milk and John, their authority regarding woodcraft and gender ideals gets challenged in the black novels' focus on recovery and communion. Morrison's and Bradley's challenges originate in their sensitivity to artistic prescriptions, the perceived need to make black writing "as close to perfect copies of white [writing] as possible" (Washington xlvi). While the admonitions toward emulation rarely emerged that bluntly, the reality was a publishing landscape that sought to fit black topic texts into white avant-garde categories. Ernest Gaines revealed that by 1993, black writers were attacking this attempt, but Morrison and Bradley show that such responses originated earlier. Revoicing modernist hunting's noncollaborative epistemology, these writers place disoriented protagonists in reach of an edifying communality. Their rescues lack tidy edges and neat corners, yet they insist that entering black archives does not entail becoming a victim of your history. This insistence surfaces in *Song's* and *Chaneysville's* incorporation of black literary precedents.

With a major character that is an undertaker, a real estate mogul, and a part owner of a bar, Richard Wright's *The Long Dream* not only anticipates the father-son and entrepreneurial plots of *Song* and *Chaneysville* but also prophesies black bourgeois disillusionment as a danger in integrated America. Published in 1959 while its author was living in Paris, *The Long Dream* prompted some reviewers to ponder whether "Wright's expatriation had caused him to lose contact with the [post–*Brown v. Board*] realities of [American] race relations" (Kinnamon viii). Medgar Evers's murder, Malcolm X's death, and Martin Luther King's assassination all suggested that Wright's meditations on black psychosis heralded a resentment that would erupt in the tumultuous 1960s. If these tragedies rocked America's landscape shaking up black complacency, then Morrison and Bradley by the 1970s considered how impugning stylists such as Wright and Chester Himes had enervated the ethics of swagger.[22] Their considerations were less about cults of charisma and more about intricate conversations that moved beyond signifying to produce ballasts amid post–civil rights absurdity. *Song's* and *Chaneysville's* treatments of love assay such movements.

22. Chester Himes's *The Third Generation* (1954) joins Wright's *The Long Dream* as a significant intertext for both *Chaneysville* and *Song of Solomon*. See Lawrence Jackson's forthcoming biography *Chronicles of the Absurd: The Life and Times of Chester Himes, 1909–1984* for a more thorough exploration of Himes's underappreciated legacy.

The Fullest Inheritance

As Milk and John strive to merge the hope of integration with the truths of their family's histories, both men contemplate how at a key moment, a division between work and love surfaced in their ancestors' approach to freedom. They conclude that the divorce of labor and intimacy diverts their forebears from liberty, a conclusion that reflects broader convictions. By stressing material wellbeing's inability to replace emotional satisfaction, Morrison and Bradley imply that black freedom is most vulnerable to racial oppression when it overlooks empathy. Milk and John's experiences reflect this finding, and their searches for love within their family archives turn up troubling emotional distances. While this remoteness begins with their parents, both men discover that stifled emotional connection may be racism's most pernicious byproduct. The irony is that in seeking to remedy dehumanization, Milk and John's families often neglected the very quality that held the possibility for healing. To remedy this oversight, *Song* and *Chaneysville*'s protagonists must reread their romantic pasts.

Milk's grasp of love's tie to liberty begins with his parent's marriage. His perception in fact may be more acute since his conception marks both the last time that his parents slept together and the final act in their bitter estrangement. Because of that convergence, Macon and Ruth treated him as a "plain" on which they "fought" out their disputes (132). This warfare accelerated Milk's flight south, but like Paul D with Beloved, it also drew him back to the obligations of empathy. His parents' defining wounds bespeak the various forms of racial terror. Whether in the clarity of a father shot from a fence post or the convolution of hypocritical elitism, the wake of white terror overwhelms the Dead marriage. The agony is not the environment that spawns such truths but the misapprehension that promotes it. Macon and Ruth are each convinced that the appurtenances of freedom are in fact freedom itself. Just as Alice Manfred's fight against Jim Crow blinds her to its insidious attack on affection, Macon and Ruth convince themselves that the epic labors of empire building dwarf the quiet rituals of soul tending. Milk's great-grandparents, Ryna and Solomon, alert him to this mindset's pitfalls, but his grandparents suggest an alternative.

While Milkman's paternal grandfather is originally called Jake, the pencil slips of a drunken Freedman's Bureau agent get him rechristened Macon Dead. Jake laments the mix-up, but he sees it differently when his future wife Sing admires the name. While his illiteracy stamps him as a former slave, a man defined by the whims of racism, Sing adjusts his situation both with education and, more tellingly, with her reading of his possibility. She believes that Jake should keep his name because it is "new and would wipe out the past" (54). Although she died before Lincoln's Heaven took its finest form, her outlook on freedom spurred her husband's efforts even beyond his death. Their intertwining of love and liberty not only inspires his work but also their daughter's. In fact, through Pilate's interpretations of the utterances of Jake's ghost, his work becomes hers.

Jake appears to Pilate shortly after her daughter's birth and says, "Sing, Sing . . . You can't just fly on off and leave a body" (147). Pilate interpreted his message as a call to go back and take full responsibility for a man that she believes she and Macon murdered, but Milk, by piecing together Solomon's story, discovers that Jake is sharing with Sing his forlorn reaction to his father's flight. This scenario proves noteworthy on two fronts. First, Jake talks to Sing about his feelings. Even in the throes of hewing a life out of Reconstruction's unshaped options, he notes that the work of liberty involves inventories of the heart. His love for his wife allows him to confess the pain of his father's absence. Second, Jake's ghost reveals that even beyond the grave, the sweetness of his marriage to Sing still persists. His confession of that sweetness' value to Pilate can only be decoded after Milk witnesses it as well. With this witnessing, his apprehension of tenderness enlarges. Such enlargement means that his past intimacies must be reviewed as well.

The defining tenderness in Milk's adult life is his relationship with Hagar, Pilate's granddaughter and his second cousin. Initially, their liaisons consist of sex fuelled by his adolescent lust and her quirky curiosity. Eventually though, his attraction cools, and she, wielding a Carlson carving knife, walks the street every thirty days determined to murder him. She cannot kill him, and eventually her pining for him leads to her death. When Milk contemplates his role in Hagar's mental unhinging, he feels ashamed of his callousness. His affair with Hagar begins in adoring glances and homemade wine, but after two decades, their desire devolved into commodity. This devolution sends them careening toward alternative fates. Using a Dear John letter as a Christmas gift, Milk insists that although separation would "deeply hurt him after all these years," he nevertheless recognized that "you couldn't be selfish with somebody you loved" (98). Feigned concern launches his Dixieland adventure. In a crude irony, Hagar's identity voyage entails a shopping spree downtown, an outing that marks irrecoverable "psychic illness" (Rushdy, *Remembering*

83).[23] Pilate unknowingly carries her father's bones for most of her life, and she must properly dispose of them to access "mercy" (317). To resurrect Jake's legacy, Milk must figuratively shoulder Hagar's body. Accepting her burden shows how a family history littered with failed bonds can eventually fuse liberty and love, and this becomes a crucial lesson for the last member of the Dead clan.

Milk's southern travels begin as an extension of his father's agenda; however, they soon take on Pilate's concerns. She detects the ways in which her brother uses greed to blunt the pain of Jake's death. While she laments Macon's materialism, she still tells Milk that "hadn't been for your daddy, I wouldn't be here today" (40). Her remembrance of how he carried her "in [his] arms" when she was a baby forever obligates her to him (51). When Pilate tells Hagar and Milk that they should treat one another as brother and sister, she is not anticipating their incestuous affair or disregarding their precise kinship; rather, she is warning them that social conventions may erode their concern for one another. Her granddaughter's death and her nephew's hand in it confirm her suspicions. Demonstrating the dangers of lapsed empathy, Hagar's demise bespeaks Milk's cultural forgetfulness. When he drives his aunt south to put down her father's bones, he offers a comfort grounded in healing memory. This generosity permeates *Song*'s conclusion even as violence punctuates its expression.

Guitar, Milk's ace, is a member of the Seven Days, a militant black organization committed to taking one white life for every black one claimed by racial terror. When the plot to rob Pilate founders, he tracks Milk through Virginia, hoping to find the treasure and fund the Days' latest endeavor—a response to the Birmingham bombing. As Pilate buries her father, Guitar, aiming for Milk, shoots and kills her. His action shows how the "deadly retribution" unleashed on "an oppressive and unjust society" produces another warped chase after freedom (Jordan 206). Where Guitar embraces a love of liberty that claims his beloved's lives, Milk taking up his aunt's refrain—"If I'd a knowed more [people], I woulda loved more"—decides that surrender is the saner reaction (336). His final act in the novel, a leap into nothingness, carries vestiges of his great-grandfather Solomon's flight; however, it truly signals a liberation

23. Susan Willis argues that Pilate's house "demonstrates the insufficiency of the agrarian social mode to provide for its members once they are transplanted to urban consumer society" (108). Thus, Hagar's purchases could be viewed as emblems of disconnection between the rural South and the urban North. Although these regional incompatibilities are evident in Morrison's portrayal, W. Lawrence Hogue has correctly suggested that if Pilate cannot teach "agrarian values to her . . . granddaughter, then she cannot pass them on to Milkman" (49).

work that attends to caring. Believing that generosity forms his family's finest legacy, Milk's gesture is less suicidal and more sacrificial.[24] Thus, he perfects what he mangles with Hagar—selflessness. John's love lessons also conjure altruism, but his curriculum requires metaphorical rather than literal leaps.

Just as Milk's survey of freedom and devotion commences with his parents, John's musings on love start with Yvette and Moses's unorthodox affections. His mother contents herself that she "had what [her husband] gave" her (308). By which perhaps she means that she had two sons, a comfortable life, and a staunch partner in the fight against Jim Crow humiliation. The dignity of Yvette's existence buffered her from certain ravages of racial prejudice, but her "emotional barrenness" fed "stoicism" and precluded intimate fellowship (Egan 276). As John studies his parent's marriage, this lack strikes him, and when he places it beside the romances, including his own, in his family's archives, he senses that his mother's imperfect consolation results from a misjudgment of love's role in freedom work. John's research on C.K., his paternal great-grandfather, sparks this insight.

C.K. Washington's escape from slavery and his Tubman-esque exploits begin as a solo project, a commemoration à la Macon and Pilate of his father's ambition, but by the 1840s, Harriette Brewer spurred a transformative collaboration.[25] Together with Harriette, a woman who possessed "the strongest moral sense he had ever encountered," he plotted and executed the theft of slaves (355).[26] They teamed up to promote the social good; however, their efforts exposed other aspects of liberation. Tying activism directly to passion, the couple united racial rescue and personal pleasure, a combination that C.K.'s son Lamen and his grandson Moses deeply misunderstood. Lamen parlayed his father's racial advocacy into bourgeois gentility. Making his living by handling dead bodies, he

24. Ashraf Rushdy argues, "What is significant about Morrison's achievement is the way she has recast Milkman's 'flight,' which would be a suicidal move according to one set of values, into a liberating act according to the set of values the novel endorses" (*Remembering* 78). If Rushdy supports a nonsuicidal view of Milk's flight, then Jeffrey Leak captures the importance of his unselfishness: "At novel's end we find Milkman engaging in sacrifice for another human being, an endeavor with which he is unfamiliar for most of his life. He progresses in his relationships with women and his understanding of history and myth. But, as with John, Milkman teaches us that even when one's consciousness experiences growth, the struggle does not end, for one must give witness to this growth or rebirth amongst kith and kin, and, yes, enemies as well" (131).

25. See Maha Marouan "Interpolating Harriet Tubman: Representing Gender and Heroism in David Bradley's *The Chaneysville Incident*" for more on Harriette and C.K.'s slave stealing.

26. Klaus Ensslen writes that C.K. led "the fugitive slaves of the local legend alluded to" in *Chaneysville*'s "title to their heroic self-immolation" and "fought his own war against the system of slavery" (280).

neglected the transactions that fed his comfort. His son Moses exhumed America's absurd racial history, but his copying of C.K. lacked the crucial perspective afforded by a colluding romantic partner. Perceiving this deficiency, John, as an adolescent, experiments with shared freedom work. The results are dismal.

Mara Jamison is the daughter of Linda Jamison, a black prostitute whose patrons are all white men. When Linda prepares Mara to enter the family business, the younger woman asks John to sleep with her and thus spoil her for the trade. This plan tries to thwart the exploitative effects of white male sexual desire, and in some ways, it recalls C.K.'s antics.[27] Despite echoing an earlier freedom fighter, John and Mara, like Moses and Yvette, discover that their rote coupling lacks revolutionary power. Klaus Ensslen speculates that the couple fails because John "resist[s] being victimized" (291). Thus, though Mara confronts a heinous fate, John will not join her vulnerability; instead, he reduces the danger to the possibility of "losing [her] body to a white man" (Leak 105). John's bitterness blocks his compassion, and this leads him to mistake togetherness for intimacy. As Pilate showed Milk, there are no gimmicks that deliver freedom. One must shoulder the burdens of empathy until caring signals deliverance. If Mara could not tutor John toward taking the weight, then in the final phases of sorting his family's legacy, he enlists his girlfriend Judith, a woman whose whiteness formidably endangers their success.

Bradley contends that the main reason he made Judith white is because nobody wants "to hear two niggers sitting around complaining about white folks" (Blake and Miller 29). While his quip betrays both irreverence and audience awareness, it also conveniently sidesteps the controversy of black-white romance. Morrison, as early as 1971, identified a "growing rage of black women over the unions of black men and white women" (*What* 26). If Bradley noted that some folks would not want to hear blacks discussing whites, he definitely knew that other people, among them a few black women, would be ticked off by a black man and a white woman who had recently made love talking about almost anything. Instead of supporting his contention that Judith is "peripheral," *Chaneysville* makes her essential, but that centrality stems less from her prodding of John's storytelling and more from her vivid illustration of the always already politicized dimensions of black existence (Blake and

27. One of the more humorous slave-stealing plans that C.K. Washington pulls off is to "liberate a whorehouse" (358). Because a fifteen-year-old John discovered his father's library, he might have been familiar with C.K.'s methods and his character.

Miller 29). Her ability to cull intimacy from that morass inspires John's reciprocity.

The insinuating energy of racial realities means that who you love is partly the work of black liberty. Because Judith embodies this permeation, she gives John the complementing perspective that Harriette offers C.K. The former couple's labor is not the same as the latter's, yet its concepts ally. John and Judith's fantastic story of Harriette and C.K.'s reunion affirms this alliance. When John finds himself out of "facts" about Moses's attempts to comprehend C.K.'s death, Judith cajoles him into using his imagination (391). Many scholars have noted how this collaboration, one that weaves a romance and a hunting plot, affirms the pair's commitment.[28] While these readings persuasively explain John and Judith's "fictional reconstruction of the unfinished story-line of history," their tendency to make her a stand-in for a broader "white reading audience" denies a crucial facet of this exchange, namely its desperate singularity (Ensslen 285). Improbably, Jack Crawley prepared John to recognize the immense importance of that feature, and he did so in the last conversation they ever shared.

As soon as Jack hears that John lives with a white woman, he feels compelled to give his pupil one last story. This account limns the border between fancy and logic conveying the costs of braiding love and black freedom work.[29] When Uncle Josh, a black man who could pass for white, proposed to Clydette, a white woman, local Ku Klux Klan members bound, tortured, and prepared him for execution. Moses and Jack saved his life, but after their rescue, he said almost nothing for the rest of his days. Jack revives Josh's vulnerability to highlight racial prejudice's indifference to love's earnestness. Just as he did not want John's book learning to blunt his survival instincts, he does not want John's relationship with Judith to consign him to the silence that enshrouded Josh's

---

28. Phillip J. Egan's "Unraveling Misogyny and Forging the New Self: Mother, Lover, and Storyteller in *The Chaneysville Incident*"; Cathy Brigham's "Identity, Masculinity, and Desire in Bradley's Fiction" (1995); Klaus Ensslen's "Fictionalizing History: David Bradley's *The Chaneysville Incident*" (1988); Missy Dehn Kubitschek's "'So You Want a History, Do You?': Epistemologies and *The Chaneysville Incident*" (1996); and Jeffrey Leak's *Racial Myths and Masculinity in African American Literature* (2005) all address the epiphany of John and Judith's collaboration. Maha Marouan and James Coleman believe that the benefits of this collaboration are temporal and the foundation of John and Judith's relationship is quite shaky. See "Interpolating Harriet Tubman" and *Black Male Fiction and the Legacy of Caliban* (2001) respectively.

29. Scholars have inveighed against the racist and sexist aspects of this tale. While there can be no gainsaying Jack's antipathy toward nearly every female in *Chanesysville,* his attitude contains textures that are often overlooked, and his last story poignantly exemplifies the broad contours and the specific crevices within his perception of women and romance.

life. His story does not impugn the sincerity of interracial love; however, it suggests that no matter how much time passes, the ghosts of bygone experiences still ride the wind, shaping the lives and the attitudes of the living. He may not bless John's relationship, but he clarifies the harrowing that will enliven it. By providing that clarification, Jack lays the burden of liberty on his mentee.

Who Profits?

Song and *Chaneysville* have been exposed to more than a quarter century of scrutiny, and despite this attention, the novels still prove difficult to grasp.[30] At the center of that difficulty is what to do with the texts' massive archives. Persuasive analyses have identified the African cosmology implicit in the novels' assorted corpses, skeletons, near dead, and ghosts, but Milk's and John's hunts for their family legacies produce libraries and living legends. Behind these men's epic amassing, Morrison and Bradley place a fundamental question: Can black freedom accommodate love? These novels meditate on this query using a privileged generation that has inherited the sacrifices and the suggestions of their elders. Through these portrayals, *Song* and *Chaneysville* also comment upon post–civil rights novelists' confrontations with black literary traditions.

The family violence that Macon and Yvette hide signals the forgetfulness that America charges for bourgeois comfort. Given the aesthetic concessions that black novelists were counseled to make, this repression connects to the shifting white estimates of Chester Himes, Ann Petry, and Gwendolyn Brooks. These writers skirted the stylistic demands for racial reconciliation and chronicled the psychoses that haunted even successful blacks. Milk and John's reliance upon Pilate and Jack suggest that while the perceptions of these elders should not cramp their autonomy, their spirits will not be displaced by mainstream mandates. The love lessons in *Song* and *Chaneysville* indicate a graceful empathy as the condition of intimacy. With the cultivation of a burden bearing concern, the novel's protagonists discovered a durable basis for fellowship. This depic-

---

30. Jane Campbell's *Mythic Black Fiction: The Transformation of History* (1986); W. Lawrence Hogue's *Race, Modernity, Postmodernity;* Ashraf Rushdy's *Remembering Generations;* and Jeffrey Leak's *Racial Myths and Masculinity in African American Literature* have all talked about both *Song* and *Chaneysville*. In addition, Madhu Dubey's *Signs and Cities,* Dolan Hubbard's *The Sermon and the African American Literary Imagination* (1996), and Valerie Sweeney Prince's *Burnin' Down the House: Home in African American Literature* (2005) have engaged *Song* while James Coleman's *Black Male Fictions and the Legacy of Caliban* treats *Chaneysville*.

tion explains why communion becomes one of the Black Archivists' most treasured resources.

Milk and John represent the fitful progress of the late twentieth-century attempt to correct the distorted black identity within the American imagination. Shaped by bourgeois respectability, intellectual activism, and pragmatic reform, these men's complicated projects demand refined fixes. Milk's materialistic maneuvering hits a dead end, and John's rationalistic tendencies offer no panacea. These developments do not mark their missions as untenable; rather, they figure them as incremental. This disposition also surfaces in Morrison and Bradley's artistic approaches. Just as John and Milk scan their pasts and presents, noticing missteps, exulting in fractional triumphs, and lamenting the incompleteness of it all, Bradley and Morrison discover that black artistic independence must necessarily be gradual and partial. For both parties, the road is not pure ascent; it harbors twists, turns, and a few cadavers. What both the characters and the novelists make clear, though, is the reward of prior and persisting failures. Failure carries artists beyond experimental technique to the humanizing possibilities of disappointment. Within that sphere, *Song* and *Chaneysville*'s string of bodies are signposts pointing to richer life. John Edgar Wideman probes narrative's negative capacities for richness in *Sent For You Yesterday* and *Philadelphia Fire*.

Measured Achievement

Sent For You Yesterday's and *Philadelphia Fire*'s Failed Artists

Critics of the African American novel rightly emphasize its successes, but this tradition also includes defining moments of failure. With the recent appearance of *Three Days Before the Shooting* (2010), Ralph Ellison's second novel, the literary world returned to one of the most discussed failures in the African American canon. Among the Black Archivists, David Bradley, with a roughly thirty-year gap between *The Chaneysville Incident* and his unfinished third novel, provokes wonderment. These examples of authors failing to produce books join fictions about artist characters failing to complete songs, stories, and paintings. From James Weldon Johnson's *The Autobiography of an Ex-Colored Man* (1912) to William Demby's *Beetlecreek* (1950), miscarried artistry forms an integral part of black literary history. Few narratives of artistic failure are as celebrated as John Edgar Wideman's *Sent For You Yesterday* and *Philadelphia Fire*.[1]

1. *Sent For You Yesterday* and *Philadelphia Fire* mark major transitions in Wideman's writing career. If *Sent* is a part of the Homewood Trilogy, a set of books—including *Damballah* (1981) and *Hiding Place* (1981)—that announced his investment in folk resources, then *Philadelphia* rounds out a middle period in that experiment. Wideman's embrace of the folk usually gets tied to his seven-year publishing hiatus from 1974 to 1980. Analyzing this lull, James Coleman has argued that by studying his family and the Homewood section of Pittsburgh where he grew up, Wideman brought the "intellectual characters [in his fiction] out of their isolation and into contact with the needs, concerns, and traditions of black people more generally" (*Blackness* 3). Although Coleman first notes this reconnection with the black community, Bonnie TuSmith (*All* 85–88), Jerry Bryant (166–69), and Raymond Janifer (60–65) all offer illuminating treatments.

As previous chapters in this study have suggested, all of the Black Archivists invest their prizewinning fiction with themes or structures that take up their professional development. Wideman, perhaps more than anyone else, has made his career a subject of his novels.[2] On the one hand, his autobiographical interpolations could be understood as a postmodernist technique. His strategies certainly partake of the authorial defamiliarization that marks texts as diverse as Frank London Brown's *The Mythmaker* (1969) and William Gaddis's *A Frolic of His Own* (1994), but his approach also harkens to the Black Archivists' fascination with submerged, obscured, and hidden black experiences. Put more precisely, Wideman's inclusion of so much about his family could be considered a reaction against American society's attempt to trivialize folks like his family. If Wideman recurrently puts his kin in his novels, then how he does so illuminates both his books and issues tied to prestige, esteem, and style.

Wideman compels writers and their readers to ask what achievement really means given the overwrought events that form black life. He inquires what results when your work of art fails the object of your love. Examining the artist figures in *Sent* and *Philadelphia,* this chapter argues that his interest in creative failure reflects his convictions about the ineffable. He experiments with literary strategies, yet he concludes that artistic mastery is a fallacy. By looking at how his prizewinning novels emphasize miscarried art, this chapter determines that the final lesson the Black Archivists pull from the black literary tradition is the yawning gap between technique and solace, a lesson that actually tightens their grasp of the ethics of swagger.

"Thwarted and Prepared"[3]

In Paule Marshall's *Brown Girl, Brownstones* (1959), Clive Springer, a black male dilettante, explains why he cannot break through into a personally, satisfying art: "[I'm] not bold enough . . . [I] don't really feel.

2. James Coleman argues that "writing about the personal has become a primary aspect of Wideman's quest to center black reality in his work and of his overall development as an experimental writer" (*Writing* xi).

3. In the introduction to *The Homewood Books,* Wideman states, "It became clear to me on those nights in Pittsburgh in 1973 that I needn't look any further than the place I was born and the people who'd loved me to find what was significant and lasting in literature. My university training had both thwarted and prepared this understanding, and the tensions of multiple traditions, European and African-American, the Academy and the Street, animates these texts" (x).

[I] was born the wrong color. . . . I have the form, the techniques, but no substance" (265). Clive notes racism's effect on his work, but his final word about failed creativity concerns technical skill and emotional depth. Throughout *Sent,* Wideman expands Clive's meditations. Using artist figures, among them pianists, a budding writer, and a painter, he considers the differences between success and failure for these black creators. Most critics have analyzed the musicians as reflections of the novel's Homewood setting, and in treating Doot, the writer, they have linked his story scavenging to the pianists' abilities to hold the community together. The galvanizing force of *Sent's* musicians and writer cannot be disputed; however, the novel's portrayal of a failed painter complicates the collision between "mainstream modernist and existentialist discourses" and black vernacular expression (Janifer 65). Wideman's interest in such a complication relates to questions separating technique and commitment.

    Sent is largely a "tri-generational" narrative that spans "a period of roughly forty years (from the 1930s to the 1970s)" (Rodriguez 137). Despite reinforcing these chronological boundaries with chapter titles such as "1941," "1962," and "1970," the novel occasionally steps outside of that frame and engages the nineteenth-century roots of Homewood,[4] the black Pittsburgh community where the book is set (159, 173, 183).[5] Just as *The Chaneysville Incident* and *Song of Solomon* tied post–*Brown v. Board* black life to the expectancy of the 1890s, *Sent* also allows readers to see the durable yet veiled networks of care that bolstered Homewood. These retrospective moments hint at the ultimate significance of black art. When elders—such as Sybela Owens—established the neighborhood, they put in place values that would refute the material and spiritual ravages of racial inequality. As each subsequent generation inherits Homewood, they wonder whether these founding principles will be preserved. Some of such wonderment centers on what function artists serve. Albert Wilkes's piano playing in the 1920s and 1930s is illustrative.

    4. When Freeda visits her Uncle Bill and Aunt Aida in 1934, the year of Albert Wilkes's return to Homewood, the episode simultaneously conveys her worry about her husband's safety and allows Wideman to push his novel's events back at least to the 1920s and perhaps further. Uncle Bill states that before he bought his house at 725, he had been playing that number for "twenty years." This means that by the time Freeda walked through the door in 1941, he had at least been around since 1921. Given that Bill is an old man in 1941 and at least old enough in 1921 to muse on "having worked all them years for O'Reilly," he perhaps pushes the chronology of *Sent* back to the nineteenth century (45).

    5. Wilfred Samuels once asked Wideman whether Homewood was a "real, physical" neighborhood and "not just a fictional community." Wideman replied, "Oh, no. Homewood is very real. As I said, [my] family history coincides with the history of the actual community" (15).

Described with blues-tinged imagery, Wilkes gets loosely associated with that musical genre. His artistic skill emerges chiefly through the way that he grants his listeners their identity. His best friend, John French, expresses this quality in Wilkes's playing: "It was after . . . the music started coming out that you could find yourself, find your face grinning back at you like in a mirror" (68). Given the vicissitudes of city life during the Roaring Twenties, Wilkes no doubt clarified the shift from rural to urban space that many Homewood blacks experienced. He took the uncertainty of new streets, new people, and new challenges and grounded them in the nervy search for selfhood. While new black residents from the south found a GPS in Wilkes's playing, John—a staunch proponent of Albert's mastery—also detected his identity there. He discovered the logic that transformed him from a put-out-the-lights woman-chaser into a family man. Even though Wilkes exposes John's reasons for changing, he also questions him about the change. Albert states, "French . . . how come you a family man?" (63). At once playful and earnest, his query shows the gap between performance and effect. The ambiguities in this gap unleash *Sent*'s major tensions, which are embodied in Freeda French, John's wife. Although many in Homewood experience Wilkes's playing as a humanizing affirmation, she sees signs of demise in it.

Freeda views the blues and the "black tide of immigrants from the South" suspiciously (41). Instead of detecting an anchor amid flux, she believes that the music is an agent of corruption. It especially threatened sexual immorality and undignified carriage, traits she perceived in "young girls" who "switched their narrow fannies" and "funky undershirts the men rolled down off their chests" (42). If these general consequences of the music disturbed her, then Wilkes's particular effect on her husband was more alarming. The two men drank together, stayed out until night became morning, and the devilment of one attached itself so closely to the other that dirt done by one could get the other killed. While Freeda's sentiments echo those of *Jazz*'s Alice Manfred, her motherhood and her multigenerational connection to Homewood make her outlook something more than self-righteousness. She sees Homewood as a place shaped by "older people who had always loved and supported her" (47). To see that love and support carried away by "Devil music" saddened her (51). More than that, thinking that the wake created by the music might leave her husband dead frenzied her. Freeda's quandary pulls virtuosic artistry out of the aesthetic realm and into the sphere of morality; through her attitude, Wideman contemplates the ethics of swagger.

Wilkes epitomizes creative swagger. He lucidly expresses black life without adjusting his style to suit white expectations. Despite his culturally astute playing, his ethics, vis-à-vis the Homewood community, are questionable. Interracial romance, as evidenced in *The Chaneysville Incident,* produces charged confrontations with America's tortured racial past; nonetheless, such a relationship is not immoral. Wilkes's affair with his white mistress, though, imperils Homewood's safety. In 1927, when a white policeman, apparently an intimate of his girlfriend, tried to shoot him, Albert murdered him while the man was wearing his uniform. Wilkes left Homewood and did not return until 1934. Upon his return, he goes to the Tate house, the place where he grew up, and with his arrival, everyone in that house lives under the threat of death. Lucy Tate, one of the orphans that Mr. and Mrs. Tate took in, described the scene: "Sometimes I think I'd be willing to die if I could play one time as fine and sweet as Albert Wilkes played that afternoon. Maybe he did know he was gon die. Maybe he didn't care. I sure didn't. Didn't nothing matter but the music" (102). While he was playing the piano, police shot Wilkes, and in that juxtaposition of white aggression and black performance, Wideman raised questions about the meaning of art that open out to the Black Archivists.

Opposition to white artistic expectations defines a noble struggle for the Black Archivists. Though each writer in the cohort personalizes his or her strategy, all of them believe that black autonomy is an ethical imperative for African American literature. Their commitment yields the canon that this study has examined; yet, Wideman asks what happens when "style and imagination," the practical fuel of swagger, run up against "a deterministic reality" (R. Miller, *Black* 97), one that threatens the very community the black artist seeks to nourish. With Wilkes's predicament at the Tate house, this rumination moves from a philosophical abstract to a literary concrete. Is Freeda correct in concluding that Albert's music robs him of the moral compass that would keep him away from a house where children and an old woman are present, or is Lucy accurate in stating "didn't nothing matter but the music"? These questions propel black novelists out of their aesthetic debates and into the controversies that raged around other black art forms in the 1980s.[6]

6. During the 1980s, Tipper Gore led a campaign that culminated in the use of "parental advisory" stickers to identify potentially offensive music. This campaign was not aimed at black music per se, although Prince's song, "Darling Nikki" sparked her efforts. Impressed by Gore's results, C. Dolores Tucker initiated scrutiny of rap music, especially so-called gangsta rap. See Robert

The night after Albert has returned to Homewood, John French makes it home and finds his worried wife waiting for him. Reprising the trio structure that surfaced in *The Women of Brewster Place* and *Jazz*, Wideman allows these three characters to range across an ideological continuum. He uses them here to contemplate communal preservation. Homewood is in John French's phrasing, Albert's "briarpatch" (79). Although he is "the traditional badman in a once stable and close-knit community," Albert's music made it his job to keep the neighborhood in place (Bryant 166). Freeda believes that preserving Homewood entails keeping it safe for the families that live there; thus, to her, playing music that drives "a bunch of drunk niggers crazier" contributes little to Homewood's survival (84). Poised between these two, John blends their positions. He acknowledged the need for safety as his children walked the streets; however, he also feels that friendship lashes individuals and communities together. The stakes of black artistry surface vividly in this triumvirate, but Wideman defers answering his provocative questions until he explores another aspect of creativity, namely contorted perception. Probing this idea requires a look at the painting career of John and Freeda's son Carl.

In the 1930s, when his mother and father struggle with the ethics of Wilkes's swagger, Carl launches his own reverie about his neighborhood's fate: "What would happen to Homewood if he ran away? What would happen to his mother and father if one morning, a bright, lazy spring summer morning, he didn't wake up and start the dream of Homewood?" (28). His questions—carrying equal traces of pubescent narcissism and existential angst—ponder imagination's power, but they do so from the perspective of a frightened boy. After World War II, Carl's musings about Homewood's future is as poignant as earlier generations.' His military experiences, including having pushed "stacks of dead Japanese marines over the edge of a cliff," tie him to Albert Wilkes's time on the lam, since in both cases the men are gone for seven years and return at a moment of crisis (115–16). Just as Wilkes did after the disorientations of his trip, Carl seeks out his woman and his best friend as reference points for a full return home.

Lucy Bruce, who "became a Tate after her mother burnt up in the fire on Hamilton Avenue," exists as a fixture of Homewood (38). Beyond that though, as Lucy matures, Freeda bestows a pejorative, "*fast Lucy,*" on

---

Siegel's "Tipper Gore and Family Values" (2005) and George Curry's "C. Delores Tucker's Fight Against Offensive Lyrics" (2007).

her that connects the younger girl to communal decline (95). In Freeda's mind, to be fast is to be "dangerous," and that danger, linked here to sexuality, threatens because of its unpredictability (50).⁷ While his mother offers one perspective on Lucy, Carl sees things differently. One of a passel of "orphans and strays" that "Old Mr. and Mrs. Tate had raised," Lucy, the putative sister of his best friend Brother, is the young lady to whom Carl loses his virginity (38–39). If that intimacy conveys personal significance, then, Lucy, who "nobody told . . . what to do so she told herself," also emerges as a communal agent who binds folks to one another (96).⁸ When she was a child, she compelled the roguish bachelor Albert Wilkes to the domesticity of administering a bath (124–25). She visits Samantha, the mother of Brother's only child, who languishes in an insane asylum amid the fallout from that child's murder by his own siblings. These offices frustrate Freeda's simple conclusions, and even though Lucy and Carl never marry, they exist as lifelong companions. Because Lucy symbolizes in many ways the horde that comes to define Homewood, Carl's love for her is affirming; however, his relationship to her as an artistic subject becomes an intriguing parable of creativity.

Carl first makes love to Lucy when both are thirteen years old. By 1970, the present of *Sent,* he tells his nephew Doot, "Been looking at [that woman] nearly fifty years now and still can't even finish her picture. Started one once . . . when you was little . . . Only thing right about [it] is one cheek and one eye" (147). He contends, "I could really draw. Ever since I was in grade school I could draw things, and they look just like real" (149). To Carl, a talent deficit did not explain his struggles with Lucy; rather, the trouble stemmed from faulty perception. Proximity, whether born of physical closeness or duration of acquaintance, convinces the brain that an individual has apprehended a subject. In justifying his flummoxed project, Carl explains, "People ain't easy to see. Can't see them cause half the time they ain't all there. I mean if you look, and look closer the way you have to do if you're trying to paint a picture . . . a person subject to go all to pieces and won't be nothing there to see" (148). His statement seems to endorse objectivity. While Carl's creative failures suggest a need for adjustments, his dilemma reflects a longer-standing hurdle. The reason that he abandoned his formal artistic training reveals that hurdle.

7. In some ways, Freeda's view of Lucy anticipates Violet's and Alice's understanding of *Jazz's* Dorcas. Both Lucy and Dorcas become daughters of the city.
8. Wideman's phrasing evokes Toni Morrison's *The Bluest Eye* where she writes about Claudia and Frieda: "Nobody paid us any attention, so we paid very good attention to ourselves" (191).

Subsequent to World War II, Carl seriously considered a fine art career. Supported by the GI Bill, he "tried some art classes at Tech," and many of his teachers used his "work to show the others how a thing could be done" (149). Despite this exemplarity, one professor, "a white dude, shit they was all white dudes" (149), delivered the following speech: "You're good. We all know that. Best student we have but you're wasting your time here. Can't earn a living with what you're learning here . . . Companies don't hire colored artists."[9] The instructor declared himself sorry to be "saying what he had to say," but in his opinion, "the rest of the teachers" were "hypocrites" who were "leading [Carl] up a blind alley" (150). On one level, this scene presents a well-worn account of segregated America's glass ceiling. That said Wideman's juxtaposition of Carl's humiliation and his inability to draw Lucy raises fascinating questions about black artistic insecurity.

The post–World War II era featured a resurgent economy, and programs such as the GI bill promised a chance for training and social advancement. Although Carl pursued these chances, his confrontation with one white instructor's version of racial reality sent him out of art school and back to the same Homewood corners where his father John had waited for day labor hanging wallpaper. Carl when he tells Doot about these events circa 1970 speculates that in the forties and fifties, the "time just weren't right" for a black man to be a fine art painter (149). While his observation captures the accumulated effects of prejudice, it ignores the example of Romare Bearden, the world-renowned black painter who went to high school in Pittsburgh in the 1920s. Perhaps, as Jerry Bryant has argued, Homewood is a community defined by generational decline. That would explain why Bearden in the 1920s might fare better than Carl in the civil rights era. The difference between Carl and Bearden no doubt reflected shifting structural realities, but Wideman by contrasting Carl's failure with the artistic successes of his main man Brother suggests that the trouble may not be seeing the subject rather it may be seeing the artist.

Despite the fact that his literary company includes Uncle Josh White from Bradley's *The Chaneysville Incident,* Brother's status as an albino orphan who barely spoke and then never spoke distinguishes him.

9. This episode recalls Charles Johnson's conversation with his father about the advisability of studying illustration with Lawrence Lariar (Byrd, *I Call* 9). Unlike Carl French, Johnson's ambitions actually ran up against his father's pessimism. Lariar actively encouraged Johnson. This perhaps unintended overlap between reality and fiction shows the pervasiveness of these sorts of encounters.

Another of his distinctions is the fact that from 1941 to 1946, he played the piano in Homewood so mellifluously that neighborhood people thought Albert Wilkes had been raised from the dead. Brother's playing roughly matches the years of America's involvement in World War II; thus, he experienced the war as an artistically fecund moment. Though this differs from Carl's time pushing dead bodies in the Pacific, it provides an interesting continuity since Brother rounds out his musical career when Carl starts his art classes. The link between Carl and Brother as artists acquires even more complexity when one considers each man's creative response to love. Even when Lucy poses nude for him, Carl's formidable technique will not yield a satisfying picture. His love provides insufficient resources for masterful expression. Untrained and unbidden, Brother swaggeringly plays the piano until his first and only son's death stills his fingers. His music exudes intimacy because it successfully documents parental ecstasy. While he does not marry the mother of his son, he—like Ciel in *The Women of Brewster Place*—mocks narratives of black urban pathology with tender gestures. These gestures cannot save his son's life, and his music cannot survive his son's death. Thus, Wideman again focuses on art's function and Homewood's survival. Though the deeply personal bond between a father and a son seems remote from preserving community, the novelist adds another dimension to Brother's art that brings *Sent*'s artistic meditations full circle.

Brother's creative efforts are often linked to his piano playing, so when the music stops in 1946, most folks felt his creative contributions to the neighborhood had ended. Shortly after his death in 1962, Lucy found a "shopping bag full of pictures" that extended his legacy. She discovered that "on one side were [Carl's] sketches of naked women from the art school, but on the back side . . . were Brother's pictures" (193). This conflation suggests that their social rituals of sharing beers, drugs, and pain intersect with the aesthetic project of making sense out of experience. Despite the convergence symbolized by these back-to-back pictures, the differences in each artist's style suggest alternate visions. Where Carl achieves a technical mastery that marks him as distinguished in the Tech professors' traditions, his virtuosity withers in the face of racism. Brother's drawings are devoid of art school virtues, yet they bring "Homewood people" to "life" (194, 195). This enlivening stems from recognition ("the faces are like cloudy photographs yet she can recognize the person right away") and independence—"Brother is saying they're my pictures and I can draw my people any way I want to." The most prominent markers of Brother's liberty are his decision to draw neighborhood people with "wings" and "old-fashioned clothes" (194). Distinct from the raucous collectivity of his piano playing, Brother's drawings constitute more solitary chronicles. They do not earn him drinks nor do they facilitate the slow dancing of couples; however, his pictures "imposed significance . . . on life" (Coleman, *Blackness* 106).

When Carl evokes a nebulous "they" to blame for Homewood's sorry state circa 1970, Lucy objects: "Ain't no they doing nothing . . . We're the ones standing by letting it happen. Those old folks *our* people" (197). She continues, "Maybe you never had a chance. Maybe it's not your fault. But you gave up too easy . . . You and me, Carl. We got scared and gave up too easy and now it's gone" (197, 198).[10] While the giving up that she references could name drug addiction, dropping out of college, or not starting a family, Lucy's comment also addresses Carl's art. Lucy romanticizes Homewood's past; nevertheless, she, better than anyone, possesses a mature grasp of life's paradoxes and ambiguities. For this reason, she knows that Albert Wilkes's sublime music spawned violence and peace. By extension, she recognizes that Brother's creativity inhabited the wounded and the healed places of the human spirit. Carl shrinks from the chaos sacrificing love to lament, and this withdrawal marks a transgression of the ethics of swagger.

When John Gardner shared with Charles Johnson his belief that great art had the capacity to change the world, he propelled his student into a full-fledged contemplation of how literature could improve black life. Similarly, Toni Morrison and Gloria Naylor's convictions that the novel could teach black people sustaining cultural wisdom reflected an optimistic view of literary work. Wideman in *Sent* registers artistic vitality, but in addition to matters of technique and topic, he engages issues of commitment. The central question regarding artistic ethics in *Sent* is are you as an artist more committed to the craft than you are to the people? The depth of a black artist's investment conditions his or her awareness of how "environment[s] influence the development of creative forms." In Wideman's mind, the cost of such environmental influence is an artist's enduring "commitment to those surroundings" that nourished him (Rodriguez 140). Carl fails because he shortchanges Homewood's investment in him. By subordinating his ambition to racial repression, he plausibly yet tragically stints the gift that would affirm his community's

---

10. Jerry Bryant views these utterances as evidence of Lucy's penchant for "nostalgia." He sees her as an "irascible and argumentative" character that oversimplifies her neighborhood's "dynamic tension" (177). I disagree since Lucy recognizes the neighborhood's tensions better than most.

concern. Art cannot reverse communal decline until the artist embodies communal worth. The Black Archivists note this reciprocity throughout the black literary tradition, and Wideman builds on these meditations by probing a site of failure in *Sent. Philadelphia Fire* expands his commentary, this time making the black writer the recipient of a lesson in defeat.

Advanced Studies in Failure

In a 2005 preface to his nonfiction classic *Brothers and Keepers* (1984), Wideman asserted, "Writing can be a means of knowing and being in the world. That kind of writing requires self-examination, self-awareness, consciousness of the process of writing and reading. I could not write my brother's story without writing mine" (xv). Though he suggested that this inextricability is especially acute in nonfiction, his fiction in the 1980s, especially *Philadelphia,* took up these very questions of who owns experience and how writing relates to such experience. The techniques that Wideman used to explore these issues, particularly the autobiographical interpolations, led some critics to place his work within the postmodern tradition of John Barth. Since his postgraduate research dealt with narrative innovators such as Laurence Stern, Thomas Mann, and James Joyce, these placements are perhaps understandable. Still, although Wideman incorporates voices as disparate as Alberto Giacometti, Mazisi Kunene, Herbert Blau, and Gaston Bachelard into *Philadelphia,* his central post-1980 concern had been with his family's role as a spur to his art. If *Philadelphia* at first glance seems a departure from that concern, the novel actually weds his testing of his family's fictional possibilities to his fuller exploration of black artistic commitment. This can be seen most vividly in the brief interludes featuring his son Jake, but the interplay between these tender, vulnerable scenes and the wistful meanderings of the novel's protagonist Cudjoe provide an intriguing index of Wideman's beliefs about what black art can and cannot do.

In "Visiting Privileges: A Journey to the Son" (2004), Wideman included some insights regarding writing about Jake: "My son has no desire to be visited by strangers. Hard enough, he said, to deal with visitors he loves, who love him. This story hasn't earned the right, quite yet, to greet him, touch him, spend the allotted three hours catching up on the nine months since the last visit, catching up on a whole life adrift in the unseason of prison time" (W14). This statement suggests that the veil between Jake as a subject and Wideman's art is purposeful, a result of the

son's disinterest in being publicized.[11] Aside from returning to quandaries
that the author articulated in *Brothers and Keepers,* this remark also estab-
lishes how *Philadelphia,* because of the primacy and the uniqueness of
its musings on Jake, is quite significant.[12] The intricate ways that Wideman chooses to meditate on the black artist's function provides a powerful testament to his talent. By registering these meditations through
the public tragedy of the Philadelphia fire and the private catastrophe
of his son's incarceration, he highlights the reasons why artistic commitment remained so crucial for the Black Archivists. He also reverses
the arc of Bradley's *The Chaneysville Incident* by taking a character back
to the big city. The journey back is shot through with angst-filled
memory.

A real historical event pulses at the center of *Philadelphia.* In 1985,
"a siege of several days" ended when "the Philadelphia police, with the
permission of the city's first black mayor, W. Wilson Goode, dropped a
bomb on the roof of . . . 6221 Osage Avenue. The house went up in
flames, killing 11 people, including several women and children" (Bray
7). The house at 6221 Osage was "home to MOVE, an armed band
of cultists with dreadlock hairstyles who had been harassing their black
neighbors" (Donohoe E1). By interjecting his fictional writer Cudjoe
into this scene, Wideman moves from *Sent'*s portrayals of family toward
equally intimate depictions of urban blight.[13] Such a shift, as the news-
paper accounts quoted above show, implies an engagement with broader
narratives of sociocultural transformations, yet Cudjoe and at times even
Wideman, who appears as a character in *Philadelphia,* show that part of
the difficulty of art is an inability to extricate one's self from the personal.
In fact the story always entails the pursuer getting in the way of its pursuit. Nowhere is this clearer than in Cudjoe's attempts to get information
about survivors of the Osage bombing.

---

11. In a 2011 conversation with the author, Wideman confirmed that he limits his disclosures
regarding Jake at his son's request.

12. Jake murders Eric Kane in 1986 and the events that led to his incarceration coincide with
John Edgar Wideman's composition of *Philadelphia Fire.* This immediacy of impact contrasts with
the space that the novelist had to digest his feelings about his brother, the subject of *Brothers and
Keepers* (1984).

13. Explaining his protagonist's name, Wideman writes, "Cudjoe, number one, was a very
common name, it's like John, that was used in slavery days. It's also a West African name day. It's an
echo of its time. There were lots of Cudjoes around" (Olander 167). The ubiquity of Cudjoe as a
moniker certainly marks the writer with allegorical qualities—specifically those tied to the African American struggle to preserve the meaning of African rituals in the face of slavery's assault. In
addition, Wideman's link of Cudjoe to his own name John reinforces a connection that is already
implicit.

Where Doot can canvas his uncle Carl, as he tries to piece together
the story of Homewood, Cudjoe must seek reconnection with his old
City of Brotherly Love stomping grounds through interactions with folks
who are inherently suspicious of his motives. His interviews with Margaret Jones, a member of MOVE who survived the fire, demonstrate
this fact. Through interactions with Margaret, Cudjoe discovers the dis-
arming contours of his role: "The woman with the bright African cloth
tied round her head had not liked him. Yet she was willing to talk, to be
taped . . . [Cudjoe] only spoke once or twice while she talked. Margaret
Jones didn't need him, care for him. She was permitting him to over-
hear what she told the machine" (9). The writer intends to operate as
an interviewer. Despite Cudjoe's intentions, both Margaret Jones and the
structure of the narrative turn him into a bystander. Wideman delivers
his account of Cudjoe's meeting via the playback of a tape, and Jones's
antipathy renders her ostensible questioner a barely tolerated intruder.
Why does such tension inhere in this encounter, and what does it mean,
at the outset of Cudjoe's quest, that he is presented as someone who has
to eavesdrop?

Ann Gaylin argues that "Eavesdropping dramatizes a primal human
curiosity to know, and to know those aspects of others' lives that we
are not supposed to know, those that they wish to keep hidden from
us" (7). Unpacking this observation, she writes, "eavesdropping represents
a version of narrative's origins, a point where curiosity takes hold and
from which storytelling springs" (8). If Cudjoe in his interactions with
Margaret Jones initially represents himself as someone who wants "to
do something about the silence [surrounding the fire survivors]" (19),
then very quickly, he changes his mind: "Cudjoe decides he will think
of himself as a reporter covering a story in a foreign country. Stay on his
toes, take nothing for granted. Not the customs nor the language. What
he sees is not what the natives see" (45). The tension between the writer
as an advocate for a black urban community and the writer as a parasite
who might be "stealing from the dead" (10) reveals not only Cudjoe's
dilemma but also the cause of what Wideman has called his own "divided
mind." He offered this account of it:

> I bring a very powerful, I hope healthy, skepticism into the [writing] pro-
> cess. One way to translate that abstraction would be to say, "Okay, here
> I am in Amherst, Mass., writing these books about Homewood, a black,
> economically depressed community in Pittsburgh—what's all that mean,
> what do all these words on the page have to do with that reality, and if

I'm really bothered by that reality—of Pittsburgh—it exists now, this moment, my people are there, my relatives are there, and suffering various forms of oppression and danger and pain, why don't I do something about it? What's it mean to make up stories about it? What's it mean to, in a sense, exploit it in a narrative? (Olander 166)

By making such a confession, Wideman not only allies his temperament to Cudjoe's but also reveals the crux of black novelists' anxieties in late twentieth-century America. In a 1980s moment when the black urbanization crises that Gaines, Morrison, and Naylor engage are metastasizing, the black novelists' attitude toward and capacity for communal advocacy is burdened by practical and aesthetic problems. How do I as a writer stem the tide of murders, incarcerations, and assaults? What story should I tell in that situation, and how should such a story be told? A consideration of how Cudjoe and Margaret Jones's interview recasts postmodern notions of play reveals how deeply his character probes questions about the artist's efficacy.

Ted Lyon—in "Jorge Luis Borges and the Interview as Literary Genre" (1994)—observes that when he met the Latin American writer in 1968, Borges took control of the conversation by slipping into "verbal play," a parodic mode that unsettled meaning and turned the questioner into a kind of toy (74). If his experiences with Borges led Lyon to conclude that the interview was a genre "caught between spontaneous overflow and meditative creation," then Margaret Jones shows that unsettling the questioner can arise from a tradition other than that of playfulness (76). In fact, her posture evokes the seething resentment that single black females traditionally reserve for welfare caseworkers.[14] The treatment that Cudjoe receives from Margaret not only reflects her cynicism about his professional motives but also marks personal insecurities. When the writer wonders whether Margaret can intuit his abandonment of his white wife and his half-white sons, he conjures issues that mock his dedication to role-playing or, as he calls it, "staying on his toes."[15] Wide-

---

14. For images of the black female response to welfare and social service caseworkers, see *Claudine, Good Times* (especially Season 1, Episode 3, "Getting Up the Rent"), and Edward P. Jones's short story "Marie" from his 1992 collection *Lost in the City*. For more on black females and government services, see Emilie M. Townes's "From Mammy to Welfare Queen: Images of Black Women in Public-Policy Formation" (2006) and Dana-Ain Davis's "Manufacturing Mammies: The Burdens of Service Work and Welfare Reform Among Battered Black Women" (2004)

15. Cudjoe's musings on Margaret Jones's knowledge about "him" especially his interracial marriage and his biracial kids take place as he is replaying her taped interview (9). On one level, the questions that he attributes to her reflect his shame—shame that he had married outside his

man's limits on his protagonist's play challenge other expressions about contemporary agony. In place of fellowship, *Philadelphia* heaps more suspicion on Cudjoe's motives.

Cudjoe interacts with the city through a telling set of activities. He stares at random panty-less white girls, gazes through windows at half-dressed female neighbors, and likewise migrates into the sex life of an anonymous white man, "Richard Corey" (173). These moments, examples of "sexual voyeurism," justify Madhu Dubey's contention that in *Philadelphia,* knowledge of fellow city dwellers is "always guilty" because such knowledge usually comes through the "pornographic modality of commodity spectacle" (*Signs* 127). While these interactions carry tremendous significance, an exclusive focus on these interracial moments of contact overlooks part of Cudjoe's dilemma, his anxiety about cultural alienation. His apprehension surfaces when he interviews Margaret and again as he remembers trying to put on a production of Shakespeare's *The Tempest* using inner-city black children. I will have more to say about the latter momentarily, but for now, I want to consider how Cudjoe counters a pornographic model of urban communion by playing basketball. In depicting this ritual, Wideman revises narratives of black male socialization by uniting transcendence and shared consciousness into a hope that momentarily creases despair.

A metaphor of Cudjoe's attempt to reclaim a space in the black community, pick-up basketball reflects the challenges of moving from spectator to player, a difficulty that captures his dilemma.[16] While waiting to run the court, the pick-up player must note each prospective teammate's distinctive skills and how he fit his talents into the game's flow. This posture, tied to the voyeurism maligned above, determines the difference between success and failure when strangers must instantly move from individuated talent to synchronized, collective effort. Cud-

---

race and shame that he had failed as a husband and a father. These dimensions of his psyche uncover the deepest implications of the personal in the professional. While Cudjoe strives to unearth a story, he must confront the ways that his own life impacts his access. This is *Philadelphia Fire's* subject.

16. Wideman's decision to depict street ball reflects tensions that erupted during his college years. Describing his time as a scholarship athlete at Penn, he states, "If the rest of the world was falling apart, at 3:30 I could go over to the gym and kick butt. Run up and down until I was exhausted. If I scored a basket, it was worth two points. If I beat my man and was on the first team, these things were unequivocal. There was a certain precision and clarity in that world that I didn't have anywhere else." While Wideman viewed the basketball court as a haven, he "was forced to pay for certain 'cultural improvements'" (Plummer). William Plummer notes, "[Wideman] was, by habit, a playground athlete, capable of electrifying ad-lib moves. At Penn his wings were clipped and he was taught to fly in formation."

joe joins a team that includes O.T., a superlative performer. Describing his teammate's prowess, he states, "O.T. a monster, operating a foot or so above everybody else. Took what he wanted. Changed gears when he wanted to. Let the other team stay close enough to believe they had a chance. Then blew them away—steals, slams, blocked shots" (38). Cudjoe's description makes O.T. sound like a one-man show, and his deftness does allow him to control the game. Despite this potential, he still needs support. Cudjoe tries to provide it. Assessing his contributions, he concludes that he "did his bit. Hit a layup and a couple jumpers from the wing. Fed the free man. Dealt the ball away from the dribble-happy dude. His legs gave out in game three" (38). Cudjoe is reduced to a role player, and there he, the old man of the cohort, finds a space for himself. Ironically, "his team retired undefeated" (38). Within the world of hoops, Cudjoe finds an urban sphere where "after the winning basket," he and his mates let "their eyes" and "their fists" meet "for a second in the core of a circle, then just as quickly," break "apart, each going his own way" (39). Such integrity within collectivity becomes the model that Cudjoe craves but cannot replicate. His failure evokes a prior instance where idealized racial unity miscarried.

Although it reprises trips that he made earlier, when he was married, Cudjoe's run on the Clark Park basketball courts takes place in the mid-1980s, after the Philadelphia fire. The park, because it hosts multifaceted examples of urban blackness, seems like a good place for Cudjoe to close the gap between Greece, the Mediterranean island to which he had escaped, and Philadelphia, the site of the grassroots struggle that he had fled. Though his ball playing restored communal fellowship better than his interviews with Margaret Jones, parks haunted Cudjoe's memory as spaces where his artistic ambitions soared and then crashed. Late in the 1960s, after his college graduation, he hatched a plot to stage Shakespeare's *The Tempest* using a cast of black children from an inner city school. His friends Timbo and Charley helped him, and although the performance was ready to go, two days of rain combined with random disruptions to derail their plans. Recalling Naylor's *The Women of Brewster Place,* which also meditates on the bard's impact on black city dwellers, this scene reinforces the Black Archivists' interest in how the Western literary canon influences black life. Naylor portrayed a successful performance of black collegians and artists for a multiracial audience that included black children. Because of the proposed cast and the attitudes of the play's sponsors, *Philadelphia*'s aborted production becomes key to Wideman's examination of failure.

Cudjoe's brainstorm evokes the nontraditional casting experiments used by Joseph Papp's New York Shakespeare Festival in the 1950s.[17] While he remembers thinking that the kids' performance would "prick pride and dignity" among the city's black population, providing an "achievement" that could not be ignored, his outlook from the 1980s features shame ("I've always felt guilty about deserting them") and an improbable vision—"I used to believe I'd hear the whole thing, start to finish, the way I rewrote it" (132, 149, 150). His retrospection acquires heightened significance since Wideman, "the fabulator," includes the following remark in his narration: "This is the central event, this production of *The Tempest* staged by Cudjoe . . . Though it comes here, wandering like a Flying Dutchman in and out of the narrative, many places at once, *The Tempest* sits dead center, the storm in the eye of the storm, figure within a figure, play within play, it is the bounty and hub of all else written about the fire" (132). On one level, Wideman's statement could be an attempt to put his readers off the trail. This possibility should not be lightly dismissed; however, the structure of part two of *Philadelphia*, the part in which Cudjoe's Shakespearean reminisces appear, casts nonlinear narration as renderings of a tortured soul rather than playfulness. Blending Cudjoe's remembrances of malfunctioning black idealism with Wideman's expressions of severed communion with his son Jake, this part of *Philadelphia* ponders pessimism's function in post–civil rights black artistry. Understanding these ponderings demands a look at two depictions of artists that appear in part one of the novel.

Upon returning to Philadelphia in the mid-1980s, Cudjoe looks up his old friend Timbo, who is now the mayor's cultural attaché. Cudjoe meets with him to walk down memory lane and to get information for the book that he wants to write about the Philadelphia fire. During these meetings, Timbo is often characterized by musical references. Cudjoe compares Timbo's pose to the "lead tenor of the Dells" and later says his friend forces him to listen like "he listens to music" (74, 83). *Sent* questioned the musician's centrality within the black community, and in *Philadelphia* Wideman uses Timbo, a politico, to extend that critique. The linking of music and politics ingenuously conjures both the racial sincerity automatically attributed to black musicians and the opportunistic postures of an incipient class of black elected officials. Seeking to capitalize on the former's cultural cache, the latter often appropriated their styles.

17. For more on Papp's New York Shakespeare Festival, see Ayanna Thompson's introduction to *Colorblind Shakespeare.*

These appropriations produced electoral success, but these victories usually heralded black officials as pragmatic survivors rather than revolutionaries.[18] If Timbo confirms the mayor as "a simple, devious, practical man," then his characterization not only reflects W. Wilson Goode's specific outlook but also the widespread perils of all who represent black constituencies (80–81). Part one's second major scene of artistry explores an alternate facet of this quandary.

Before they divorced, Cudjoe and his wife Caroline took a trip to visit his mentor, Sam, a man he described as "the tough new critical priest of the text speaking for itself" (67). Cudjoe brought a manuscript for Sam to read, and while he awaits the older white man's response, he wonders, "Would [Sam] know what the fuck he was reading?" (61). Where representing blackness, for the politician/musician, carries threats of exploited authority, Cudjoe, the writer, shows how black expression—even for someone as sympathetic as Sam—could be unintelligible, either because of inadequacies of the composer or the reader. *Philadelphia* never clarifies how Cudjoe's manuscript fares; nonetheless, the text's repeated inclusions of these scenes of literary evaluation are always paired with episodes of familial stress. By combining these elements, Wideman reveals how the traumatic discontinuities that test the artist's faith and feed his fears are precisely the reservoirs that he must draw on to retain relevance.[19] Thus, his turns to Jake and the ways that he frames these turns through King, the leader of the MOVE cult, and J.B., a homeless man, provides interesting answers to Cudjoe's artistic struggle, a struggle figured prominently in the never performed script of *The Tempest* that he wrote.

King and J.B. are the unfulfilled promises of America's post–civil rights experiments.[20] The former, a dreadlocked Gramscian intellectual,

18. As mayors from Carl B. Stokes to Maynard Jackson rose to power, questions arose about whether their black faces would mean a better representation of black interests. Timbo as an attaché to a black mayor focuses Wideman's exploration of this issue. For more on blacks and mainstream politics, see Carol M. Swain's *Black Face, Black Interests: The Representation of African Americans in Congress* (1995) and Cedric Johnson's *Revolutionaries to Race Leaders: Black Power and the Making of African American Politics* (2007).

19. Grant Wiggins and John Washington are prime examples of black intellectuals who are paralyzed by lack of faith. While Grant repudiates religion, John's problems stem from hyperrationality. These ideological positions, agnosticism and positivism, connect intriguingly with what Eddie S. Glaude and Cornel West see as the natural philosophy of black existence, pragmatism. See Glaude's *In A Shade of Blue* (2007) and West's *The American Evasion of Philosophy (1989)*. For a consideration of black pragmatism's aesthetic consequences, look at Walton Muyumba's *The Shadow and the Act: Black Intellectual Practice, Jazz Improvisation, and Philosophical Pragmatism* (2009).

20. Wideman's decision to name his cult leader King produces several interesting resonances. First, the monarchal imprimatur that inheres in the title creates a paradox. On the one hand, King

possesses an Afrocentric orientation, and the latter symbolizes an "urban zone of scarcity" where "inhabitants have no choice but to feed on waste" (Dubey, *Signs* 61).[21] Though these two men differ in ideology and behavior, they are united in their remoteness from the governmental authority symbolized by Timbo. This distance makes them "a thorn in [the] side" of the powers that be and insures that they will eventually be pushed "off the map" (81, 79). Although Timbo seemingly supports renovating the black community's consciousness, he, for the sake of dignity, would literally burn up offending aspects of urban blackness. His convictions relate to adults like King and J.B. and "little runty-assed no-hair-on-their-dicks neophytes" who "ain't twelve years old yet" (89). While Timbo's remark addresses the youth gangs such as "*Kaliban's Kiddie Korps*" that want to "run the world their way," his sentiments also reflect the twentieth century's final generational tension (88, 89). *The Chaneysville Incident* and *Song of Solomon* represent the conflict between the civil rights generation and the Black Power vanguard, but *Philadelphia* examines Black Power's clashes with the hip hop generation.[22] When Timbo engages the juvenile court system and youth's murderous capacities, he not only references a new delinquency fear but also evokes the cynicism that surrounds Jake's situation.[23]

In one of *Philadelphia*'s most direct references to his son's fight for justice, Wideman laments "the unmitigated cruelty of the legal system," a system that will not render a decision on an "appeal to remove [Jake's] case from adult to juvenile court" and will not allow him to be treated for the "childhood personality disorders" that are "almost certainly coalesc[ing] into incurable adult schizophrenia" (115, 116). This lamenta-

---

is an anti-establishment figure, an antagonist to mainstream authority. Alternately, his claims for divinely inspired wisdom connect him directly to notions such as "deo de los reyes." Of course, the civil rights leader Martin Luther King, Jr., also lurks within the morality that King cultivates. Blending these connotations allows Wideman to reinforce notions of unforeseen cultural braiding and anticipates Charles Johnson's interest in the Buddhist dimension of King's thought. See John Whalen-Bridges "Waking Cain: The Poetics of Integration in Charles Johnson's *Dreamer*" (2003) and John Malkin's "Buddhism is the Most Radical and Civilized Choice" (2004).

21. For more on Gramsci's relation to black radicalism, see Cornel West's "Black Theology and Marxist Thought" (1979).

22. Bakari Kitwana "established 1965–1984 as the age group for the hip hop generation" (xiii). While Wideman's inclusion of rap lyrics in *Philadelphia Fire* signals his engagement with this group's culture, his depiction of middle-aged former black student radicals and their grappling with the hip hop generation is one of the first of its kind.

23. America's preoccupation with juvenile delinquency emerged powerfully in the 1950s, and their effects were evident in both academic and popular venues. What I am calling the new delinquency discourse focuses on African American youth and their involvement in the legal system. For more on this idea, see Janice Joseph *Black Youth, Delinquency, and Juvenile Justice* (1995).

tion, a quiet impugning of American civility, joins with musing on "the emptiness" of a loss, an "absence" that is like an amputation "without a name" (120). Braiding these two themes, the writer defines language's expressive limits. He notes the difference between felicitous execution and "consolation," ultimately concluding that though it is his most earnest aim, he is incapable of the latter (151). Recognizing these facts, Wideman writes prayers for renewed hope. Cudjoe's dispersed drama troupe swirls around these prayers, signaling the mysteries of battles with canonical power.

August Wilson once observed that "colorblind casting is an aberrant idea that has never had any validity other than as a tool of the Cultural Imperialists . . . It is inconceivable to them that life could be lived and even enriched without knowing Shakespeare" (A. Thompson 1). Although Wilson's remark emphasizes a generic scuffle where white culture-brokers wield Shakespeare as an artistic gold standard, his statements also clarify the specific stakes of Cudjoe and Wideman's focus on black children who are deemed expendable. Cudjoe wrote a script for his troupe that he thought would compel a mainstream world to take notice. Betting on the unlikely confluence of inner city blackness and an iconic English playwright, he tried to translate emotional maelstroms through language. He discovers the intersection of experiences and emotions where ineffability marks failure, a spot haunted by the schoolchildren who never performed his play. At that crossroad, he, like John Edgar Wideman, abandons epic gestures of rescue and consolation and settles for hope that is a flickering candle in gale winds. This commitment becomes the artist's most fruitful gift.

Failure's Swag

The distance from Carl French's wasted talent to Cudjoe's fractured narrative could be explained as a journey from the deceptive comforts of post–World War II blackness to the bankruptcy of post–civil rights self-delusion. While Wideman accepts this premise, he likewise documents both via his characters and his autobiographical renderings a more coherent tradition. Lucy indicts Carl not because his attention to racial prejudice is inexplicable but because he allows that foul incursion to occlude his view of her—the person that he claims as his most precious company. When Carl and Cudjoe are examined in light of their compromises of such intimacy, Wideman's thoughts about failure and the way forward both for his own writing and for black writing more broadly can be detected.

In both *Sent* and *Philadelphia,* the struggling artist is confounded by faulty perception. The difficulties here are not technical; rather, they result from discounting empathy. As much as Doot receives a lofty ordination, only in his reincarnation as Cudjoe does the arsenal of black expressivity get fully stocked. For if Doot represents the post–civil rights generation's discovery of their families' legacies, then Cudjoe, marking Wideman's return to Morrison's depictions in *Beloved,* reflects how the basis of community is never experiential commonality. Rather, the cultural connection begins with love and the vulnerability of caring. Michael Cooke contends that intimacy "takes the form of reaching, or being invited, out of the self and into an unguarded and uncircumscribed engagement with the world" (9). Wideman believes that artistic failure destroys the final hurdles to such communion. In many ways, this is the final lesson that he learned from trolling through the black literary tradition, and the autobiographical interludes in *Philadelphia* suggest why.

The interpolations related to Jake intrude on Wideman's worthy commemoration of the Philadelphia fire. Though these passages chop up the narrative, they do so with talk about elemental aspirations—"I breathe into the space separating me from my son. I hope the silence will be filled for him as it is filled for me by hearing the nothing there is to say at this moment . . . Not because it is enough but because it's all we have" (104). This passage grapples with the ineffable, yet it casts that struggle, that site of failure, as the crux of intimacy. In place of technical felicity, it situates a gesture toward fellowship, a commitment to connection. The necessity of this substitution becomes Wideman's finest legacy. His main characters walk along the avenues of refulgent inspiration and, hemmed in by their failures as husbands, fathers, and lovers, experience the humiliation of art that will not give. Notwithstanding these realities, Cudjoe, like Carl, gets another chance, a chance that hinges on a studious exploration of "all we have." It is here that both the character and the author overcome their insecurities. In a 2001 essay, Wideman observed that "one of the worst trials for Americans of visible African descent (and maybe for invisible crossovers too) is the perpetual fear of not measuring up to standards established by so-called white people" ("More" 1204). By shedding such self-consciousness and attending to the simple exigency of breathing, he replaced the tangled measurements of literary merit with the ethics of swagger. Ironically, this replacement inspired mainstream applause.

Swagger's Afterlife

As a cohort, the Black Archivists possess excellent balance. They were all born between 1931 and 1950; thus, the life experiences of the oldest and the youngest members are separated by a generation.[1] Age is not the only factor that produces this group's diversity. One writer spends her childhood in the South and another splits his formative years between Dixie and the Bay area; one is from the East Coast, while four have Midwestern roots.[2] Finally, gender falls out roughly even: four men, three women. Although any of these attributes—age gaps, varied geographic hailing, and gender difference—could promote fracture, the Black Archivists allow their variety to strengthen them. They belie views of African American writing as acrimonious and confound white expectations with range rather than unanimity. Needing to locate cultural moorings during America's post–civil rights era, the Black Archivists achieve the ethics

1. David Bradley and Gloria Naylor were both born in 1950 while Ernest Gaines and Toni Morrison were born in 1933 and 1931 respectively. John Edgar Wideman was born in 1941, three years before Alice Walker (1944) and seven in front of Charles Johnson (1948).

2. Alice Walker and Ernest Gaines spend formative years in Georgia and Louisiana respectively. Gaines leaves the South and lands in California while Walker goes to New York to finish college. By contrast, John Edgar Wideman and Gloria Naylor mature within the urban spheres of Pittsburgh and New York. For college, he goes to Philadelphia, Iowa City, and Oxford. She stays in the Big Apple. Completing this composite, David Bradley, Toni Morrison, and Charles Johnson—a trio of Midwesterners—grow up respectively in Bedford, Pennsylvania; Lorain, Ohio; and Evanston, Illinois. Bradley and Johnson stay in the region for college; however, Morrison attends Howard University in Washington, DC, and Cornell University in Ithaca, NY.

of swagger through individuated yet principled representations of their tribe.[3] Their accomplishments institutionalize the study of black literature and expand the literary options for subsequent black writers. This conclusion considers the impact of these developments.

Ronald A. T. Judy argues that a Yale symposium in 1977 signaled a key moment in the academic study of African American literature. Contending that this symposium used "Afro-American canon formation" to challenge prevailing models of "American cultural history," he concludes that there black literary criticism reconstructed its instruction (2). Judy echoed Houston A. Baker, Jr., who suggested that Yale was where the "newly emergent" experiment with "poststructuralist" theory discovered black writing (xvi).[4] At the moment that the Yale symposium convened, the MLA Division on Black Literature and Culture did not exist.[5] *Negro American Literature Forum* had been published since 1967, MELUS first met in 1974, and the NEH summer seminars convened by Darwin T. Turner flourished, but the heyday of black literature's entry into academia was yet to come.[6] While commentators such as Deborah McDowell note that slave narratives served as the earliest guinea pigs in the critical experiments that led to this heyday, as "the race for theory" intensified, black novels gained popularity as analytical targets.[7] This

3. My phrasing here borrows an idea from Toni Morrison's "Rootedness: The Ancestor as Foundation," in which she stated, "There must have been a time when an artist could be genuinely representative *of* the tribe and *in* it; when an artist could have a tribal or racial sensibility and an individual expression of it" (*What* 56). Her sentiment overlooks just how successful the Black Archivists were in producing the kind of epoch that she mourned as post.

4. Houston A. Baker talks about the Yale scene, if not this symposium, in the revised edition of *Long Black Song: Essays in Black American Literature and Culture* (1990). Noting "the generational shift in black literary criticism," he observes that the "project of such analysts as Henry Louis Gates, Jr., and Robert Stepto was grounded in a newly emergent project in literary theory. This project was specifically poststructuralist; it had its origins in Paris, but its United States supporters were legion at Yale" (xvi). For a brief, incisive treatment, see Maurice Wallace's "Print, Prosthesis, (Im)Personation: Morrison's *Jazz* and the Limits of Literary History" (2008).

5. The MLA, or Modern Language Association, is a leading professional organization connected to the academic study of literature. Organized around a structure of divisions, the MLA lacked a division devoted to black literature until the early 1980s. SallyAnn Ferguson observed, "R. Baxter Miller attended [the 1982 MLA Convention] and solicited signatures to help found" the Black Literature division (543). The Black Literature division was ratified in 1983.

6. Regarding the history of *Negro American Literature Forum* aka *Black American Literature Forum* aka *African American Review,* see Joe Weixlmann's "*African American Review* at 40: A Retrospective" (2007). Katherine Newman discusses MELUS, or the Society for the Study of Multi-Ethnic Literature of the United States, in "MELUS Invented: The Rest is History" (1989). Richard Lloyd-Jones's "A Basket of Pies: The University of Iowa School of Letters" (1980) briefly mentions Darwin Turner's National Endowment for the Humanities summer seminars.

7. My phrasing takes its cue from Barbara Christian's "The Race for Theory" (1988), an essay that offers trenchant observations regarding academia, black literature, and interpretive expectations.

development led to the Black Archivists' crucial role in the institutional-
ization of African American literature.

During the 1980s, academic fashion demanded that tenure-seekers
perform theoretically aware literary analyses. Scholars who studied black
literature were often forced to juggle their commitments to interpret-
ing neglected texts and their need to endorse difficult ones. This was
true across all genres, but the trend was especially acute in the study of
the novel. Beginning with Robert Stepto's *From Behind the Veil: A Study
of Afro-American Narrative* (1979), expectations for analyses that incor-
porated avant-garde literary theory heightened.[8] Critics of the African
American novel noted these expectations, and repeatedly their articles,
book chapters, and monographs used works from the Black Archivist
canon to cut their critical teeth. Suggesting this trend, consider a few
examples: Jane Campbell's *Mythic Black Fiction: The Transformation of History* (1986), Valerie Smith's *Self-Discovery and Authority in Afro-American
Narrative* (1987), and Henry Louis Gates, Jr.'s *The Signifying Monkey: A
Theory of African American Literary Criticism* (1988). If prizewinning black
novelists fed this tributary of academic study, then they also contributed
their own literary commentaries.

Charles Johnson's study *Being and Race* and Toni Morrison's *Playing in
the Dark: Whiteness and the Literary Imagination* (1992) are the most obvious examples of the Black Archivists' forays into literary criticism; however, John Edgar Wideman and Alice Walker both write influential essays
about black literature that reflect not only a thorough grasp of literary
history but also an impressive understanding of literary theory. In some
ways, the Black Archivists' analytical competencies reflect their encounters with colleges and universities as both students and employees. Unlike
the towering novelists of the indignant generation, the Black Archivists
were all college educated.[9] In addition, many of them earned advanced
degrees including Masters in English, Masters in Fine Arts, and, in the
case of Charles Johnson, a PhD in philosophy. These folks were crea-
tures of higher education environments, and their entrée into white elite

8. For meditations on the development of African American literary analysis from 1977
to 1993, see Dexter Fisher and Robert Stepto's edited volume, *Afro-American Literature: The Reconstruction of Instruction* (1979); J. Edgar Tidwell's review, "The Birth of a Black New Criticism";
Houston A. Baker's article, "Generational Shifts and the Recent Criticism of Afro-American Literature" (1981); and Ronald A. T. Judy's introduction to *(Dis)Forming the American Canon.*

9. Lawrence Jackson uses "indignant generation" to describe black writers whose careers
crested between 1934 and 1960. When I speak of novelists who lack an undergraduate degree,
I refer to Ralph Ellison, Richard Wright, Chester Himes, and James Baldwin. The most accom-
plished female novelists, Ann Petry and Paule Marshall, were college graduates.

spaces not only exposed them to African and African American studies but also heightened their comfort with questioning received wisdom. In addition to studying at colleges and universities, the Black Archivists also instructed at them.

As early as the mid-1950s, Toni Morrison taught at Texas Southern University and then moved on to Howard University. Her career included stints at Yale, SUNY-Albany, and Bard. When she accepted the Robert F. Goheen professorship at Princeton, she became the first black woman to occupy a named chair at an Ivy League institution. Morrison's experience proves the rule among the Black Archivists. Wideman taught at Penn, Amherst, and Brown. Johnson recently retired after more than thirty years at the University of Washington. Alice Walker has held teaching positions at more than twenty schools, and David Bradley, who worked at Temple University, has taught at the University of Oregon since 2003. In part, these realities reflect the sort of shifts that Mark McGurl chronicles in *The Program Era: Postwar Fiction and the Rise of Creative Writing* (2009), but for black novelists it also means that they were more than ever in direct conversation with the folks who interpreted their work. This contact yielded diverse results among them a deep investment in the academic profile of black literature.

From editing and teaching to reviewing and completing scholarship, the Black Archivists promoted the cause of black fiction.[10] This promotion and the professional networks that it established convinced black novelists to risk greater autonomy in their writing. When their risks yielded fruit, they—in modest numbers—achieved enough renown to participate in the mainstream prize-granting system.[11] This blend of independence and assimilation seemingly would have resulted in continued black prizewinning during the last decade of the twentieth

10. Charles Johnson published *Being and Race* just years before *Middle Passage,* and John Edgar Wideman published a series of articles on the problems of black representation in the *American Poetry Review* and in *Callaloo.* Although Morrison's *Playing in the Dark* comes after most of her fictional production, her master's thesis on Faulkner reveals her interest in literary critical matters. The tendency of black writers to publish literary critical pieces is not confined to the Black Archivists. Melvin Dixon published *Ride Out the Wilderness: Geography and Identity in African American Literature* (1987) and Gayl Jones wrote *Liberating Voices: Oral Tradition in African American Literature* (1991). These works continue the efforts of Sherley Anne Williams's *Give Birth to Brightness: A Thematic Study in Neo-Black Literature* (1972), Ralph Ellison's *Shadow and Act* (1964) and *Going to the Territory* (1986), and Amiri Baraka's essays.

11. I have already discussed Gloria Naylor's efforts on the National Book Award selection committee. By the 1990s, Toni Morrison, Charles Johnson, Ernest Gaines, and John Edgar Wideman were all in demand as judges for literary awards. These writers rarely joined a black majority in their service on these committees; nonetheless, their presences signal an important development.

century and the first twelve years of the twenty-first. Notwithstanding such expectations, it should be noted that the only major literary prizes to go to a black novelist since 1993 have been Edward P. Jones's 2004 Pulitzer and National Book Critics Circle Award for *The Known World* and Jesmyn Ward's 2011 National Book Award for *Salvage the Bones* (2011).[12] This development indicates that 1977 to 1993 constituted a singular epoch for the black novel. With the rise of post-soul/post-black novelists such as Trey Ellis, Martha Southgate, Shay Youngblood, Paul Beatty, Colson Whitehead, April Sinclair, Mat Johnson, Alice Randall, and Jeffrey Renard Allen, the Black Archivists' unique legacy can be explored.[13]

In George Wolfe's *The Colored Museum* (1988), there is a vignette entitled "The Last Mama on the Couch Play." This irreverent send-up of Lorraine Hansberry's *A Raisin in the Sun* (1959) signaled that a younger generation of African American dramatists was no longer averse to lampooning the hang-ups, the aesthetics, or even the ethics of their elders. Wolfe's statements dealt with the stage, but arguably the manifesto of this attitude was written by a novelist, Trey Ellis. In his 1989 essay "The New Black Aesthetic," Ellis identified a group of young black "cultural mulatto[s]" who were all born after 1960 and tasked with carving out a worldview and an artistic outlook that would capture the precise realities of their suspension between white and black worlds (235). Eventually linked to the post-soul aesthetic, this group becomes the most direct inheritor of both the thematic and aesthetic achievements of the Black Archivists and of the labors that this group made to make both earlier black writers' and their own works agents of light in what they felt to be a dark world. Of this group, Bertram Ashe has stated, "Many post-soul writers critique the events or the mindset of the Civil Rights Movement in their fiction . . . and it is important . . . that these writers have no lived, adult experience with that movement" (611). The post-soul writer

---

12. In 2010, Jones also received the PEN/Malamud in recognition of his achievements in the short story.

13. Darryl Dickson-Carr asserts that "post-soul" gained currency as a "way of describing the works emerging from the generation of writers that were born during or after the Civil Rights/ Black Power eras or who reached personal and artistic maturity from the late 1970s forward. [Post-Soul] is virtually synonymous with the new black aesthetic that author Trey Ellis outlines in his 1989 *Callaloo* essay of the same name" (190). Although the term post-black was not immediately applied to late twentieth- and early twenty-first century African American culture, with Barack Obama's presidency and other pressures impelling America toward a post-racial future, there is a growing tendency to view the literature of this moment as both post-soul and postblack. For a thoughtful overview, see Bertram D. Ashe's "Theorizing the Post-Soul Aesthetic: An Introduction" (2007).

constructs the civil rights movement as a distortion; its period and priorities cloud the understanding of a thoroughly pluralistic world.[14] Contrasting the Black Archivists' belief that the civil rights struggle clarified their art, the younger generation's outlook dramatizes conflicts about contemporary black fiction. Their freedom gains its force from their elders' ethics of swagger.

Often focusing on theme and representational strategy, recent studies decry the homogeneity of black literature and argue for more elastic literary canons. These books revive old debates, and with regard to African American novels, they raise the prickly question of whether such a thing does or should exist. At the heart of their analyses, there is a fear that scholars of black literature are politically motivated to overlook nuances in favor of facile solidarity. While it may be true that earlier cultural movements thus distorted blackness, the Black Archivists suggest that from the rural to the urban, from the poor to the rich, and from the experimental to the conventional, fictional accounts of African American identity manifest distinctness even as they coalesce around signature moments. Such coalescence attained full expression in the works of the Black Archivists, and this group inclined American literary prize grantors toward a more complex engagement with blackness. This feat and this simultaneity held broad significance.

Major prizes symbolize one yardstick of artistic command, and their uneasy place in the Black Archivists' minds reflects a conundrum with inter- and intraracial dimensions. All of the Black Archivists spent formative years in black environments; however, each of them also attended majority white institutions for either undergraduate or graduate education. While the writers' experiences on these campuses were varied, one commonality was exposure to Eurocentric curriculums. This exposure fuelled cosmopolitan outlooks and hybrid aesthetics, and it clarified the significance of black culture's home spaces. By addressing the stress of balancing these factors while retaining artistic authority, the Black Archivists and their novels spoke eloquently about democratic possibil-

14. Jeffrey R. Allen, a budding black writer, captures the post-soul outlook: "African Americans have always been cultural mulattos, but when you have a new generation of black writers who don't see race in the same way, the racial landscape is transformed. The other thing here is that, frankly, people are tired of writing about how badly white folks are treating us. Where can you go from there? I mean, hasn't that all been said?" (Antonucci). Paul Taylor's "Post-Black, Old Black" (2007) provides a less binary discussion of the post-black/post-soul notion. While his insights are compelling, the fact that they are needed points to the intensity of this black intergenerational conflict. Stuart Hall prophesied these types of conflicts in his 1993 essay "What Is This 'Black' in Black Popular Culture?".

ity and black citizenship. Their achievements and the controversies they aroused also exposed gaps in the nation's meritocracy discourse. With these developments, they provoked and participated anew in America's soul-searching.

The Black Archivists were not crusaders. Their determination to chronicle the signature themes that informed twentieth-century blackness—slavery, segregation, the Great Migration, and the urban blight—arose from a simple wish to see themselves and their people reflected in art. Despite these motives, the Black Archivists refused to eschew the textures that characterized African American experience. They spoke as novelists who strived to "preserve the uniqueness of the African American sensibility, establish a sense of communal independence, and participate in the American mainstream on [their] terms" (Bryant 179). With moral daring and stylistic flair, they amplified the country's vision. They did so because they discovered the ethics of swagger. When, in a post-Vietnam moment, black culture was called to account by both civil rights elders and mainstream society, the Black Archivists produced prize-winning, game-changing fictions. In doing so, they consolidated a black artistry that neither abdicated nor lamented its protean contours.

bibliography

Abbandonato, Linda. "A View From 'Elsewhere': Subversive Sexuality and the Rewriting of the Heroine's Story in *The Color Purple.*" *PMLA* 106 (1991): 1106–15.

Angelo, Bonnie. "The Pain of Being Black." In *Conversations with Toni Morrison,* ed. Danille Taylor-Guthrie, 255–61. Jackson: University Press of Mississippi, 1994.

Anonymous. "Black Writers in Praise of Toni Morrison." *New York Times Book Review* 24 January 1988: 36.

———. "Morrison, duCille, Baquet, Pulitzer Prizewinners." *Jet* 18 April 1988: 14.

———. "Story of a Prize." *Rutgers Magazine* 67.4 (1988): 36.

———. "Walt Whitman's New Poem." *The Cincinnati Daily Commercial* 28 December 1859: 2.

———. "What is the Best Work of American Fiction of the Last 25 Years?" *New York Times* 21 May 2006. Web. 20 January 2012.

Antonucci, Michael A. "Walking Sebold's Spider: Michael A. Antonucci Talks with Jeffrey Renard Allen." *Other Voices* 18.43 (2005): n.pag. Web. 29 February 2012.

Ashe, Bertram. "Theorizing the Post-Soul Aesthetic: An Introduction." *African American Review* 41 (2007): 609–23.

Awkward, Michael. *Inspiriting Influences: Tradition, Revision, and Afro-American Women's Novels.* New York: Columbia University Press, 1989.

Baker, Houston A., Jr. *Long Black Song: Essays in Black American Literature and Culture.* Charlottesville: University of Virginia Press, 1990.

Bakerman, Jane. "The Seams Can't Show: An Interview With Toni Morrison." In *Conversations with Toni Morrison,* ed. Danille Taylor-Guthrie, 30–42. Jackson: University Press of Mississippi, 1994.

Baraka, Amiri. Liner Notes for *Woody III* by Woody Shaw. Columbia Records, 1979. LP.

———. "The Revolutionary Theatre." In *The Norton Anthology of African American Literature,* 1st ed. Ed. Henry Louis Gates, Jr., and Nellie Y. McKay, 1899–1902. New York: Norton, 1997.

————. "State/meant." In *The LeRoi Jones/Amiri Baraka Reader*, ed. William J. Harris, 169–70. New York: Thunder's Mouth Press, 1991.

Barksdale, Richard. *Praisesong of Survival: Lectures and Essays, 1957–89*. Urbana: University of Illinois Press, 1992.

Bates, Gerri. *Alice Walker: A Critical Companion*. Westport, CT: Greenwood, 2005.

Beavers, Herman. "Prodigal Agency: Allegory and Voice in Ernest J. Gaines's *A Lesson Before Dying*." In *Contemporary Black Men's Fiction and Drama*, ed. Keith Clark, 135–54. Urbana: University of Illinois Press, 2001.

Bender, Thomas, et al. "Thinking in Public: A Forum." *American Literary History* 10.1 (1998): 1–83.

Berger, James. "Ghosts of Liberalism: Morrison's *Beloved* and the Moynihan Report." *PMLA* 111.3 (1996): 408–20.

Berlant, Lauren. "Race, Gender, and Nation in *The Color Purple*." In *Bloom's Modern Critical Interpretations: Alice Walker's* The Color Purple, ed. Harold Bloom, 21–50. New York: Infobase, 2008.

Bey, Dawoud. "Swagger." In *Black Cool: One Thousand Streams of Blackness*, ed. Rebecca Walker, 147–54. Berkeley: Soft Skull, 2012.

Black Creation Annual. "Conversation With Alice Childress and Toni Morrison." In *Conversations with Toni Morrison*, ed. Danille Taylor-Guthrie, 3–9. Jackson: University Press of Mississippi, 1994.

Blair, Sara. *Harlem Crossroads: Black Writers and the Photograph in the Twentieth Century*. Princeton, NJ: Princeton University Press, 2007.

Blake, Susan, and James Miller. "The Business of Writing: An Interview with David Bradley." *Callaloo* 21 (1984): 19–39.

Bogan, Lucille. "Drinking Blues." Banner Records. 1934. LP.

Bonetti, Kay. "An Interview with Gloria Naylor." In *Conversations with Gloria Naylor*, ed. Maxine Lavon Montgomery, 39–64. Jackson: University Press of Mississippi, 2004.

————. "Interview with John Edgar Wideman." In *Conversations With John Edgar Wideman*, ed. Bonnie TuSmith, 42–61. Jackson: University Press of Mississippi, 1998.

Boudreau, Kristin. "Pain and the Unmaking of Self in Toni Morrison's *Beloved*." *Contemporary Literature* 36.3 (1995): 447–65.

Bouson, J. Brooks. *Quiet As It's Kept: Shame, Trauma, and Race in the Novels of Toni Morrison*. Albany: State University of New York Press, 2000.

Bradley, David. *The Chaneysville Incident*. 1981. New York: Harper & Row, 1990.

————. "Novelist Alice Walker Telling the Black Woman's Story." *New York Times Magazine* 8 January 1984: 25–37.

Bray, Rosemary L. "'The Whole City Seen the Flames.'" Review of *Philadelphia Fire*. *New York Times Book Review* 30 September 1990: 7, 9.

Bryant, Jerry. *Born in a Mighty Bad Land: The Violent Man in African American Folklore and Fiction*. Bloomington: Indiana University Press, 2003.

Buchanan, Robert Williams. *David Gray and Other Essays, Chiefly on Poetry*. London: Sampson Low, Son, and Marston, 1868.

Buell, Lawrence. "Observer-Hero Narrative." *Texas Studies in Literature and Language* 21.1 (Spring 1979): 93–111.

Byerman, Keith E. *Remembering the Past in Contemporary African American Fiction*. Chapel Hill: University of North Carolina Press, 2005.

Byrd, Rudolph. *Charles Johnson's Novels: Writing the American Palimpsest*. Bloomington: Indiana University Press, 2005.

————, ed. *I Call Myself an Artist: Writings By and About Charles Johnson.* Bloomington: Indiana University Press, 1999.

Carden, Mary Paniccia. "Models of Memory and Romance: The Dual Endings of Toni Morrison's *Beloved.*" *Twentieth Century Literature* 45.4 (1999): 401–27.

Carter, Tom. "Ernest Gaines." In *Conversations with Ernest Gaines,* ed. John Lowe, 80–85. Jackson: University Press of Mississippi, 1995.

Christian, Barbara. "Naylor's Geography: Community, Class and Patriarchy in *The Women of Brewster Place* and *Linden Hills.*" In *Gloria Naylor: Critical Perspectives Past and Present,* ed. Henry Louis Gates, Jr., and K. A. Appiah, 106–25. New York: Amistad, 1993.

Coleman, James W. *Blackness and Modernism: The Literary Career of John Edgar Wideman.* Jackson: University Press of Mississippi, 1989.

————. *Faithful Vision: Treatments of the Sacred, Spiritual, and Supernatural in Twentieth Century African American Fiction.* Baton Rouge: Louisiana State University Press, 2006.

————. *Writing Blackness: John Edgar Wideman's Art and Experimentation.* Baton Rouge: Louisiana State University Press, 2010.

Conner, Marc, and William Nash, eds. *Charles Johnson: The Novelist as Philosopher.* Jackson: University Press of Mississippi, 2007.

Cooke, Michael. *Afro-American Literature in the Twentieth Century: The Achievement of Intimacy.* New Haven, CT: Yale University Press, 1984.

Crouch, Stanley. "Ralph Ellison's Endless Blues." *The Daily Beast* 6 February 2010. Web. 18 January 2012.

Cutter, Martha J. "Philomela Speaks: Alice Walker's Revisioning of Rape Archetypes in *The Color Purple.*" In *Bloom's Modern Critical Interpretations: Alice Walker's* The Color Purple, ed. Harold Bloom, 145–60. New York: Infobase, 2008.

Daley, Katherine, and Carolyn M. Jones. "Ernest J. Gaines' *A Lesson Before Dying:* Freedom in Confined Spaces." In *From the Plantation to the Prison: African American Confinement Literature,* ed. Tara T. Green, 83–117. Macon, GA: Mercer University Press, 2008.

Daniels, Jean. "The Call of Baby Suggs in *Beloved:* Imagining Freedom in Resistance and Struggle." *Griot* 21.2 (2002): 1–7.

Dickson-Carr, Darryl. *The Columbia Guide to Contemporary African American Fiction.* New York: Columbia University Press, 2005.

Donohoe, Cathryn. "Bust A MOVE: John Edgar Wideman Sifts Through 'Philadelphia Fire.'" *Washington Times* 15 October 1990: E1–E2.

Douglas, Susan, and Meredith Michaels. *The Mommy Myth: The Idealization of Motherhood and How It Has Undermined All Women.* 2004. New York: Free Press, 2005.

Dowling, Colette. "The Song of Toni Morrison." In *Conversations with Toni Morrison,* ed. Danille Taylor-Guthrie, 48–59. Jackson: University Press of Mississippi, 1994.

Doyle, Laura. *Bordering on the Body: The Racial Matrix of Modern Fiction and Culture.* New York: Oxford University Press, 1994.

Doyle, Mary Ellen. *Voices from the Quarters: The Fiction of Ernest J. Gaines.* Baton Rouge: Louisiana State University Press, 2002.

Dreifus, Claudia. "Chloe Wofford Talks about Toni Morrison." In *Toni Morrison: Conversations,* ed. Carolyn C. Denard, 98–106. Jackson: University Press of Mississippi, 2008.

Dubey, Madhu. *Black Women Novelists and the Nationalist Aesthetic.* Bloomington: Indiana University Press, 1994.

————. *Signs and Cities: Black Literary Postmodernism*. Chicago: University of Chicago Press, 2003.

Duvall, John. *The Identifying Fictions of Toni Morrison: Modernist Authenticity and Postmodern Blackness*. New York: Palgrave, 2000.

Egan, Philip J. "Unraveling Misogyny and Forging the Self: Mother, Lover, and Storyteller in *The Chaneysville Incident*." *Papers on Language and Literature* 33 (1997): 265–87.

Ellis, Trey. "The New Black Aesthetic." *Callaloo* 12 (1989): 233–43.

Ellison, Ralph. *The Collected Essays of Ralph Ellison*. Ed. John Callahan. New York: Modern Library, 2003.

————. "What America Would Be Like Without Blacks." *Teaching American History.org* 20 April 1970. Web. 26 February 2012.

Ellison, Ralph, Michael Harper, and Robert Stepto. "Study and Experience: An Interview with Ralph Ellison." *The Massachusetts Review* 18 (1977): 417–35.

Emerson, Ralph Waldo. "Self-Reliance." In *The Essential Writings of Ralph Waldo Emerson*, ed. Brooks Atkinson, 132–53. New York: Random House, 2000.

English, James. *The Economy of Prestige: Prizes, Awards, and the Circulation of Cultural Value*. Cambridge, MA: Harvard University Press, 2005.

Ensslen, Klaus. "Fictionalizing History: David Bradley's *The Chaneysville Incident*." *Callaloo* 11 (1988): 280–96.

Faulkner, William. *Absalom, Absalom!*. 1936. New York: Vintage International, 1990.

Ferguson, SallyAnn H. "Remembering Katherine Newman." *MELUS* 29.3/4 (2004): 542–45.

Fitzgerald, Gregory, and Peter Marchant. "An Interview: Ernest J. Gaines." In *Conversations with Ernest Gaines*, ed. John Lowe, 3–15. Jackson: University Press of Mississippi, 1995.

Folks, Jeffrey. "Communal Responsibility in Ernest J. Gaines' *A Lesson Before Dying*." *Mississippi Quarterly* 52 (1999): 259–71.

Fowler, Virginia C. *Gloria Naylor: In Search of Sanctuary*. New York: Twayne, 1996.

Fraser, Celeste. "Stealing B(l)Ack Voices: The Myth of the Black Matriarchy and *The Women of Brewster Place*." In *Gloria Naylor: Critical Perspectives Past and Present*, ed. Henry Louis Gates, Jr., and K. A. Appiah, 90–105. New York: Amistad, 1993.

Fulton, Lorie Watkins. "Hiding Fire and Brimstone in Lacy Groves: The Twinned Trees of *Beloved*." *African American Review* 39 (2005): 189–99.

Gaines, Ernest. "Ernest Gaines Interview: *A Lesson Before Dying*." *The American Academy of Achievement* 4 May 2001. Web. 31 July 2009.

————. *A Lesson Before Dying*. 1993. New York: Vintage, 1994.

————. *Mozart and Leadbelly: Stories and Essays*. New York: Vintage, 2005.

Gates, Henry Louis, Jr. "Preface." In *Gloria Naylor: Critical Perspectives Past and Present*, ed. Henry Louis Gates, Jr., and K. A. Appiah, ix–xii. New York: Amistad, 1993.

————. *The Signifying Monkey: A Theory of African American Literary Criticism*. New York: Oxford, 1989.

Gates, Henry Louis, Jr., and Cornel West. *The Future of the Race*. New York: Vintage, 1997.

Gayle, Addison. "Cultural Strangulation: Black Literature and the White Aesthetic." In *The Addison Gayle Jr. Reader*, ed. Nathaniel Norment, Jr., 101–6. Urbana: University of Illinois Press, 2009.

Gaylin, Ann. *Eavesdropping in the Novel from Austen to Proust.* Cambridge: Cambridge University Press, 2002.

George, Nelson. *Post-Soul Nation: The Explosive, Contradictory, Triumphant, and Tragic 1980s as Experienced by African Americans (Previously Known as Blacks and Before That Negroes).* New York: Penguin, 2004.

Gikandi, Simon. "Race and the Idea of the Aesthetic." *Michigan Quarterly Review* 40.2 (2001): 318–50.

Glass, Loren. *Authors Inc.: Literary Celebrity in the Modern United States, 1880–1980.* New York: New York University Press, 2004.

Goldstein, William. "A Talk with Gloria Naylor." In *Conversations with Gloria Naylor,* ed. Maxine Lavon Montgomery, 3–6. Jackson: University Press of Mississippi, 2004.

Goodman, Amy. "Alice Walker on the 'Toxic Culture' of Globalization." *Democracy Now!* 27 October 2004. Web. 19 March 2010.

Goodman, Walter. "The Lobbying for Literary Prizes." *New York Times* 28 January 1988: C26.

Gray, Herman. *African Americans and the Politics of Representation.* Berkeley: University of California Press, 2005.

Griesinger, Emily. "Why Baby Suggs, Holy, Quit Preaching the Word: Redemption and Holiness in Toni Morrison's *Beloved.*" *Christianity and Literature* 50.4 (2001): 689–702.

Hans, James S. *The Golden Mean.* Albany: State University of New York Press, 1994.

———. *The Sovereignty of Taste.* Urbana: University of Illinois Press, 2002.

Hansen, Drew D. *Martin Luther King, Jr. and the Speech That Inspired a Nation.* New York: Ecco, 2003.

Harris, Jessica. "I Will Always Be A Writer." In *Toni Morrison: Conversations,* ed. Carolyn C. Denard, 3–9. Jackson: University Press of Mississippi, 2008.

Harris, Norman. *Connecting Times: The Sixties in Afro-American Fiction.* Jackson: University Press of Mississippi, 1988.

Harris, Trudier. *Fiction and Folklore: The Novels of Toni Morrison.* Knoxville: University of Tennessee Press, 1991.

———. "On *The Color Purple,* Stereotypes, and Silence." *Black American Literature Forum* 18.4 (1984): 155–61.

Hayden, Robert. "Those Winter Sundays." In *I Am The Darker Brother: An Anthology of Modern Poems by Negro Americans,* ed. Arnold Adoff, 10. New York: Macmillan, 1968.

Hegel, Georg Wilhelm Friedrich. *The Philosophy of History.* 1837. Translated by J. Sibree. New York: Dover, 1956.

Heinich, Nathalie. "The Sociology of Vocational Prizes: Recognition as Esteem." *Theory Culture Society* 26.5 (2009): 85–107.

Henderson, Stephen. *Understanding the New Black Poetry: Black Speech and Black Music as Poetic References.* New York: William Morrow, 1973.

Henry, DeWitt. "About James Alan McPherson." *Ploughshares* 34.2–3 (Fall 2008): 187–91.

Hicks, Heather. "'This Strange Communion': Surveillance and Spectatorship in Ann Petry's *The Street.*" *African American Review* 37.1 (2003): 21–37.

Hirsch, Marianne. "Knowing Their Names: Toni Morrison's *Song of Solomon.*" In *New Essays on Song of Solomon,* ed. Valerie Smith, 69–92. New York: Cambridge University Press, 1995.

Hogue, W. Lawrence. *Race, Modernity, Postmodernity: A Look at the History and the Literatures of People of Color Since the 1960s.* Albany: State University of New York Press, 1996.

Holloway, Karla. *Passed On: African American Mourning Stories.* Durham, NC: Duke University Press, 2003.

hooks, bell. *Killing Rage, Ending Racism.* New York: Henry Holt, 1995.

———. *Yearning: Race, Gender, and Cultural Politics.* 1990. Boston: South End Press, 1999.

Hughes, Langston. "The Negro Artist and the Racial Mountain." In *The Norton Anthology of African American Literature*, 1st ed. Ed. Henry Louis Gates, Jr., and Nellie Y. McKay, 1267–71. New York: Norton, 1997.

Hurston, Zora Neale. *Their Eyes Were Watching God.* New York: Harper & Row, 1990.

Iannone, Carol. "Literature By Quota." *Commentary* March 1991: 50–53.

———. "Toni Morrison's Career." *Commentary* December 1987: 59–63.

Isaacs, Harold. "Five Writers and Their African Ancestors." In *Conversations With Ralph Ellison*, ed. Maryemma Graham and Amritjit Singh, 63–69. Jackson: University Press of Mississippi, 1995.

Iton, Richard. *In Search of the Black Fantastic: Politics and Popular Culture in the Post–Civil Rights Era.* New York: Oxford University Press, 2008.

Jablon, Madelyn. *Black Metafiction: Self-Consciousness in African American Literature.* Iowa City: University of Iowa Press, 1997.

Jackson, John. *Real Black: Adventures in Racial Sincerity.* Chicago: University of Chicago Press, 2005.

Jackson, Lawrence. *The Indignant Generation: A Narrative History of African American Writers and Critics, 1934–1960.* Princeton, NJ: Princeton University Press, 2011.

———. *Ralph Ellison: Emergence of Genius.* New York: Wiley, 2002.

Jackson, Richard. *Black Literature and Humanism in Latin America.* Athens: University of Georgia Press, 2008.

Janifer, Raymond E. "Looking Homewood: The Evolution of John Edgar Wideman's Folk Imagination." In *Contemporary Black Men's Fiction and Drama,* ed. Keith Clark, 54–70. Urbana: University of Illinois Press, 2001.

Jarrett, Thomas D. "Toward Unfettered Creativity: A Note on the Negro Novelist's Coming of Age." *Phylon* 11.4 (1950): 313–17.

Johnson, Charles. *Being and Race.* 1988. Bloomington: Indiana University Press, 1990.

———. "John Gardner as Mentor." *African American Review* 30.4 (1996): 619–24.

———. *Middle Passage.* New York: Scribner, 1990.

———. *Oxherding Tale.* 1982. New York: Plume, 1995.

———. "The World According to John Gardner." *E-Channel* 4 June 2011. Web. 7 February 2012.

Johnson, James Weldon. *The Book of American Negro Poetry.* New York: Harcourt, Brace and Company, 1922.

———. "The Dilemma of the Negro Author." In *The New Negro: Readings on Race, Representation, and African American Culture, 1892–1938,* ed. Henry L. Gates, Jr., and Gene Andrew Jarrett, 378–81. Princeton, NJ: Princeton University Press, 2007.

Jordan, Margaret I. *African American Servitude and Historical Imaginings: Retrospective Fiction and Representation.* New York: Palgrave, 2004.

Judy, Ronald A. T. *(Dis)Forming the American Canon: African-Arabic Slave Narratives and the Vernacular.* Minneapolis: University of Minnesota Press, 1993.

Juneja, Om P. "The Purple Colour of Walker Women: Their Journey From Slavery to

Liberation." In *Bloom's Modern Critical Interpretations: Alice Walker's The Color Purple,* ed. Harold Bloom, 79–88. New York: Infobase, 2008.

Kang, Nancy. "To Love and Be Loved: Considering Black Masculinity and the Misandric Impulse in Toni Morrison's *Beloved.*" *Callaloo* 26.3 (2003): 836–54.

Karenga, Maulana. "Black Art: Mute Matter Given Force and Function." In *The Norton Anthology of African American Literature,* 1st ed. Ed. Henry Louis Gates, Jr., and Nellie Y. McKay, 1972–77. New York: Norton, 1997.

Keizer, Arlene R. *Black Subjects: Identity Formation in the Contemporary Narrative of Slavery.* Ithaca, NY: Cornell University Press, 2004.

Killens, John Oliver. *Black Man's Burden.* New York: Trident Press, 1975.

King, Wilma. *Stolen Childhood.* Bloomington: Indiana University Press, 1995.

King James Bible. Uhrichsville, OH: Barbour Publishing, 2003.

Kinnamon, Kenneth. Foreword. *The Long Dream.* By Richard Wright. Boston, MA: Northeastern University Press, 2000. vii–xiv.

Kitwana, Bakari. *The Hip Hop Generation: Young Blacks and the Crisis in African-American Culture.* New York: BasicCivitas, 2002.

Knight, Margaret R. "He Must Return to the South." In *Conversations with Ernest Gaines,* ed. John Lowe, 69–71. Jackson: University Press of Mississippi, 1995.

Koenen, Anne. "The One Out of Sequence." In *Conversations with Toni Morrison,* ed. Danille Taylor-Guthrie, 67–83. Jackson: University Press of Mississippi, 1994.

Kubitschek, Missy Dehn. "'So You Want a History, Do You?': Epistemologies and *The Chaneysville Incident.*" *Mississippi Quarterly* 49 (1996): 755–74.

Kuhne, Dave. *African Settings in Contemporary American Novels.* Westport, CT: Greenwood, 1999.

Laney, Ruth. "Southern Sage Savors His Rise to Success." In *Conversations with Ernest Gaines,* ed. John Lowe, 293–96. Jackson: University Press of Mississippi, 1995.

Leak, Jeffrey. *Racial Myths and Masculinity in African American Literature.* Knoxville: University of Tennessee Press, 2005.

Lewis, Catherine E. "Sewing, Quilting, Knitting: Handicraft and Freedom in *The Color Purple* and *A Woman's Story.*" In *Bloom's Modern Critical Interpretations: Alice Walker's The Color Purple,* ed. Harold Bloom, 161–74. New York: Infobase, 2008.

Lewis, George E. *A Power Stronger Than Itself: The AACM and American Experimental Music.* Chicago: University of Chicago Press, 2008.

Lewis, Rudolph. "An Interview With Keith Gilyard." *Chicken Bones: A Journal for Literary & Artistic Themes* N.d. Web. 29 February 2012.

Little, Jonathan. *Charles Johnson's Spiritual Imagination.* Columbia: University of Missouri Press, 1997.

Love, Heather. "Close but not Deep: Literary Ethics and the Descriptive Turn." *New Literary History* 41 (2010): 371–91.

Lowe, John. "An Interview With Ernest Gaines." In *Conversations with Ernest Gaines,* ed. John Lowe, 297–328. Jackson: University Press of Mississippi, 1995.

Lyon, Ted. "Jorge Luis Borges and the Interview as Literary Genre." *Latin American Literature Review* 22.44 (1994): 74–89.

Mandle, Jay R. *The Roots of Black Poverty: The Southern Plantation Economy After the Civil War.* Durham, NC: Duke University Press, 1978.

Marks, Kathleen. *Toni Morrison's Beloved and the Apotropaic Imagination.* Columbia: University of Missouri Press, 2002.

Marshall, Paule. *Brown Girl, Brownstones.* 1959. New York: Feminist Press, 1981.

Martin, Reginald. "An Interview with Ishmael Reed." *Review of Contemporary Fiction* 4.2 (1984): 176–87.

Mayberry, Susan Neal. *Can't I Love What I Criticize?: The Masculine and Morrison.* Athens: University of Georgia Press, 2007.

McCluskey, Audrey T. "A Conversation with Toni Morrison." In *Toni Morrison: Conversations,* ed. Carolyn C. Denard, 38–43. Jackson: University Press of Mississippi, 2008.

McDowell, Edwin. "48 Writers Protest by Praising Morrison." *New York Times* 19 January 1988: C15.

———. "Book Awards are Pondered." *New York Times* 12 November 1987. Web. 20 March 2010.

McGurl, Mark. *The Program Era: Postwar Fiction and the Rise of Creative Writing.* Cambridge, MA: Harvard University Press, 2009.

Miles, Jack. "The 'Dictatorship of Mediocrity.'" *Los Angeles Times* 7 Jul. 1991. Web. 7 Feb. 2012.

Miller, R. Baxter, ed. *Black American Literature and Humanism.* Lexington: University of Kentucky Press, 1981.

———. "A Deeper Literacy: Teaching *Invisible Man* from Aboriginal Ground." In *Approaches to Teaching Ellison's Invisible Man,* ed. Susan Resneck Parr and Pancho Savery, 51–57. New York: MLA, 1989.

———. *A Literary Criticism of Five Generations of African American Writing: The Artistry of Memory.* Lewiston, NY: Edwin Mellen Press, 2008.

———. *On the Ruins of Modernity: New Chicago Renaissance From Wright to Kent.* Champaign, IL: Common Ground, 2011.

Miller, William Robert. "The Broadening Horizons: Montgomery, America, the World." In *Martin Luther King, Jr.: A Profile,* ed. C. Eric Lincoln, 40–71. New York: Hill and Wang, 1984.

Minutes of "The Sisterhood." 20 March 1977. TS. June Jordan Papers. Schlesinger Library, Radcliffe Institute, Harvard University, Cambridge, MA.

Mitgang, Herbert. "For Morrison, Prizes Silence Gossip." *New York Times* 1 April 1988: B5.

Mobley, Marilyn Sanders. "Call and Response: Voice, Community, and Dialogic Structures in Toni Morrison's *Song of Solomon.*" In *New Essays on Song of Solomon,* ed. Valerie Smith, 41–68. New York: Cambridge University Press, 1995.

Montgomery, Maxine L. "The Fathomless Dream: Gloria Naylor's Use of the Descent Motif in *The Women of Brewster Place.*" In *The Critical Response to Gloria Naylor,* ed. Sharon Felton and Michelle C. Loris, 42–47. Westport, CT: Greenwood, 1997.

Morrison, Toni. *Beloved.* 1987. New York: Vintage, 2004.

———. "A Bench by the Road: *Beloved.*" In *Toni Morrison: Conversations,* ed. Carolyn C. Denard, 44–50. Jackson: University Press of Mississippi, 2008.

———. *The Bluest Eye.* 1970. New York: Vintage, 2007.

———. *Jazz.* New York: Knopf, 1992.

———. *Song of Solomon.* 1977. New York: Plume, 1987.

———. *Sula.* 1973. New York: Vintage, 2004.

———. *What Moves at the Margins: Selected Nonfiction.* Ed. Carolyn C. Denard. Jackson: University Press of Mississippi, 2008.

Murchison, Gayle. "Mary Lou Williams's Hymn *Black Christ of the Andes (St. Martin de*

Porres):Vatican II, Civil Rights, and Jazz as Sacred Music." *The Musical Quarterly* 86.4 (2002): 591–629.

Murray, Rolland. *Our Living Manhood: Literature, Black Power, and Masculine Ideology.* Philadelphia: University of Pennsylvania Press, 2006.

Nash, William. *Charles Johnson's Fiction.* Urbana: University of Illinois Press, 2003.

Naylor, Gloria. "A Conversation: Gloria Naylor and Toni Morrison." In *Conversations with Toni Morrison,* ed. Danille Taylor-Guthrie, 188–217. Jackson: University Press of Mississippi, 1994.

———. *The Women of Brewster Place.* New York: Penguin, 1982.

Neal, Larry. "The Black Arts Movement." In *The Norton Anthology of African American Literature,* 1st ed. Ed. Henry Louis Gates, Jr., and Nellie Y. McKay, 1959–72. New York: Norton, 1997.

Neal, Mark Anthony. *Soul Babies: Black Popular Culture and the Post-Soul Aesthetic.* New York: Routledge, 2002.

Nielsen, Aldon L. *Writing Between the Lines: Race and Intertextuality.* Athens: University of Georgia Press, 1994.

Norman, Brian. *Neo-Segregation Narratives: Jim Crow in Post–Civil Rights American Literature.* Athens: University of Georgia Press, 2010.

O'Brien, John. *Interviews with Black Writers.* New York: Liveright, 1973.

Olander, Renée. "An Interview with John Edgar Wideman." In *Conversations With John Edgar Wideman,* ed. Bonnie TuSmith, 165–79. Jackson: University Press of Mississippi, 1998.

Page, Philip. *Dangerous Freedom: Fusion and Fragmentation in Toni Morrison's Novels.* Jackson: University Press of Mississippi, 1995.

———. *Reclaiming Community in Contemporary African-American Fiction.* Jackson: University Press of Mississippi, 1999.

Parker, Betty Jean. "Complexity: Toni Morrison's Women." In *Conversations with Toni Morrison,* ed. Danille Taylor-Guthrie, 60–66. Jackson: University Press of Mississippi, 1994.

Patterson, Orlando. *Slavery and Social Death: A Comparative Study.* Cambridge, MA: Harvard University Press, 1982.

Piacentino, Ed. "'The Common Humanity That Is In Us All': Towards Racial Reconciliation in Gaines's *A Lesson Before Dying.*" *Southern Quarterly* 42 (2004): 73–85.

Plummer, William. "John Edgar Wideman." *People.com* 11 February 1985. Web. 27 February 2012.

Price, Kenneth, ed. *Walt Whitman: The Contemporary Reviews.* Cambridge: Cambridge University Press, 1996.

Pruitt, Bernadette. "'For the Advancement of the Race': The Great Migration to Houston, Texas, 1914–1941." *Journal of Urban History* 31 (2005): 435–78.

Rampersad, Arnold. *Ralph Ellison: A Biography.* New York: Knopf, 2007.

Ransom, John Crowe. "Criticism, Inc." *Virginia Quarterly Review* 13.4 (1937): 586–602.

Rodgers, Lawrence. *Canaan Bound: The African American Great Migration Novel.* Urbana: University of Illinois Press, 1997.

Rodrigues, Eusebio L. "Experiencing *Jazz.*" *Modern Fiction Studies* 39.3–4 (1993): 733–54.

Rodriguez, Denise. "Homewood's 'Music of Invisibility': John Edgar Wideman's *Sent for You Yesterday* and the Black Urban Tradition." In *Critical Essays on John Edgar Wide-*

man, ed. Bonnie TuSmith and Keith Byerman, 127–44. Knoxville: University of Tennessee Press, 2006.

Ross, Michael. "The Root Interview: Charles Johnson." *The Root* 7 Jan. 2010. Web. 7 Feb. 2012.

Rowell, Charles. "This Louisiana Thing That Drives Me: An Interview With Ernest Gaines." In *Conversations with Ernest Gaines,* ed. John Lowe, 86–98. Jackson: University Press of Mississippi, 1995.

Ruas, Charles. "Toni Morrison." In *Conversations with Toni Morrison,* ed. Danille Taylor-Guthrie, 93–118. Jackson: University Press of Mississippi, 1994.

Rukeyser, Muriel. Letter to Alice Walker. May 1975. TS. Muriel Rukeyser Papers. Library of Congress, Washington, DC.

Rushdy, Ashraf. *Neo-Slave Narratives: Studies in the Social Logic of a Literary Form.* New York: Oxford University Press, 1999.

———. *Remembering Generations: Race and Family in Contemporary African American Fiction.* Chapel Hill: University of North Carolina Press, 2001.

Russell, Kathy, Midge Wilson, and Ronald Hall. *The Color Complex: The Politics of Skin Color Among African Americans.* New York: Harcourt, 1992.

Samuels, Wilfred. "Going Home: A Conversation With John Edgar Wideman." In *Conversations With John Edgar Wideman,* ed. Bonnie TuSmith, 14–31. Jackson: University Press of Mississippi, 1998.

Santamarina, Xiomara. "'Are We There Yet?': Archives, History, and Specificity in African-American Literary Studies." *American Literary History* 20.1–2 (2008): 304–16.

Schappell, Elissa. "Toni Morrison: The Art of Fiction." In *Toni Morrison: Conversations,* ed. Carolyn C. Denard, 62–90. Jackson: University Press of Mississippi, 2008.

Scott-Heron, Gil, and Brian Jackson. *Winter in America.* Strata-East Records, 1974. LP.

Seelye, Katherine. "Writer Tends Land Where Ancestors Were Slaves." *New York Times* 20 October 2010. Web. 7 February 2012.

Selzer, Linda. *Charles Johnson in Context.* Amherst: University of Massachusetts Press, 2009.

———. "Race and Domesticity in *The Color Purple.*" *African American Review* 29 (1995): 67–82.

Shakespeare, William. *Macbeth.* 1606. Ed. William J. Rolfe. New York: American Book Company, 1918.

Shange, Ntozake. *Nappy Edges.* 1978. New York: St Martin's Press, 1991.

Skerrett, Joseph. "Recitation to the Griot: Storytelling and Learning in Toni Morrison's *Song of Solomon.*" In *Conjuring: Black Women, Fiction, and Literary Tradition,* ed. Majorie Pryse and Hortense J. Spillers, 192–202. Bloomington: Indiana University Press, 1985.

Stepto, Robert. "Intimate Things in Place: A Conversation With Toni Morrison." In *Conversations with Toni Morrison,* ed. Danille Taylor-Guthrie, 10–29. Jackson: University Press of Mississippi, 1994.

Storhoff, Gary. *Understanding Charles Johnson.* Columbia: University of South Carolina Press, 2004.

"Strut, v.1." *OED Online.* September 2012. Web. 12 September 2012.

Takaki, Ronald. *Violence in the Black Imagination: Essays and Documents.* Expanded edition. New York: Oxford University Press, 1993.

Tally, Justine. *The Story of Jazz: Toni Morrison's Dialogic Imagination.* Hamburg: LIT, 2001.

Tarshis, Jerome. "The Other 300 Years: A Conversation With Ernest J. Gaines, Author of *The Autobiography of Miss Jane Pittman.*" In *Conversations with Ernest Gaines,* ed. John Lowe, 72–79. Jackson: University Press of Mississippi, 1995.

Tate, Claudia, ed. *Black Women Writers at Work.* New York: Continuum, 1983.

———. *Domestic Allegories of Political Desire: The Black Heroine's Text at the Turn of the Century.* New York: Oxford University Press, 1992.

———. *Psychoanalysis and Black Novels: Desire and the Protocols of Race.* New York: Oxford University Press, 1998.

———. "Toni Morrison." In *Conversations with Toni Morrison,* ed. Danille Taylor-Guthrie, 156–70. Jackson: University Press of Mississippi, 1994.

Taumann, Beatrix. *Strange Orphans: Contemporary African American Playwrights.* Würzburg: Königshausen & Neumann, 1999.

Thompson, Ayanna, ed. *Colorblind Shakespeare: New Perspectives on Race and Performance.* New York: Routledge, 2006.

Thompson, Carlyle V. "From a Hog to a Black Man: Black Male Subjectivity and Ritualistic Lynching in Ernest J. Gaines's *A Lesson Before Dying.*" *CLA Journal* 45 (2002): 279–310.

Tooker, Dan, and Roger Hofheins. "Ernest J. Gaines." In *Conversations with Ernest Gaines,* ed. John Lowe, 99–111. Jackson: University Press of Mississippi, 1995.

Touré. "What If Michael Vick Were White?" *ESPN.* 25 Aug. 2011. Web. 8 Mar. 2012.

Trevor-Roper, Hugh. *The Rise of Christian Europe.* London: Thames and Hudson, 1964.

TuSmith, Bonnie. *All My Relatives: Community in Contemporary Ethnic American Literatures.* Ann Arbor: The University of Michigan Press, 1993.

———, ed. *Conversations with John Edgar Wideman.* Jackson: University Press of Mississippi, 1998.

Walby, Celestin. "The African Sacrificial Kingship Ritual and Johnson's *Middle Passage.*" *African American Review* 29.4 (1995): 657–69.

Walker, Alice. *The Color Purple.* 1982. Orlando: Harcourt, 2003.

———. *In Search of Our Mother's Gardens: Womanist Prose.* Orlando: Harcourt, 2003.

———. Letter to Muriel Rukeyser. 19 May 1975. TS. Muriel Rukeyser Papers. Library of Congress, Washington, DC.

———. Letter to Muriel Rukeyser. N.d. MS. Muriel Rukeyser Papers. Library of Congress, Washington, DC.

Walker, Melissa. *Down From the Mountaintop: Black Women's Novels in the Wake of the Civil Rights Movement, 1966–1989.* New Haven, CT: Yale University Press, 1991.

Wall, Cheryl. *Worrying the Line: Black Women Writers, Lineage, and Literary Tradition.* Chapel Hill: University of North Carolina Press, 2005.

Walling, William. "Ralph Ellison's *Invisible Man:* 'It Goes a Long Way Back, Some Twenty Years.'" *Phylon* 34.1 (1973): 4–16.

Warren, Kenneth. *What Was African American Literature?* Cambridge, MA: Harvard University Press, 2011.

Washington, James Melvin, ed. *Conversations With God: Two Centuries of Prayer by African Americans.* New York: HarperCollins, 1994.

Watson, Wilbur H. "The Idea of Black Sociology: Its Cultural and Political Significance." *The American Sociologist* 11.2 (1976): 115–23.

Watterson, Zachary. "Literary Mentors & Friends: An Interview With Charles Johnson." *Fiction Writers Review* 9 April 2010. Web. 7 February 2012.

Whalen-Bridge, John. "'Whole Sight in Review': Reflections on Charles Johnson." *ME-LUS* 31.2 (2006): 244–267.

Whitaker, Thomas. "Committee on Negro Housing." In *Organizing Black America: An Encyclopedia of African American Associations,* ed. Nina Mjagkij, 160–61. New York: Garland, 2000.

White, Evelyn C. *Alice Walker: A Life.* New York: Norton, 2004.

Whitt, Margaret Earley. *Understanding Gloria Naylor.* Columbia: University of South Carolina Press, 1999.

Wideman, John Edgar. *Brothers and Keepers.* 1984. New York: Mariner, 2005.

———. *The Homewood Books.* Pittsburgh: University of Pittsburgh Press, 1992.

———. "More." *Callaloo* 24.4 (2001): 1198–1209.

———. "*Of Love and Dust:* A Reconsideration." *Callaloo* 3 (1978): 76–84.

———. *Philadelphia Fire.* 1990. New York: Vintage, 1991.

———. *Sent for You Yesterday.* Boston: Houghton Mifflin, 1983.

———. "Visiting Privileges; A Journey to the Son." *Washington Post* 11 July 2004: W14.

Wilentz, Gay. *Binding Cultures: Black Women Writers in Africa and the Diaspora.* Bloomington: Indiana University Press, 1992.

Williams, Dana. *In the Light of Likeness-Transformed: The Literary Art of Leon Forrest.* Columbus: The Ohio State University Press, 2005.

Williams-Forson, Psyche. "I Ain't Singing Nothing Without My Coca-Cola: Women and the Politics of Food in the Work of August Wilson." *Baltimore Centerstage* N.d. Web. 20 February 2012.

Willis, Susan. *Specifying: Black Women Writing the American Experience.* Madison: University of Wisconsin Press, 1987.

Wilson, August. *King Hedley II.* New York: Theater Communications Group, 2005.

index

Abbandonato, Linda, 50n7
Achebe, Chinua, 20n45
aesthetics: black writers' questioning of
    white, 2, 13, 17, 26, 41, 44, 61, 70,
    88; sources for black literary, 5, 12,
    15, 16, 121. *See also* modernism;
    naturalism; New Criticism; post-
    modernism
affirmative action, 15, 45n35, 48n2, 62,
    68
Africa: black American return to, 19,
    55n22, 61, 130–31; independence
    movements in, 47–48; missionaries
    in, 72; rape survivors in, 51n8. See
    also *The Color Purple; Middle Passage*
African American cultural formation:
    debates about, 48, 48n2, 63n37,
    64n38
African American literature: academic
    study of, 3, 11, 46, 46n36, 166–67;
    anthologies of, 11n29; autonomy of
    writers of, 2, 18, 69, 89, 117, 121,
    148, 168; compared to black music,
    33, 33n14, 95n7; and gender, 12,
    12n30, 17n42, 37, 37n22, 66n43,
    73–74; and pleading black human-
    ity, 10n26; and racial injustice, 1, 8,

8n21; traditions of, 5, 11–12, 16, 19,
    27n5, 32–33, 69; and transnational-
    ism, 14, 14n36; white authentication
    of, 69n51
African American novelists: and artistic
    fellowship, 3n6, 10n25, 11, 12, 36,
    41, 69, 93, 95, 117, 119; and black
    cultural archives, 5, 11, 12, 17, 100,
    110, 120, 121, 128, 135; and cos-
    mopolitan criticism, 13, 14, 93; and
    historiography, 13n35; and inter-
    racial readership, 7–8, 8n19; in the
    post–civil rights era, 2, 3, 5n11, 49,
    54, 66–69, 74, 89, 94n4, 95, 95n7,
    95n8, 95n9, 95n10, 118, 120, 120–
    21n1, 122n5, 135; post-soul cohort
    of, 169–70, 169n13, 170n14; and
    social science accounts of black life,
    6, 7n15, 32, 95n10, 100; and voca-
    tion 6, 11
Allen, Jeffrey R., 169n14
Amadi, Elechi, 58n26
American Book Award, 4n9, 17, 17n42.
    See also National Book Award
American Book Award (Before Colum-
    bus Foundation), 4n9
Amistad, 72n4

Ransom, John Crowe, 8n22

Reagan, Ronald, 28n7, 87; black views of, 27n4, 95n8

Reconstruction, 19, 27, 31, 38, 43, 123, 137

Reed, Ishmael, 16–17, 17n40, 17n42, 37; *Mumbo Jumbo,* 17

Robinson, Jackie, 81n18, 86

Rodgers, Lawrence, 118

Rukeyser, Muriel, 52–53, 52n13, 52n14, 53n17, 54, 54n18, 57, 68, 68n49

rural: black men in fiction, 131–32; folk culture, 76n11; homelands, 121; grace, 19; South and agrarian values, 138n23; South and black survival, 17, 110; South as literary setting, 54, 73, 73n6, 131

Rushdy, Asraf, 10n25, 62n33, 139n24

Santamarina, Xiomara, 14

Sarah Lawrence University, 47n1, 52, 62 52n12, 53, 53n16, 58, 58n26

Schomburg Library, 12n31

Scott-Heron, Gil, 87n26

segregation, 2, 6, 13, 14, 17, 17n43, 19, 58, 63, 86, 120–21n1, 125n9, 151, 171

Selzer, Linda, 62n32, 64, 64n39, 67n45

Sent For You Yesterday (Wideman), 4, 16, 18n43, 19, 20, 108n41; artistic failure, 144, 145–46, 150–51, 153–54, 163–64; autobiographical elements, 145, 145n2146n5; black community, 146, 147, 148, 149–50; black vernacular versus white mainstream aesthetics, 145n3, 146, 148, 152, 164; chronology, 146, 146n4; painting, 150–51, 152–53; piano playing, 146, 147–48, 152; technique versus solace, 145–46, 147–48, 152, 153, 164

Shakespeare, William: See *Macbeth; Philadelphia Fire; Women of Brewster Place*

Shange, Ntozake, 33n14; *For Colored Girls,* 10n27

single motherhood, 27, 28, 28n7, 29

Skerett, Joseph, 131n16

slavery, 2, 13, 17, 17n43, 19, 27, 29,
35n19, 45–46, 49, 62, 63–64, 72, 87–88, 118, 119n53, 121

Smith, Tommie, 15n38

social death, 35, 35n19, 36

Song of Solomon (Morrison), 4, 18n43, 19, 20, 28n8, 142n30; alcohol in, 99, 99n18; and African cosmology, 130–31, 130n15, 131n16, 142; and black literary traditions, 120–21n1, 121, 121n3, 128, 131n16, 131n18, 135, 142, 143; cultural amnesia/editing in, 120, 121, 124, 125, 128, 128n13, 138; democratic access in, 120, 123–24, 124n7, 124n8, 125, 135, 136, 137, 138, 142, 143; entrepreneurship in, 123, 123n6, 135; familial bequeathal in, 120, 121, 123–25, 129–31, 132, 136–37, 138–39; hunting in, 115n51, 121, 129, 130, 132; inheritance in, 104n30, 121, 124–25, 129; intimacy in, 114n50, 122, 124–25, 130, 131–32, 131n17, 135, 136–38, 139, 139n24; narrative structure of, 120–21n1; racial terror in, 136, 138; search for black selfhood in, 125, 128, 130; urban to rural journeys in, 121, 129–32, 129n14, 138, 138n23; and white expectations, 34, 122n4, 125, 129, 135, 142; work versus pleasure in, 122–23, 122n5, 124, 125, 128, 136–37, 142

Southern Illinois University, 47n1, 60

Spelman College, 47n1, 51–52, 51n11, 58, 58n26

Stegner, Wallace, 87

Steinem, Gloria, 17n42

Stepto, Robert, 166n4

The Street (Petry), 94, 97–98, 97n14, 106, 106n37, 106n38

Sula (Morrison), 5n10, 28n8, 34, 45, 104, 104n29, 114n50

swagger, the ethics of: and black artistic freedom, 1, 5, 14, 16, 84, 164, 171; and black cultural recovery, 2, 17, 19, 121–22, 135; compared to elegance, 3; and creative fellowship, 10n26, 36, 41; individual flair and collective discipline in, 94, 147–48, 165–66;